To

Tom Pocock has been described as one of the foremost writers on the Napoleonic Wars and Nelson. He is the author of eight books about the admiral and his time including *Horatio Nelson*, runner-up for the Whitbread Biography Award in 1987. He has written the biographies of three diverse writers – Captain Marryat, Rider Haggard and Alan Moorehead – and his other books include two about his own experiences as a newspaper war correspondent. During many years in Fleet Street, he was also Naval Correspondent of *The Times* and Defence Correspondent of the London *Evening Standard*. Tom Pocock's most recent book is *The Terror Before Trafalgar*. He is married with two daughters and lives in London.

By the same author

Nelson and His World
Chelsea Reach
Fighting General
Remember Nelson
The Young Nelson in the Americas
1945: The Dawn Came Up Like Thunder
East and West of Suez
Horatio Nelson
Alan Moorehead
Sailor King
Rider Haggard and the Lost Empire
Norfolk
A Thirst for Glory
Travels of a London Schoolboy, 1826–1830 (ed.)
Battle for Empire
Nelson's Women
Captain Marryat
The Terror before Trafalgar
London Walks
Essential Venice

STOPPING NAPOLEON

War and Intrigue in the Mediterranean

Tom Pocock

JOHN MURRAY

© Tom Pocock 2004

First published in Great Britain in 2004 by John Murray (Publishers)
A division of Hodder Headline

Paperback edition 2005

The right of Tom Pocock to be identified as the Author of the Work has been asserted
by him in accordance with the Copyright, Designs and Patents Act 1988.

1 3 5 7 9 10 8 6 4 2

A CIP catalogue record for this title is available from the British Library

ISBN 0 7195 6604 5

Typeset in Monotype Bembo by Servis Filmsetting Ltd, Manchester

Printed and bound by
Clays Ltd, St Ives plc

Hodder Headline policy is to use papers that are natural, renewable and recyclable
products and made from wood grown in sustainable forests. The logging and
manufacturing processes are expected to conform to the environmental regulations of
the country of origin.

John Murray (Publishers)
338 Euston Road
London NW1 3BH

For Robert and Sue Key

Contents

Contents

Illustrations

The author and publisher would like to thank the following for permission to reproduce illustrations: Plates 1, 5, 6, 7 and 28, courtesy of the Director, National Army Museum, London; 2, 4, 10, 19 and 22, National Maritime Museum, London; 3, 11, 12, 13, 29 and 30, Musée national de la Marine, Paris; 8, 15, 20, 21, 23, 24, 25 and 26, Private Collection; 9, Museo Civico Gaetano Filangieri, Naples; 14, Prince Napoleon Collection; 16, 17 and 18, Das Innsbrucker Riesenrundgemälde, Innsbruck; 27, Museo Borghese, Rome.

Every effort has been made to contact holders of all copyright illustrations reproduced in this book but in the event that any has been inadvertently overlooked the publishers would be pleased to hear from them.

Preface

This is a book about war. The naval and military operations here described were fought in the Mediterranean and Adriatic and on their shores during the decade following the Battle of Trafalgar. Much has been written about the Peninsular War, but that might not have been fought in the Iberian peninsula because, for several of those years, it seemed probable that the main British effort against Napoleonic France would be through another peninsula: Italy. That did not happen as expected, and changing strategic plans led to the events described in this book. Seldom are these stories told and rarely in any detail; when they are, they tend to be seen as dramatic sideshows to the main events in Europe. Yet all — the successful, the disastrous, the gallant, the farcical and the bizarre — were linked by a grand concept: the prevention of the eastward expansion of the Napoleonic empire. There were interludes in the torrent of violent history too, and even a little light relief; particularly in Venice and on the island of Elba.

Once Trafalgar had been fought, the Emperor Napoleon knew that, whatever he might boast, he could never invade the British Isles. But he required a grand design, an ultimate aim, and that, it was believed, would be the acquisition of the Ottoman Empire and, finally, the conquest of British India. This gave rise to counter-moves, rarely centre-stage in the course of global war, yet often preoccupying statesmen and commanders when they tried to cast their minds forward months, or years. But for this, the

British would not have found themselves in the narrows of the Dardanelles, the vineyards of Capri, the hot alleys of Rosetta, scaling Balkan mountains, or scanning the Arsenale of Venice through their telescopes – all with the aim of stopping Napoleon.

The long war in the Mediterranean, even then sometimes forgotten by the British public, threw up some remarkable characters. Among the naval commanders there were former friends of the dead Nelson: Collingwood, Tom Fremantle, William Hoste and the maverick Sir Sidney Smith; notable among the soldiers, Sir John Moore. Nor were the protagonists all British: others included the dashing Joachim Murat and Caroline Bonaparte, the exotic and infuriating King Ferdinand and Queen Maria Carolina of the Two Sicilies and the robust Tyrolese patriot Andreas Hofer. Even Napoleon himself makes two appearances in the theatre: one in Venice and the other, of course, on Elba.

The story of this sweep of action has not, I think, been told in this way before; indeed, books in English that concentrate on this aspect of the Napoleonic Wars have been few. The political and military history of much of this period was comprehensively described in *The War in the Mediterranean, 1803–1810*, by Piers Mackesy (1957), and events have been the subject of such studies as Richard Hopton's *The Battle of Maida* (2002), Norman MacKenzie's *The Escape from Elba* (1982) and the earlier *The British in Capri, 1806–1808* (1918) by Sir Lees Knowles. Otherwise they have formed part of books with a wider scope, such as Rory Muir's *Britain and the Defeat of Napoleon* (1996), Sir Harold Acton's *The Bourbons of Naples* (1990) and Desmond Gregory's *Sicily: The Insecure Base* (1988). Individuals sometimes contributed their own memoirs – Donat Henchy O'Brien's *My Adventures During the Late War* (1902), Sir Neil Campbell's *Napoleon at Fontainebleau and Elba* (1869) and Montgomery Maxwell's *My Adventures* (1845) being particularly vivid – or wrote diaries and letters, as did Sir John Moore and Sir Thomas Fremantle. Others became the subject of biographies, including Carola Oman's *Sir John Moore* (1953), Ann Parry's *The Admirals Fremantle* (1971) and two of my own books, *Remember Nelson: The Life of Captain Sir William Hoste* (1977) and *A Thirst for Glory: The Life of Admiral Sir Sidney Smith* (1996). A selection of books I consulted is listed in the bibliography.

I am grateful to several distinguished historians for advice, including David Chandler, John Ehrman, Flora Fraser, Christopher Hibbert, Richard Hopton and Elizabeth Sparrow. Ann Parry, the historian of the Fremantle family, gave me her archive of notes and cuttings about Admiral Fremantle and I am also grateful to Lord Cottesloe, Tom Fremantle, Nigel Foxell, Michael Nash and to Elizabeth Imlay and Anne Petrides of Parapress Ltd for allowing me to quote from *Sea Soldier: The Letters and Journals of Major Marmaduke Wybourn, R.M.*, published in 2000. For permission to reproduce paintings by Lieutenant William Pocock, I am grateful to his direct descendants, Patrick and Richard Bryan. I have been able to visit almost all of the places where the events in this book took place, either on recent travels or, in the past, as a journalist. In Venice I was guided through the Arsenale thanks to introductions from Philip and Jane Rylands and shown Fort Marghera by Robert Morgan, while Sarah Quill and Anna Wayman helped with translation; Viscount Norwich kindly lent me the wonderfully detailed *I dieci giorni di Napoleone I a Venezia*, by Ugo Fugnagnollo. Fernando Savarese and Violetta Elvin were hospitable hosts and guides on my visits to the Bay of Naples.

In the past I enjoyed the company of two naval historians, David Woodward and Richard Hough, when exploring Dubrovnik and Vis, while my father, Guy Pocock, inspired my interest in naval history and long ago took me to see the Andreas Hofer statue on Berg Isel outside Innsbruck and the extraordinary nineteenth-century panorama of the battle fought there. I am, as always, grateful to the staff of the London Library, the British Library, the Public Record Office, the National Maritime Museum and the National Army Museum for their help.

Caroline Knox of John Murray has been a wise and kind editor, Roger Hudson gave useful historical advice and I am also grateful for help from Andrew Lownie, Caroline Westmore, Christine Highmoor and my wife, Penny.

Tom Pocock
Chelsea, 2004

Maps

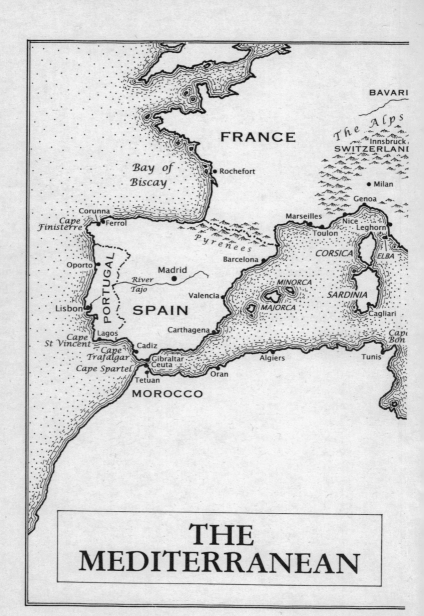

THE
MEDITERRANEAN

RUSSIA

A

Salzburg
Vienna
AUSTRIA
Budapest
Trieste
Fiume
(now Rijeka)
Venice
Belgrade
Zara
River Danube
Ancona
Ragusa
(now Dubrovnik)
LISSA
(now VIS)
Cattaro
(now Kotor)
Rome
Sofia

River Dniester

Black Sea

Constantinople
The Bosphorus

Naples
Apennines
Taranto
KINGDOM OF THE
TWO SICILIES
Salonika
Sea of
Marmara
CORFU
Larissa
Dardanelles
TURKEY
Maida
IONIAN
ISLANDS
Palermo
SICILY   Messina
Athens
MOREA
Cape
Passaro
Cape
Matapan
MALTA
RHODES
CYPRUS
Mediterranean
CRETE
Sea
Tripoli
Derna
Rosetta
Alexandria
Cairo
River Nile
N
W   E
S
EGYPT
Red Sea

0   miles   500
0   kilometres   800

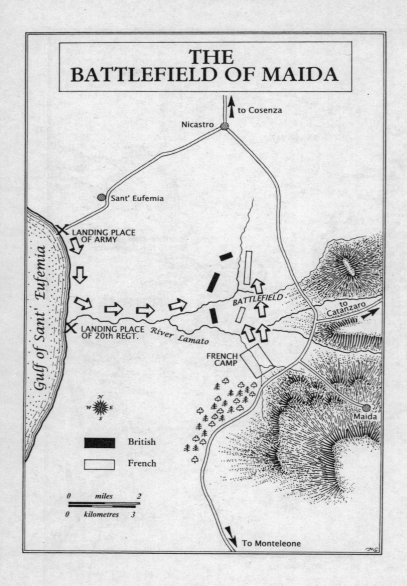

THE
BATTLEFIELD OF MAIDA

to Cosenza

Nicastro

Sant' Eufemia

LANDING PLACE
OF ARMY

Gulf of Sant' Eufemia

BATTLEFIELD

to Catanzaro

LANDING PLACE
OF 20th REGT.

River Lamato

FRENCH
CAMP

Maida

N
W E
S

British

French

0   miles   2

0   kilometres   3

To Monteleone

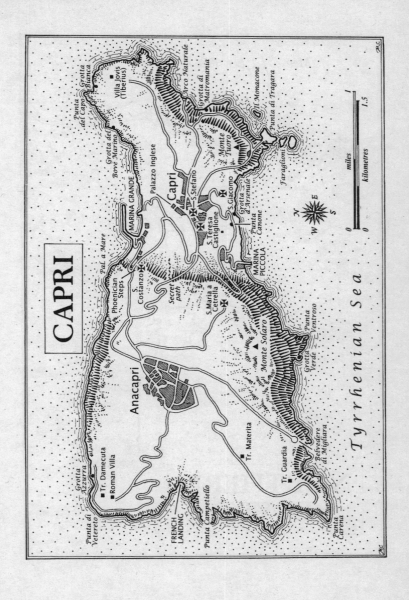

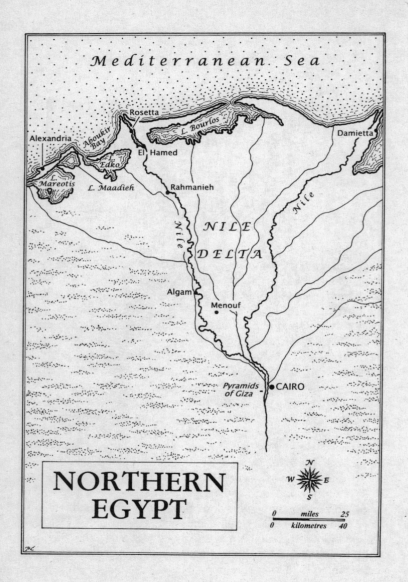

Mediterranean Sea

Rosetta
L. Bourlos
Alexandria
Aboukir Bay
Damietta
El Hamed
Edko
L. Maadieh
Rahmanieh
L. Mareotis
Nile

NILE

DELTA

Nile

Algam
Menouf

Pyramids of Giza
CAIRO

NORTHERN EGYPT

N
W—E
S

0 — miles — 25
0 — kilometres — 40

Prologue

A T THIRTY-THREE and a half minutes past five o'clock on the
afternoon of 9 January 1806 a lever was released in the crypt of
St Paul's Cathedral in London and what was known as the 'secret
machinery'[1] began to move. As a counterweight sank, a section of
the cathedral floor began to descend by a system of pulleys, bearing a coffin, bound in black velvet fixed with gilt nails and decorated with heraldic emblems. Within, was another made from
the mainmast of a French battleship, which had blown up off the
Egyptian coast more than six years earlier. The outer coffin also
bore a gold plate inscribed with the words, 'DEPOSITUM. The Most
Noble Lord HORATIO NELSON, Viscount and Baron NELSON of the
NILE, and of Burnham Thorpe in the County of Norfolk . . .
Duke of Bronte in Sicily . . . Born September 29, 1758.'

The nation's hero and, as he was regarded, saviour, had ended
his passage from Cape Trafalgar. Fourteen minutes later, as the
choirs sang and the organ thundered in the cathedral above, the
funeral service ended and the four thousand who had attended
began to file from the west door into the cold night air. It took
three hours for them all to leave and go in search of their carriages,
which had packed the narrow streets on Ludgate Hill. They had
been up and dressed since the early hours, and most had identified
and boarded their carriages in St James's Park before it was light.
Now they were exhausted and silent.

Prominent among the departing crowds were the naval officers

1

— more than thirty admirals and a hundred captains — wearing black breeches instead of white as a sign of mourning, on whose gold epaulettes and brass buttons the candlelight in the cathedral had glittered all day. There were those who had known Nelson in the Caribbean and the Mediterranean, watched him steer into the heart of the Spanish fleet at St Vincent, seen him in the glare of the exploding French flagship at the Battle of the Nile, and amid the dangers and triumphs of Copenhagen and Trafalgar. For them, the grief they had shared since October was giving way to a great question: what next?

It was not that the man who had focused the patriotism and determination of the nation, the one man to match the dynamism and charisma of their enemy, the Emperor Napoleon, was dead. It was that there now seemed to be no aim that could be identified. At Trafalgar, Nelson had known, as he died from his wound, that by destroying the enemy's fleet he had achieved domination of the seas and saved his country from the threat of invasion. But, soon afterwards, Napoleon had achieved the same dominance on land, by breaking his Austrian and Russian enemies in the great battles of Ulm and Austerlitz. France, with double the population of Britain, dominated the Continent, either by military occupation or by intimidation. Prussia remained uneasily neutral. The northern Italian states, together with Dalmatia, were directly ruled by the French, who were in the process of occupying Naples and the south, driving King Ferdinand and Queen Maria Carolina of the Two Sicilies to exile in their secondary capital, Palermo, for the second time in eight years. So the two principal opponents still faced each other, the one commanding the sea, the other the land. What more could one achieve against the other?

One admiral — albeit a newly promoted rear-admiral — was notable by his absence from St Paul's. He might have been expected to be there because, a few weeks before his death, Lord Nelson had appointed him to command his inshore squadron off Cadiz. Sir Sidney Smith had, six years before that, completed the destruction of Napoleon Bonaparte's dreams of eastern conquest. The year after Nelson had destroyed the French fleet in Aboukir Bay, Smith had halted Bonaparte's planned march homeward via Constantinople and Vienna at the Levantine fortress-city of Acre and had forced him to turn back to Egypt and eventual disaster. That feat had endeared him to Nelson, who had hitherto seen him as a mercurial braggart.

The two men had much in common. Both were imaginative, brave and inspiring leaders but were also as ruthless, vivid and vain as they were ambitious. Neither had hesitated to make use of connections outside the Navy: Nelson with his ties to the Bourbon rulers of the Kingdom of the Two Sicilies – southern Italy and Sicily – through Sir William Hamilton, the British ambassador, and his wife, Emma, who had become his mistress; Smith through his involvement with secret intelligence, which he regarded as 'an occupation of a superior sort',[2] and his cousin William Pitt, the Prime Minister. Nelson had been instantly recognizable by his missing right arm and the decorations embroidered on his uniform coat; Smith, by his shock of dark hair and striking, Semitic-seeming face, sometimes wearing 'mustachios . . . which fashion he had adopted when so much associated with the Turks'.[3] Both had been touched by scandal: Nelson by his affair with Emma Hamilton, the wife of his friend Sir William; Smith by his affair with Princess Caroline, the estranged wife of the Prince of Wales. Both men were charming: Smith was 'extremely gentlemanly . . . and had a good-humoured, agreeable manner with him with a certain dash and turn of chivalry that was very taking with the ladies . . . he was generally very showily dressed, perhaps with some singularity'.[4]

The two men had almost become rivals, while appearing friends. Smith had on several occasions tried to attract more attention than Nelson and, even when the latter had invited him to join his command, he had had plans to snatch the laurels for himself. He had not been present at the climactic battle off Cape Trafalgar because he had been hoping to make that unnecessary. With his inshore squadron he had planned to attack the combined French and Spanish fleets within Cadiz harbour with rockets and torpedoes, burning and sinking them before they could emerge to be fought by Nelson on the high seas. Rehearsals off Boulogne and the preparation of what were called his 'infernals' had delayed his departure and the battle had been fought and won before he could launch his own attack.

Now, it seemed to him, there was room for a successor to Lord Nelson and it would be himself. So instead of attending the obsequies of the dead hero, Rear-Admiral Sir Sidney Smith was reported to be at Plymouth, preparing his flagship for sea, a task that should be the responsibility of his flag-captain. The *Pompée* – a 74-gun ship of the line captured when Smith was burning the French fleet in Toulon twelve years earlier – was commanded by Captain Richard Dacres, who was supervising work in the ship, moored in Cawsand Bay, buffeted by 'strong gales and heavy squalls'.[5] They were busy at this time taking in cables, painting the yards and loading fresh beef. Captain Dacres was also concerned about the health of his ship's company; men were being sent to hospital and in an attempt to maintain some level of hygiene, the lower deck was being washed down and the ratings' bedding aired.

But on the day of Nelson's funeral Sir Sidney Smith was not, in fact, on board. Indeed, he did not hoist his rear-admiral's flag in the *Pompée* to the salute of thirteen guns for another six days and did not occupy his cabins until two days after that. So where was he? Wherever he was, he was drafting his own answer to the question, 'What next?' He wrote his letter not to his superiors at the Admiralty but, as had long been his custom, to the men of power, with whom he had made contact and over whom the admirals had no jurisdiction. His justification was that the subject was beyond the comprehension of most admirals because Napoleon Bonaparte was now in central Europe, far from the sea. So he wrote to his friend William Windham, Secretary for War, and despatched it to London three days after Nelson's funeral.

He began by urging an offensive spirit to guide the conduct of the war: 'Surely Lord Nelson's death ought not to operate so disadvantageously to us as to change our system into a simple and passive one of defence, when active, offensive operations towards destroying the enemy's means of annoying us and our allies are so much more efficacious to that end.' Then he came to the point. 'Knowing Bonaparte as I know him,' he wrote,

I can easily imagine his thirst to realize a *speculation manqué* on Constantinople and the route to India. He cannot fail to find it increase on being nearer to the capital of the eastern Empire

than he is to his own. He will be surrounded by Polish adven-
turers and Venetian navigators of the Black Sea, who will suggest plans . . . These he will propose in dictatorial style to the
Porte [The Sublime Porte, the colloquial term for the government of the Ottoman Empire, named after the Imperial Gate at
Constantinople] . . . He will send his army to garrison
Byzantium and the Dardanelles, while his Venetian flotilla
creeps along the coast of the Morea [Greece] and carries sailors
to man the Turkish fleet by way of balancing his loss at Trafalgar.
All this he can do if not counteracted . . . I dare say I shall be
looked to for the Herculean labour when the difficulties are
found.[6]

Sir Sidney, as prescient as he was presumptuous, was following
the gaze of the Emperor Napoleon, which was no longer fixed on
the cliffs of England but on the Levant and beyond. As Smith
was later to be told, Napoleon's Foreign Secretary, Charles de
Talleyrand-Périgord, said, when discussing the Emperor, that 'the
great end of his views was the wresting of India from England.'[7]

I

The spirit of Lord Nelson

A T THE beginning of April 1806 the *Pompée* passed between the Pillars of Hercules — the Rock of Gibraltar and Mount Hacho in Morocco — and entered the Mediterranean. To those officers with a smattering of classical education, this was the sea of the Ancient World: Greeks and Romans, Egyptians and Israelites, Phoenicians and Assyrians, more recently Crusaders and Venetians, all seen through a miasma of myth. To the practical seamen it was a perilous sea, deep and stormy, but the most acute dangers came from enemies because most of its shores were hostile.

Spain was allied to France and the French now occupied all of Italy — except for one fortress on a rocky headland — and the coasts of the Adriatic. Greece, Turkey, the Levant and Egypt were nominally ruled by the Ottoman Empire but it exerted a shaky hold over its diverse and quarrelsome peoples. Westward from Egypt, North Africa was ruled by a succession of beys and sultans, who still indulged in, or condoned, piracy and slavery but had to be humoured for the sake of the need to provision and water British ships in their ports.

Far to the north-east was the unpredictable colossus Russia, which could sway the balance of power and decide the future of Europe. Alliance, or at least friendship, with Russia was high in the priorities of British policy, for without Russian support the eventual defeat of France in continental Europe could not be imagined.

If Tsar Alexander I were to emulate his predecessor, the assassi-nated Tsar Paul I, and support Napoleon, they could, together and without undue difficulty, divide the Ottoman Empire between them.

So Russia was an ally, but an uneasy one. Partly this was due to Russian activity and ambition in the Mediterranean; and partly it was because of their longing for ice-free ports outside the Black Sea and the Baltic, both of which could be closed by a maritime enemy. Also it was due to fear of France and a unilateral move by Napoleon into the Ottoman Empire. This fear prompted their own moves for containing any French plan to reach Constantinople overland through the Balkans. So Greece and the Adriatic were of particular interest to the Tsar. He had despatched an expeditionary force as a strategic reserve and a strong naval squadron to the Adriatic, where it was based on Corfu and the Ionian Islands, which they had occupied – with British and Ottoman agreement – since 1799. Thus, when the British studied their strategic options in the Mediterranean, Russian power was part of the equation. At present, they were allies but they might not always remain so. The Mediterranean was, as in its distant, mythological past, fraught with strange and unexpected dangers.

Sir Sidney Smith knew these waters well. He had seen action here since the wars with Revolutionary and then Napoleonic France had begun thirteen years earlier. In 1793, in the western basin of the sea, he had burned most of the French squadron in Toulon before the port fell to the revolutionaries. In the eastern basin, six years later, he had held the port of Acre against General Bonaparte. With his brother Spencer Smith he had exerted power-ful influence at Constantinople; Spencer as British minister and himself, although a serving British officer, as nominal commander of the Sultan's armies and warships, when he was allied to Britain in the fight with aggressive France. This was much to the annoy-ance of Sir Sidney's naval superiors Admirals Nelson and Keith, who disliked divided loyalties and considered Smith an ambitious, albeit brave, upstart. Perhaps they were unaware, or only sus-pected, that Smith was, in fact, as much an intelligence officer, answerable directly to Whitehall, as a naval officer under their command.

The two basins of the Mediterranean were divided by the Italian peninsula and the islands of Sicily and Malta, both held by the British. It was Sicily that was considered the strategic key to the Mediterranean and that was Smith's destination. This large, triangular, mountainous island of 10,000 square miles seemed the keystone of future possibilities. Eight years earlier, young General Bonaparte had led a French army to Egypt to establish a French colony and open the way to India. When Nelson and Smith had expelled him, he had returned to become First Consul – in effect, dictator – of the French Republic. In 1801 the war had petered out in stalemate, with France dominant on land, Britain at sea; there was nothing one could achieve against the other. The dreamlike lull of the Peace of Amiens followed, to be broken in 1803 when Bonaparte had completed his rearmament and the rearrangement of his European allies.

Preparations for the invasion of England had begun and a *Grande Armée* of some 150,000 men assembled on the Channel coast. While waiting for his fleets to escape from their Mediterranean and Atlantic ports, Bonaparte crowned himself Emperor Napoleon, founding his own dynasty and addressing the monarchs of Europe on equal terms. The invasion threat had been ended by Nelson at Trafalgar. Although Napoleon had then already marched east to break the Austrian and Russian armies – the former at Ulm and both at Austerlitz – in the final months of 1805 he had intended only to postpone the invasion of England for perhaps a year. This was now an impossibility, but it was known that he still dreamed of conquest in the grandest, most heroic, style. The Corsican conqueror, who had mesmerized British visitors to Paris during the year of peace either as 'a profoundly studious and contemplative man'[1] or 'as a rattlesnake',[2] was noted by all as smiling with his mouth but not with his eyes. Now, like Alexander the Great, his eyes would turn eastward.

In consequence, the eyes of the British government were looking east, too. They were apprehensive. When William Pitt, the great Prime Minister of the wars with Revolutionary and Napoleonic France, had died on 23 January 1806 at the age of only forty-six, the country had seemed leaderless. He was replaced by a political coalition, a governing committee that was to be known optimistically as 'The Ministry of All the Talents'. Its members were indeed as talented as they were varied in view: their leader, Lord Grenville, a former Foreign Secretary, had been in government for most of the past quarter-century and had always supported the war against France, while his Foreign Secretary, Charles James Fox, the former Leader of the Opposition, had originally been opposed to war. All had become aware of rising danger in the east and it was they who had ordered the reinforcement of British strength in the Mediterranean.

So, on 21 April, the *Pompée* came in sight of Monte Pellegrino, the angular mountain that stands above Palermo. Fifty days out from England, she had arrived off Cadiz at the end of March and Smith had reported to the commander-in-chief, Lord Collingwood, whose command stretched from the Atlantic approaches to the Straits of Gibraltar to the Levant. Nelson's successor was aware of Smith's plan to pre-empt the climactic battle of Trafalgar by attacking the Cadiz anchorage with his 'infernals'. Nelson had been tolerant of such newfangled ideas, while distrusting them, but Collingwood had made his views clear to the First Lord of the Admiralty, Charles Grey. He reported his meeting with Smith when, as he put it:

> I endeavoured to impress upon him the inefficacy of that mode of war which is carried on by explosion-vessels and sky-rockets. I know no instance of a favourable result from them. They serve merely to exasperate, to harass our own people . . . As a general mode of warfare, they are unworthy of the English.[3]

In any case, Admiral Smith would have no use for such weaponry where he was going. The inshore squadron would be needed in the Mediterranean to protect Sicily from French invasion.

The two men were so different that it seemed they might prove uneasy as superior and subordinate. Collingwood, who had led the British fleet into action at Trafalgar, was now fifty-five, ten years the senior and the opposite of his restless friend Nelson. All were in awe of him as a hard-driving seaman. 'The fractious old admiral, ever on the fidget, is hurrying us to be ready for sea', complained one officer.[4] 'He should be transformed into a fish, or a sea monster, for his delight is in gales of wind and buffeting about – worrying all the other admirals, captains and crews to death.'[5] Described by one of his officers as 'thin and spare in person', he was

> slightly bent and in height about five feet ten inches. His head was small with a pale, smooth, round face, the features of which would pass without notice were it not for the eyes, which were blue, clear and penetrating, and the mouth, the lips of which were thin and compressed, indicating firmness and decision of character. He wore his hair powdered and tied in a queue.[6]

Collingwood could be witty and charming in the company of women and longed for his wife and daughters waiting in Northumberland, but was duty-bound to serve until recalled by the Board of Admiralty. But his officers often thought him 'an old bear', deploring that 'Old Collingwood likes *quiet* people.'[7] Some saw him more harshly; one frigate captain said, 'In body and mind he was iron and very cold iron – in heart, I believe, the same, except for one small, soft corner, accessible only to his family.'[8]

Smith, bright-eyed and shock-headed, vivid as a gypsy, was far from quiet. He talked so much about his exploits at the siege of Acre that he had been nicknamed 'Long Acre'. He sparkled with witticisms, wrote clever, sometimes *risqué*, doggerel and flirted outrageously, all in several languages, including fluent French. This he had perfected during the two years he had been held in Paris as a spy before being rescued from the Temple prison by French royalists acting on orders from Smith's superiors in the Aliens Office, the cover name for the headquarters of the secret intelligence organization in London.

But Collingwood was aware that beneath Smith's braggadocio was an imaginative officer, even if one more at home in the palaces of Europe and the Levant than on a quarterdeck. He might prove to be the ideal officer to send into the welter of intrigue swirling around the Bourbon court at Palermo. Whichever allies he encountered – be they Sicilians, Neapolitans, or Russians – or whichever neutrals – perhaps Turks and their subject peoples, or the unruly beys of North Africa – all would have something in common. All would be assessing the threats, or the favours, they could expect from the man who dominated Europe.

The place and the people that Smith was about to encounter were suited to his own theatricality; indeed, they verged on pantomime. The Kingdom of the Two Sicilies had been composed of the whole of Italy south of a border between Rome and Naples, which was its capital, and Sicily. Everything about this island, where both people and buildings bore the mark of Phoenicians, Greeks, Carthaginians, Romans, Vandals, Byzantines, Saracens, Normans and corsairs, seemed different and exotic: Greek temples and Norman cathedrals; lava and mosaics; sweet wine and blood oranges; traditions of generosity and secrecy. The Spanish Bourbon dynasty, which had ruled the double kingdom for the past seventy years, had twice been driven from Naples by the French during the past decade and had had to take refuge in Palermo. On the first occasion, in 1798, they had been rescued by Nelson, who had restored them in a bloody counter-offensive within a year. On the second, in February of this year, the Queen had abandoned Naples to join the King, who was finding the hunting and shooting in Sicily more congenial than affairs of state.

Queen Maria Carolina was the real ruler of what survived of the kingdom. The daughter of the Empress Maria Theresa of Austria and the sister of Queen Marie Antoinette, who had died by the guillotine in Paris thirteen years earlier, she was formidable. She had Habsburg looks: a long, pale face with bridged nose and determined chin, but pouchy-eyed, and a down-turned, thin-lipped mouth. Baron Alquier, when French ambassador to her court in Naples, had described her thus:

The Queen is neither good nor bad. Burns with a great deal of intelligence and natural grace and, thanks to her education, endowed with more knowledge than women usually possess, she had a fair claim to govern when she came to Naples and found a man on the throne incapable of governing. A relish for pleasure was mingled with a passion to dominate, hence the double intrigues of politics and gallantry . . . The Queen's life is a prolonged crisis of vapours.

Yet the ambassador marvelled at 'all this extraordinary woman can say in the course of an hour, things agreeable and strange, ingenious and absurd, surprising in their wisdom, or their folly'. Once handsome, noted for her stately carriage and the elegant poise of her neck, she was now aged fifty-four, and Alquier described her as 'this famous wreck of bygone graces and gallantries'.[9]

Since their first exile in Palermo, King Ferdinand IV had found that his own plebeian tastes – fishing with local fishermen and selling his catch in the market, hunting and shooting driven game in blood sports of almost Roman frenzy – could be enjoyed as fully in Sicily as around Naples, so he was seldom to be seen in the halls of the colossal Palazzo Reale, built by the Saracens and Normans and aglitter with mosaics. He was a gangling man with deep-lined face, a prow of a nose dropping straight from his 'low brow, pig's eyes'[10] to his large mouth with jutting lower lip, and nicknamed *Il Re Nasone* or, to British sailors, 'Old Nosey'. He was happy to leave the business of government to his domineering wife.

For her part, the Queen still missed the stimulating company of Lady Hamilton, the energetic, enthusiastic, overweight but handsome wife of the British minister to her court, Sir William, and their friend Lord Nelson. She had used Lady Hamilton as confidante and to influence Nelson, when he became Emma's lover, but for him she had particular gratitude and affection. Indeed, at the end of 1805 she had known that he was dead as soon as the first reports of a battle had arrived because he had not written to tell her about it. 'I shall regret him all my life', she mourned; 'for him it is happiness, for us a heavy misfortune,'[11] For Sir Sidney Smith, too, the dead hero held a special meaning. As he arrived at Palermo to meet the royal family, Sir Sidney was determined to 'show the government and the people that the spirits of Mr Pitt and Lord Nelson were still alive'.[12]

On going ashore, Admiral Smith was escorted past Baroque palaces and churches of golden stone, fountains and statues of nymphs and tritons and up the long, straight street paved with black lava to the Palazzo Reale. Some British officers found this disconcerting – the vast, painted salons, gazed down upon by wild-eyed, hunted deer and sad-eyed saints in mosaic, all under the tangible pressure of the Sicilian past – but not Sir Sidney, who was familiar with the exoticism of Constantinople. He was presented to the King, who was not hunting that day, and then to the Queen. At the sight of Smith – slightly built, alert as a terrier and sparkling with decorations – Maria Carolina responded as to the return of a friend and hero, although they had never before met. This was to be a second Nelson.

Radiating charm, talking rapidly in broken English and in French, she took the admiral on a *tour d'horizon*. Naples, her lost capital, set in its lovely bay, its own horizon bounded by the volcanic cone of Vesuvius, the dragonback mountains of the Sorrento peninsula and the island of Capri heaving out of the sea, haunted her. She missed the social activity, drawing so much from other European capitals – her mother's Vienna in particular – and on the procession of rich English visitors making the customary Grand Tour of Italy. But the tour seldom extended to the barren hills of Sicily. The Sicilian aristocracy, while it might be ancient, was poor company and coarse in comparison to the Neapolitan, and underlaid with a sulphurous tradition of intrigue and vendetta.

The Queen told Smith how Nelson had recaptured Naples with the help of her loyal subjects in Calabria, the mountainous, almost roadless south-western peninsula of Italy. He, Smith, must do the same. This was the cue for him to declare that he was the right man for the task. Had he not defeated General Bonaparte himself by stiffening the Turkish and Syrian garrison of Acre with a mere 800 seamen and marines? This he could repeat, raising the Calabrian peasantry and restoring Naples to her.

The Queen and the admiral established an immediate rapport and she spoke of him henceforth as 'the loyal Schmidt'.[13] She would receive him sometimes in the forbidding mass of the Palazzo Reale but more often in the elegant little oriental folly of a summer palace the Palazzina Cinese, in the park of La Favorita below Monte Pellegrino. There, amid the charming chinoiserie of a salon hung with English prints given to her by Nelson, they could weave their political fantasies. Their intimacy quickly aroused the suspicion and resentment of Hugh Elliot, the British minister in Palermo. The brother of Nelson's friend Sir Gilbert Elliot, the former Viceroy of Corsica and later Earl of Minto, he understandably assumed that politics and strategy were matters for himself. Smith spent much time ashore, often visiting the Queen twice a day, leaving Captain Dacres in charge of the *Pompée*, busy with the administration of punishment – two days after their arrival there were three floggings, two of them of two dozen lashes apiece – and preparations for the admiral's reception of the Queen's son the Hereditary Prince, to a salute of twenty-one guns.

Sometimes he would accompany the Queen at celebrations ashore, as for a royal birthday, such as described by one of his officers:

> This being the King of Sicily's birthday, the ceremonies, pomp, court and churches, etc., created such a bustle in the town . . . High Mass was performed by the Bishop in the great church, everybody in court dress, carriages driving about, bells deafening, cannon firing, etc., etc. Drums beating, both English and Sicilian, marching to all the alarm posts of the garrison, great guns and small arms, fireworks, more praying, bells, music and confusion occupied the whole day, which closed with a brilliant opera . . . At one o'clock went on board quite tired.[14]

Although Smith's meetings with the Queen overshadowed all else, he was made aware that he was not to be the only taker of operational decisions. The admiral would have to contend with a British general. Sicily had become the keystone of British strategy in the Mediterranean largely on the advice of Nelson, and in 1805 Sir William Hamilton and William Pitt had sent a small expeditionary force to the Mediterranean as a strategic reserve to protect Naples, Sicily and even Egypt from French attack. Four battalions with small detachments of cavalry and artillery had reached Malta on 18 July that year. It had been commanded by Lieutenant-General Sir James Craig, described by a contemporary as 'a pocket Hercules but with sharp, neat features as if chiselled in ivory'. An experienced professional, Craig was nonetheless 'not popular, for he was hot, peremptory and pompous',[15] favouring those he liked; he was also in poor health. At Valetta he received orders to co-operate with Russian troops – the Tsar was currently an ally – to protect Naples itself, cut the communications of the French in southern Italy and act in concert with Austrian allies in the north.

A combined Anglo-Russian army – some ten thousand Russians from Corfu and more than double that number from Black Sea ports – would combine with six or seven thousand British from Malta and land at Naples to support the Neapolitan army. The allied force had landed in the Bay of Naples in November 1805, to be greeted with news that the strategic outlook had been transformed by the defeat of the Austrians by Napoleon at Ulm and Nelson's victory at Trafalgar. There was now no clear plan, and British officers whiled away the days visiting the excavations at Pompeii and Herculaneum. An attack on Venice involving a voyage around Italy into the Adriatic was being considered when news arrived of the final defeat of the Austrians and Russians at Austerlitz in December. It was over. The Russians sailed for Corfu. King Ferdinand and his Queen again fled, abandoning Naples in February 1806 for Palermo. The British, too, re-embarked and sailed for Sicily. There Craig had found himself caught in the web of the Queen's intrigues and emotions.

So was Sir Sidney Smith, but he was content to be so for he, too, saw himself as the heir to Nelson and not only as a fighting admiral. He was aware that a fleet needed to be kept active and that long stays in port sapped morale, even when kept hard at work preparing for sea. One of his officers noted this:

> The usual routine of business going on in the fleet, all bustle, confusion and hurry to get water, provisions, repair ships, set rigging to rights, painting, etc., etc. This generally lasts for some days; the poor sailors fagged to death from daylight till after dark and frequently all night, and, when all is complete, *they* are the *only* class not permitted to enjoy a few hours on shore; so much for the brave fellows who are so conspicuous in their Country's cause – how these undaunted men submit is a matter of astonishment.[16]

No such restrictions applied to officers, and the same one described a picnic in Sicily at the same time, when at

a wild, retired spot a sumptuous entertainment was provided. Everyone pursued his plan of amusement till two o'clock, the

hour named to dine – some fishing, the water as clear as crystal
. . . and multitudes of fish, the appearance on the whole most
gratifying . . . Many amused themselves shooting and others
lounging around the tent, reading and superintending the display of eatables . . . We all did great justice to our collation and
drank out 20 bottles of wine, three dozen of porter and two
Noyau [a fruit liqueur]; of course we were merry enough and
some famous songs contributed to our hilarity.[17]

Aware of Nelson's concern for morale and the need for activity
at sea – as well as his own ambitions – Sir Sidney drew up a plan of
action and sent it to London, although it might well arrive after it
had been implemented. He wrote directly to his friend John
Barrow, the Second Secretary to the Admiralty, and the latter's son
was to record Smith's plans at this time: 'Of course, the plan of
operations was grounded on the minute of Lord Nelson placed in
the hands of Mr Pitt, which the latter had confidentially commu-
nicated generally to Sir Sidney Smith; the principal object being
that of recovering Naples and its territories from the French . . .
Sir Sidney lost no time in commencing operations.'[18]

2

Tally-ho, said I!

O N 3 May 1806 Monte Solaro, the highest point of the island of Capri, standing 2,000 feet above the Gulf of Naples, an echo of the cone of Vesuvius twenty miles away, was sighted from the deck of the *Pompée*. Sir Sidney Smith was heading not for Naples, however, but for a point forty miles north of the city, and he turned north-east towards the coast. Soon he could see the long, gentle curve of a bay below the shadowy mountains and, at its far end, a massive fortress crowning a rocky headland. This was Gaeta, the only scrap of Italy remaining in the control of King Ferdinand and Queen Maria Carolina.

Next day, as the ship drew nearer, it could be seen to be start-lingly reminiscent of Acre, where Smith had ended Napoleon Bonaparte's dreams of eastern conquest. Around the citadel on the summit huddled a small town and the domes and *campanili* of churches. This was ringed by ramparts with bastions and curtain walls of grey and honey-coloured stone rising sheer from the rock to hundreds of feet above the sea that surrounded it on three sides. The isthmus below was rocky, then flat and sandy and there could be seen the enemy's siege-works, which had now crept to within 250 yards of the outer defences: entrenchments, fascines, batteries and, beyond the range of the guns of Gaeta, rows of tents. Occasionally a flash and a gout of smoke and the thump of gunfire would carry across the water.

The *Pompée* anchored in the deep, clear water below the castle walls and Smith ordered ammunition to be sent ashore, starting with a hundred 24-pounder cannon-balls from his ship. When they were joined next day by another ship of the line, the *Excellent*, he ordered her captain to land four of his heavy main-deck guns and, as at Acre, British gunners. Soon Smith himself went ashore to meet the King's general, Prince Louis of Hesse-Philipstadt, a Westphalian mercenary, said to be the most effective general in the King's service. He commanded a garrison of some 6,000 men, two-thirds of whom were Neapolitan infantry, one-third, freed prisoners and galley-slaves, and a few trained artillerymen. Climbing to one of the fortress's seaward sally-ports, the admiral was told that the general was on the ramparts and that, indeed, he never left them, again a reminder of his own galvanizing of the defenders of Acre. He was led through a warren of alleys, steep flights of steps and tunnels to a bastion overlooking the scene of action. When they met, Admiral Smith and the Prince of Hesse could be seen to be kindred spirits, if different in looks. Like Smith at Acre, the Prince waged psychological warfare against the besiegers, although in far less subtle ways, shouting at them through a speaking-trumpet, 'Gaeta is not Ulm! Hesse is not Mack!'[1] (referring, to the French victory in 1805 and the defeated Austrian general), and he particularly enjoyed ordering a brisk bombardment of the enemy after dinner. Also like Smith, he was described by a contemporary as 'wild-brained'; he was small, rotund, rubicund, moustachioed and, it was said, 'though drunken and eccentric to the very verge of insanity, he was faithful, active and brave even to rashness . . . While his eye was on them, his men did their duty for they were more afraid of him than of an enemy; and his occasional buffoonery made him a favourite with the soldiers', whom he inspired as 'his daring example mastered their fears, their affection and their admiration.'[2] A British colonel described him as 'half crazy . . . dissolute and regardless of rules; but he was unsparingly active and unconquerably brave'.[3] He expected to be addressed as 'your Serene Highness', yet beneath the bluster was a sad figure, suffering from an unfaithful wife and aware of his own weakness for drink; remorseful after a heavy bout of drinking, he gave the key of his wine cellar to the Bishop of Gaeta with instructions that he ration him to one bottle a day. Like Smith, he was an optimist and did not seem perturbed that Marshal André Masséna, the senior French Officer in Italy, had just tripled the force on the isthmus to some 12,000 men, including, it was said, fourteen generals, and with more heavy artillery to follow.

At once the Prince of Hesse made use of the ammunition Smith had landed by ordering a bombardment of the enemy's entrenchments. Smith's little squadron had been joined by a convoy escorted by the *Intrepid*, bringing Neapolitan infantry to reinforce the garrison. The admiral responded to the Prince's enthusiasm when he returned to his flagship by ordering the boats of the squadron to be manned and armed for a seaborne raid. The boats landed sixty of the Prince's best soldiers behind the French lines to spike their guns and re-embark without loss. Three nights later the garrison of Gaeta made a sortie, supported by British and Neapolitan gunboats. In the two actions the British lost four seamen killed, but the French suffered about a hundred more casualties, added to the thousand already lost to cannon-fire, including two generals killed.

Confident that the Prince of Hesse could, with British naval support, hold the fortress indefinitely, Smith looked for other activity. He was aware that defence against a French attack on Sicily must be accorded higher priority than raising the siege of Gaeta, although he did not, of course, know that the Emperor Napoleon himself had written to his generals in Italy, 'La Sicile est tout et Gaete n'est rien;[4] and berated them for the unnecessary losses, while being aware that the siege was luring British warships away from the Straits of Messina, where the invaders would cross.

Naples might be Smith's next target. He knew that the Emperor's brother Joseph had been declared King of Naples and was about to arrive there, where he would be vulnerable to harassment from the sea. The siege of Gaeta had drawn French troops and artillery from Naples; if he attacked Naples, they would be ordered back again. So, leaving the Prince of Hesse in fine fettle, Smith led a squadron of four sail of the line south to the Bay of Naples, where he was joined by a fifth, the *Eagle*.

As it grew dark on the evening the ships came in sight of the city and its three castles, Ouvo and Nuovo on the waterfront to either side of the royal palace and Sant' Elmo on the hill above, it became apparent that their arrival had coincided with another. 'The city was illuminated on account of Joseph Bonaparte proclaiming himself King of the Two Sicilies!' reported Smith in his despatch to Collingwood.

> The junction of the *Eagle* made us five sail of the line and it would have been easy for their fire to have interrupted this ceremony and show of festivity but I considered that the unfortunate inhabitants had evil enough on them; that the restoration of the capital to its lawful sovereign . . . would be no gratification if it should be found a heap of ruins, ashes and bones . . . Not a gun therefore was fired.[5]

So, as the music drifted across the water from the windows of the Palazzo Reale, the squadron sheered away into the night.

At dawn the next day it lay some fifteen miles west of Naples, between the islands of Ischia and Capri, and Smith could see through his telescope the *tricolore* flying from the flagstaff of the little castle on one of the peaks of the latter. This then would be his next objective. The high, humped back of the island had long been a seamark for the Royal Navy but it had not been thought of strategic value. There was no port worth the name and it was only possible to anchor off the Marina Grande to the east, or the Marina Piccola to the west, in calm weather, or when one or other offered a lee shore. When the wind changed, it would be necessary to move to the other side; if from the north, or south, there would be no shelter whatsoever when the wind blew. Lying some twenty miles west of Naples, Capri, four miles long by two miles wide, rose to the summit of Monte Solaro. Otherwise the highest ground was the plateau where stood the village of Anacapri, separated from the town of Capri by a precipice of at least 1,000 feet. This could only be climbed by flights of narrow steps cut in its face by the Phoenicians, or, it was rumoured, by a goat track known only to the Caprese. The little capital of flat-roofed, whitewashed houses lay among the fig trees, vineyards and olive groves across a saddle between this cliff and a lesser mountain on which the Roman Emperor Tiberius had built a villa. Above the town on the seaward side stood the Castiglione on a peak of rock, guns on its ramparts commanding the little harbours to either side of the island.

Despite Napoleon's maxim that an island under threat should be defended either strongly or not at all, Capri was known to be held by a garrison of only about a hundred French infantry, commanded by a Captain Chervet. It seemed to Smith that, while the capture of the island would hamper, but not stop, the trade of Naples, it would be a useful observation post for the gathering of intelligence; as importantly, it would be a dramatic gesture of defiance since King Joseph would see British territory when he looked out of the windows of the Palazzo Reale. So Admiral Smith decided to summon Chervet to surrender; otherwise, he would attack.

Smith enjoyed the chivalrous etiquette of war and on 11 May he wrote a formal summons to surrender. If Captain Chervet refused to evacuate the island, he would be

> forced to yield upon terms more or less favourable, according to the degree of force and time which you oblige me to employ to reduce you to this extremity. Thus, sir, you see that the terms of the surrender of the post depend upon yourself *today*; in the hope of an answer which will spare blood on both sides. I have the honour to be, etc.

He received an immediate reply from Chervet declaring that 'a true soldier does not surrender till he has tried his force with that which attacks him. You are, sir, too good and brave a soldier to blame me if I do not accept your polite invitation.'[6]

So Smith ordered the attack to begin next morning. Captain Charles Rowley of the *Eagle* was to command it, with the admiral sending him his own marines and some seamen to help. At nine o'clock the ship glided close inshore, followed by two Neapolitan mortar-boats, and opened fire on the Marina Grande. The French seemed to have no artillery, but their infantry was deployed in vineyards outside the walls that surrounded the town of Capri above and they replied with musket fire, wounding the *Eagle*'s first lieutenant and killing a seaman. The ship fired for an hour and, when the sniping ceased, Rowley ordered the assault. The boats pulled ashore, the landing-parties scrambled on to the quay and 'mounted the steps, for such was their road'[7] between the houses and through the vineyards towards the town, led by Captain Bunce of the Royal Marines.

Captain Chervet had regrouped his men below the Castiglione for a counter-attack. British marines, led by a Captain Stannus, then gained the crest of the saddle where the town stood and made for what they called Castle Hill. There they met the French. Chervet was leading his men downhill to attack when Stannus shot him dead and his men wavered, halted and ran. There was a lull until a French drummer was heard to beat the signal for a truce and parley and a letter was delivered to Captain Stannus. It was an offer to surrender on the terms offered the day before. Admiral Smith disputed whether the terms offered yesterday applied today and finally agreed that, so long as the surrender was complete by midday, it would be accepted. The French marched down to the Marina Grande to the beat of their drums to embark in Neapolitan ships for the passage back to Naples. Capri was British. Realizing that his marines were few and could not be left to garrison the island, Smith at once wrote to Major-General Sir John Stuart, second-in-command to General Craig, asking for garrison troops to be sent urgently to the island.

On 6 May the *Pompée* was back at Messina. She was not a happy ship. While ashore, the crew of her barge vanished into the town, were then rounded up by British soldiers and sent back to the ship; next day twelve of them were given two dozen lashes each and the day after three more were flogged, while two other deserters suffered three dozen each. Captain Dacres regularly mustered the ship's company in the waist of the ship to witness punishment, usually for drunkenness and neglect of duty, sometimes for insolence, theft or just suspicion of theft. Admiral Smith kept aloof from this, staying in his cabin, which he had furnished in Turkish style with cushions and shawls festooned across the bulkheads, immersed in his plans for taking the offensive against the French.

He reported on the operations at Gaeta and Capri, sending ashore plans of the French siege-works before the former to be copied. General Stuart gave these to an engineer officer, Captain

Charles Boothby, for copying, saying, 'When you have finished the plan, Boothby, you will like an opportunity to meet with the hero of Acre. You will admire him of all things, but be sure, when you see him, he will take you to Acre.' Boothby took his copies on board the flagship and handed them to Smith, who, as the former later reported,

> good-naturedly said, 'So you are the young officer who has had the goodness to copy this for me. Well now, sir, just look here. They pretend to tell me this place is indefensible – *me*, who knows pretty well what determined hearts can do behind very simple barriers – who has seen a handful of men behind the angle of a wall bid defiance to the bravest troops led by the finest general in the world – I mean Mr Bonaparte at Acre.' Tally-ho! said I. I was really in pain lest a smile should be detected on my features . . . and that anxiety gave me an air of deeper attention to the inferences of strength and capability of Gaeta, which he drew from the defence of Acre.[8]

At Messina was the headquarters of General Stuart and his army of some 10,000 men – including mercenaries, notably Corsicans, with some British officers – mostly deployed there and along the coast to the west and south. Soon after Smith arrived, he and the general met to discuss the next naval and military moves. Despite the admiral's undoubted successes at Gaeta and Capri, the mood of the army officers was resentful because he had been indulging in warfare ashore, which was their element.

The admiral now asked the general for British troops to employ in coastal raids. But Stuart refused, dismissing the idea as 'too trivial' and declaring that, if he was to use his army on the mainland, it would be, as he grandly put it, for 'a descent on Calabria'.[9] Stuart's change in attitude from defensive to offensive was not, it was thought, so much due to the influence of the Queen but his own view that the Army should not be inactive while the Royal Navy's exploits would be reported in the London newspapers.

His new pugnacity delighted Smith and they began to assess the options. The French were scattered throughout the southern half of Italy. The bulk of Joseph Bonaparte's Army of Naples was in the trenches before Gaeta, while another 10,000 men plus the same number of irregulars were in the south. Those in Upper Calabria, commanded by General Verdier, were enmeshed in counter-insurgency since the Calabrese peasantry, the *massi*, enraged by French looting and attempts to conscript them for military service, were attacking their outposts and ambushing patrols. The French in Lower Calabria, commanded by General Jean-Louis Reynier, who had fought with Bonaparte in Egypt, were scattered between his headquarters at Cosenza and Reggio across the straits from Messina. Like most French armies, Reynier's had been told to live off the land and as Calabria was poor, barren, mountainous country they had also resorted to seizing food from villages. This, of course, had roused the anger of the hot-tempered Calabrese mountain men, who had been described as being as fierce as the Sicilians but without their redeeming qualities of generosity and loyalty; yet not all were hostile to the French, as local feuds set village against village and some sought the invaders' help in settling their own vendettas. French patrols were ambushed and captured, French soldiers castrated and roasted over bonfires; in revenge, the French burned villages and rounded up Calabrese men for execution; a state of confused war existed throughout the southern ranges of the Apennines. Despite this, Reynier managed to advance to the point of the south-western peninsula. There were no roads, and heavy weapons and ammunition transported by sea were vulnerable to attack by the British and Neapolitan navies. So his engineers managed to build a rudimentary road through Calabria to Reggio in the far south and along this, that summer, the first heavy weapons – two 24-pounder naval guns – were dragged. At Reggio, Reynier established a garrison of a thousand men, who from their nearby outpost at the castle of Scilla on the rocky coast were able to see the red coats of the British on the Sicilian shore.

If Smith's squadron could put a large force ashore between Cosenza and Reggio, Stuart would be able to cut Reynier's communications with the south and force his withdrawal northward, while also seeming to threaten Naples and drawing Masséna's army south from Gaeta. The most suitable landing-place would be the Gulf of Sant' Eufemia, a twelve-mile stretch of sandy beach at the point where the Calabrian peninsula narrows to only twenty miles between the Tyrrhenian and Ionian seas, its narrowest point. Smith promised Stuart his full support, but first it was essential that he visit Palermo and report to the British minister there, Hugh Elliot, and, more importantly, to the Queen.

At Palermo he was, as expected, given a hero's welcome and was entertained by the royal couple. The image of him as a second Nelson was now reinforced by official glorification. Nelson had been rewarded with a Sicilian dukedom and Smith with the Swedish knighthood in reward for his services as a mercenary in the Baltic – and now the latter was accorded a new rank with which he was familiar. Seven years earlier the Sultan of Turkey had appointed him commander-in-chief of all Ottoman forces in the Levant. Now, on 28 June, Smith, after many audiences with the Queen, invited her and the King to dine on board the *Pompée* when the King marked the occasion with a characteristically flamboyant gesture. Ignoring his earlier appointment of General Stuart as commander of the defences of the north-east and east coasts of Sicily, he created Smith Viceroy of Calabria, so, in effect, commanding all operational naval and military forces. This came as no surprise to one British officer, who wrote, 'I can easily believe, remembering their worship of Nelson, that it was a much easier thing for the King and Queen to give such a commission to a renowned naval officer, whom they might view as Nelson's successor, than to a British general.'[10] So, while Stuart would directly command British troops in Sicily and any landed on the mainland, Smith would not only be responsible for the Calabrese irregulars and Neapolitan troops as well as all naval forces but, apparently, could act as the commander in the theatre.

When Stuart was told that he might require Smith's authority to take action, he replied that he needed no higher authority than that of King George III, which he already had, and would continue to 'act perfectly independent of the Court of Palermo and its Councils'.[11] The Queen could now inspire, if not direct, military operations on the mainland, and Lieutenant-Colonel Henry Bunbury, the quartermaster-general, wrote, 'Sir Sidney Smith entered at once into her wild schemes of raising the Calabrese; and, without the slightest communication with Sir John Stuart, our naval commander was invested with unlimited authority on the land . . . as well as on the sea.'[12]

At this moment a despatch arrived from William Windham ordering offensive action as 'an enterprise on a larger scale, which could offer permanent advantage'.[13] This was exactly what Stuart and Smith had agreed, but the general and the admiral would have to co-operate. Even so, Stuart in Messina awaited word from Smith in Palermo about the reaction of Elliot and the King and Queen, or further orders from Collingwood, and he waited in vain.

Meanwhile there were changes in the British military command. General Craig had resigned because of failing health, leaving Stuart in temporary overall command. The new army commander, now on his way, was to be Lieutenant-General Henry Fox, the brother of Charles James Fox, the Foreign Secretary, who had been commanding a slovenly garrison at Gibraltar. At fifty-one, he seemed old, unhealthy and lacking in military flair. But he was to be followed by a new second-in-command, Lieutenant-General Sir John Moore, an innovative officer who had developed the techniques of light infantry fighting; moreover, he was to be accompanied by a reinforcement of four more battalions. So General Stuart's enthusiasm for 'a descent on Calabria' could also be due, it was being said, to his hope 'to give éclat to this command before the arrival of General Fox'.[14]

On 23 June an exasperated Stuart had written to Smith:

I have been much disappointed at not having had the pleasure of hearing from you since your arrival at Palermo on the subject of our discussions previous to your departure . . . Under these circumstances I have determined upon the immediate execution of the plan upon which we reciprocally agreed before our separation . . . St Euphemia, I before mentioned to you, had been the point of our observations. In every view it is the most favourable for our landing . . . Our movements will begin from hence on the 27th and should I not hear from you, or see your protecting flag with us before that period, I shall commit myself to the escort and assistance of your representative, Captain Fellowes, who tells me he has your full and kind deputation to concur with me in all objects of service.[15]

On the day after Stuart and his army embarked at Messina, Sir Sidney Smith was entertaining the royal family on board the *Pompée* and assuring the Queen that active moves to recover her lost capital were about to begin. Then he sailed, not to meet the convoy from Messina but north, towards Naples and his own adventures.

3

The glitt'ring bayonets shine

THE NORTH and east coasts of Sicily were busy in the last week of June 1806. British troops had become familiar to the Sicilians around their barracks and the billets in the coastal towns and villages of the north-east. There they paraded in red coats with coloured facings, white linen trousers and cross-belts, black shackoes with brass badges, while their officers wore dark blue trousers, having discovered a thin Sicilian silk that was comfortable in the heat. After more than a year in Sicily they were so deeply sunburned that one officer joked that 'that black visage of mine' had given him the looks of 'a Captain of Banditti'.[1] Increasingly, the silence of the mountainside was broken by the rasp of volleys as they exercised the rapid loading and firing of muskets on a shouted order when they deployed from column into two long, parallel lines with the aim of firing three volleys a minute. They had enjoyed garrison life in Sicily; although hot in summer, in winter it was, as one officer wrote, 'not as in England . . . amidst snows and frosts but delightful verdure, shady lanes and groves of oranges, the trees at this moment in full bearing blossom, green and ripe fruit on the very same tree, such is the orange and lemon at this period. It is winter at sea but summer in Sicily.'[2]

Now they were marching away and clearly something was afoot. Finally, on the evening of 26 June, the dapper little General Stuart left his headquarters and, as Captain Boothby recalled, 'A nice military figure, he jumped gaily into his carriage, laughing

with his aide-de-camp, and, nodding kindly, drolly and signifi-
cantly to the viva'ing Messinese, who, notwithstanding the pro-
foundest secrecy, had a pretty good guess what he was after, drove
rapidly off.'[3] The barouche swept him along the coast road to the
point of Faro, north of Messina, where the frigate *Apollo* was lying
offshore and he embarked. Meanwhile his troops boarded the
transports, fully provisioned and loaded with ordnance and stores,
anchored off Faro and at Milazzo to the west. That night they
sailed. As one officer of the 27th Foot speculated, 'Something
dashing is expected.'[4]

Isolation from the court at Palermo and the imaginative ideas of
Sir Sidney Smith, wherever he might be, had had its advantages.
General Stuart had an exceptionally able staff and regimental commanders, and together they had planned the coming operation. If
more than half of his army, about 5,000 men, embarked and the
rest remained to defend Sicily, he would probably outnumber any
force that the French could muster to meet him, which he thought
might amount to 4,000, although Sir Sidney had estimated it at
double that. All were now acclimatized because Sicily, although
hot in summer and cold in winter, was dry and healthy, and even
those who had never seen action were well trained. There would
be five infantry battalions: two of them, the 20th from Devonshire
and the 27th, the Inniskillings from Ireland – were veterans of the
campaign in Egypt seven years earlier – and three of them – the
58th, recruited in Rutland, the 78th Highlanders and the 81st from
Lincolnshire – were recently raised and untested, including the
young Scots of the 78th whose kilts and feather bonnets had
amazed the Sicilians.

There would also be foreign mercenaries: a battalion of Swiss
infantry, detachments of the tough Royal Corsican Rangers and
the footloose Royal Sicilian Volunteers. The artillery would con-
sist of a dozen small four-pounder guns, but there would be no
cavalry, although a few of the officers would be mounted and there
would be some horses and mules to carry the light guns and the
ammunition. Most importantly, Stuart formed a light infantry brigade from about a thousand specially trained sharpshooters drawn
from all the British battalions and the Corsicans. This was quickly
welded into an efficient force by Lieutenant-Colonel James

Kempt, a small, slightly built, spirited officer. His adjutant, Captain Richard Church, commented, 'In my whole life I never saw such harmony as pervades the whole.'[5] Stuart also formed a special grenadier battalion drawn from different regiments. The grand total was some 5,400 men, and this would leave Stuart's second-in-command, Brigadier Broderick, with four battalions for the defence of Sicily.

The bulk of the expedition would sail that night under convoy of Captain Fellowes in the frigate *Apollo* and two Neapolitan ships for the Gulf of Sant' Eufemia. Meanwhile 550 men of the 20th Regiment under Lieutenant-Colonel Robert Ross would embark in small sailing-ships and cruise off Reggio and south to the point of Cape Spartivento as if about to land, in the hope of convincing the French that that was their intention. So the main convoy sailed on the evening of 26 June, steering westward at first to keep out of sight of land on a passage expected to last three or four days.

They had passed the Lipari islands and then the steep cone of Stromboli when, on the northern horizon, they sighted what could only be a ship of the line. This proved to be the *Pompée*, but Sir Sidney Smith was not about to join their escort for he had different activities in mind. Although he had announced that he was going to cruise off Gaeta and Naples, he was, in fact, making for the coastal town of Amantea, to the north of the Gulf of Sant' Eufemia, which was held by a small French garrison and was under attack by Calabrese partisans.

Late on the hot, moonlit night of 30 June the convoy closed with the mainland; Captain Boothby later recalled that

> big with expectation and imagining the eventful future did I walk the deck, contrasting the fair heaven, refreshing sea and noiseless vessels with the dire principles of destruction and slaughter within them. Wistfully I looked towards the bold outline of the Italian shore, on which the condensing fleet was bearing with unflagging wing.[6]

Then phosphorescent surf was sighted, breaking on a long, pale beach, and the ships turned into the wind and dropped anchor. They had arrived off Sant' Eufemia.

General Stuart had planned the landing for two o'clock in the morning. However, it was seen that a thick, dark belt of scrub stretched the whole length of the beach beyond the sand, and that might conceal enemy guns. He decided to await daylight. As the sun rose, a small boat was seen pulling from the shore: on board were two armed Calabrese, who reported that there were no French troops on the beach, or in the bushes. So the landing began. Surf was heavy and the troops, scrambling up the sand, were soaked and much of their ammunition spoiled, but the boats returned to the transports for the second division. Soon the sun was hot and high and the sodden soldiers steamed in the midsummer heat.

They had come ashore near a small, deserted fort at the northern end of the beach named the Bastione di Malta, which became the principal rendezvous. They could now see from the ships' tops (platforms on the masts by the main yards) that inland there spread a wide arena, a plain bounded by *massifs* on the slopes of which small, whitewashed villages clung like scraps of cloud. To the east foothills and mountains gradually closed together in a jumble of summits, beyond which they knew that, only twenty miles from their beach, lay the Adriatic.

In the first light of day there was no sign of the enemy. Stuart ordered Lieutenant-Colonel John Oswald to take the first wave of troops – seven companies and the Royal Corsican Rangers – inland to the village of Sant' Eufemia, about a mile to the northeast and just below the lower slopes of the foothills. They advanced through the belt of scrub and low, wind-shaped trees and into a flat country of olive groves, vineyards and coppices. There was a sudden sputter of musket-fire. The Corsicans stopped, then fell back. As the British deployed and advanced from tree to tree, the enemy began to retreat. Oswald gave the order to charge and, as Captain Boothby described it, 'No fox-hunters after a long frost could appear to enjoy their sport more than our soldiers as they ran at the enemy with shouts and cries of delight.'[7] The enemy were outflanked and some captured. They proved to have been some 400 skirmishers, French and Polish. Twenty had been wounded, and two officers and about a hundred men were captured; one British soldier had been wounded.

From the prisoners it was discovered that the French commander, General Reynier, had taken up a position on high ground at the head of the valley about ten miles from Sant' Eufemia; one prisoner claimed that his army numbered between 27,000 and 30,000. Stuart decided that it would be prudent to fortify his beachhead in case of a hasty evacuation under fire and he ordered Boothby, the engineer, to dig an entrenchment on the beach, using a nearby stream to create a moat; this and the nearby tower were to be held by the Swiss battalion. The main force was then marched forward and entered the village of Sant' Eufemia to take up positions between there and Nicastro, on the lower foothills of the mountains to the north. The villagers gave them a cautious welcome, fearing the return of the French, but some 200 armed Calabrese, described by Bunbury as 'ruffians of the lowest type',[8] did volunteer to join the British.

More intelligence began to reach Stuart. Reports put Reynier's strength at only 2,000 to 3,000. If this was true, an immediate advance and attack would be essential before reinforcements could reach him from French garrisons in the south. After dark that night the mystery of his exact whereabouts was solved. At the head of the wide valley, on high ground below the hilltop village of Maida, could be seen the lights, lanterns and camp fires of the French. Reconnaissance was required and Stuart and a small staff and escort mounted some of the few horses and cantered across the plain towards the distant hills. Across the levels spread olive groves and vineyards; there were scattered copses and the several narrow water-courses winding towards the sea, fringed with rushes and bamboo. As they rode east, they saw that the trees and foliage thinned and beyond there appeared to be open country, where buffalo were grazing. To the south rose the foothills of the Apennines, thickly wooded with evergreen oak, and these they began to ascend. At the same time General Reynier and his staff were also on reconnaissance in the same wooded hills, but so intent were both parties on their mission that neither sighted the other. Had they done so, decision by battle might have proved unnecessary.

When Stuart returned, he saw that Captain Fellowes had shifted the *Apollo* close inshore to cover the beachhead with her guns; but of Sir Sidney Smith there was no sign. He was still off Amantea, summoning the French garrison to surrender. On 1 July he had bombarded their positions, then sent muskets and ammunition to the Calabrese partisans, who were hovering outside the village. He also put ashore one of the most notorious of the Queen's agents, Colonel Michele Pezza, known as 'Fra Diavolo' because of his devilish reputation.* But the French did not surrender, and next day he went ashore himself with his marines but with no more success, as is suggested by the flogging of seven of them for drunkenness on board the *Pompée* next morning. He also spent much of the day composing a long letter to General Stuart, explaining why he was not supporting him in his 'present manly and, I will venture to say, glorious undertaking,'[9] adding his explanation as to why he had been appointed Viceroy of Calabria. This was as vague as it was long-winded, blaming the divided commands of the Neapolitan forces for his inability to relieve Gaeta, where, he said, the Prince of Hesse might have to surrender. Smith's critics now suggested that he and Stuart had become rivals and that Sir Sidney thus preferred to concentrate on igniting revolt in Calabria. In any case, having signed this letter, the admiral at last ordered Captain Dacres to steer for the Gulf of Sant' Eufemia.

Three days had passed since the landing. Sant' Eufemia itself, near the beach, and Nicastro, in the foothills, offered relatively healthy bivouacs for the troops while the plain itself looked unhealthy with its marshes and thick greenery. General Stuart assessed intelligence reports that Reynier, ten miles away in the hills across the plain, could field about 4,000 infantry, 300 cavalry and 4 guns but was daily expecting 3,000 reinforcements from the south. The danger was that he would move north to join General Verdier's army and together they would return to attack the British with overwhelming force. So Stuart decided that he should attack Reynier's army immediately to prevent such a concentration and that his objective must be a valley running past the enemy's left, or southern, flank, which seemed vulnerable.

There was no further sign of the enemy until, on 3 July, it was reported, 'a sergeant, who was straggling from the camp, was shot through the head by a Frenchman, who had concealed himself in a bush.'[10] Although Colonel Ross's 20th Foot had not yet arrived,

---

*He was later captured and executed by the French.

Stuart decided to attack. Before the advance could begin, Stuart marched his army along the beach as far as the widest of the streams flowing across the plain and into the sea, the Lamato (or Amato). The beach was of coarse, soft, silver-grey sand, scattered with pumice-stones, across which the soldiers trudged, each carrying his musket, sixty rounds of ammunition, rations and pack. By the time they reached the mouth of the Lamato, they were exhausted.

The British army – 4,570 men and three horse-drawn guns (the rest being left to defend the beachhead) but, of course, no cavalry – then turned inland, marching in columns, first through trees and undergrowth, then over marshes by the streams towards open ground below the distant heights of Maida, keeping to the north bank of the Lamato. They did not know what to expect. Captain Thomas Dyneley of the Royal Artillery noted that, after receiving orders at ten o'clock the night before to advance with two guns under his command, he had marched all night and 'at daybreak found myself on the plain of Maida'. It had been hard going over rough, scrubby, sometimes boggy ground, but now the bulk of the British were deployed across open country. Ahead they could see the French camp on the hillside, 'in a most beautiful position in a wood of full-blown myrtle bushes as white as snow'.[11]

From the hillside General Reynier watched their advance with satisfaction, believing in his superior numbers and the experience of his army. His reinforcements had arrived – some from Reggio, having marched eighty miles in three days – and his force was now at least 6,500 strong, including 300 cavalry. He wanted a quick decision, catching the British off-balance and before they could rally the Calabrese; in any case, the partisans already presented a threat, particularly by sniping from the woods to the rear of the French positions. So he gave the order to strike camp and march down the hillside to meet the British on the plain. Reynier was confident of victory. His troops were acclimatized, hardened by fighting in rough country against the Calabrese, and many of them were seasoned by other campaigns; some had fought the British in Egypt. Their morale was high and the night before striking camp they had been drinking to an expected victory. Reynier was particularly proud of his light infantry and one of its two regiments, the *1ère Régiment d'Infanterie Légère*, was commanded by Général de

Brigade Compère, who had fought throughout the wars of the Revolution and in Bonaparte's Italian campaign. These men, accustomed to victory and brimming with confidence, marched downhill, building up momentum and pace. The British, who had expected to have to storm the heights, were amazed. Major Roverea, aide-de-camp to Brigadier Cole, who commanded the British left flank, recalled, 'Imagine our surprise and joy when we saw the French troops leave their advantageous position to descend into the plain!'[12]

As the armies began to close, those on the beachhead turned and saw approaching the beach a ship of the line with open gun-ports. This was, at last, the *Pompée*. Sir Sidney Smith ordered that she be moored close inshore so that the guns could cover the beach in case of a precipitate retreat. Officers climbed to the tops and from there, as the ship's log recorded, 'At 5, observed the British Army advancing towards the Enemy, who were observed in a line and marching to meet them. Weighed and made sail inshore to assist the right wing of the Army in case of need.'[13] The French had been seen debouching from the scrub in two columns 'with drums playing and colours flying'.[14] This was their custom but Reynier, expecting the British to fight in line and recognizing the vulnerability of columns to the concentrated fire from extended lines of infantry, ordered deployment on the march into line formation, three-deep.

Keeping the Lamato and its boggy banks to their right, the British had moved east in echelon towards the hills of Maida in four divisions, with Colonel Kempt's light infantry on the right flank and in advance of the others. The river could easily be waded and Kempt took the precaution of sending Corsican skirmishers across it and into the woods beyond to guard against surprise attack. Reynier had also sent skirmishers into the woods but his main force had forded the stream and now faced the British on its northern side, also advancing in echelon with light infantry – Compère's 1st *Légère* – in advance. The British had also deployed into line, but two-deep.

Then Dyneley, accompanying Kempt's force, heard 'a slight "poppery" '.[15] Skirmishing had started in the woods on the far, southern side of the river. Kempt's Corsicans were first to come under fire and were charged and driven back, while British reinforcements splashed across the stream to join the fight. A British company commander was shot dead before the French fell back and the army's right flank was secured. The two armies were now in sight of each other, both advancing steadily. The guns of both opened fire, the light French field-pieces sending their shot whirring overhead, or falling short, while the British, firing from the right flank, made better shooting. The two armies, less than a mile apart, were, as Major Roverea put it, 'in parallel lines, in march towards each other, on a smooth and clear plain, and in dead silence only interrupted by the report of the enemy's guns; it was more like a chosen field fixed upon by a general officer for exercise, or to exhibit a show fight.'[16]

Now they heard the drumming of hoofs, first as startled herds of buffalo stampeded to ironical cheers from the French army, then as the French cavalry charged. The *Chasseurs* did not attack but galloped between the lines in whirlwinds of dust, trying to shake the nerve of the infantry they threatened. It was now nearly nine o'clock, the sun was high and a heat haze was gathering across the plain.

Kempt halted his men and ordered them to drop their packs and rolled blankets. They stood in the two ranks in which they would meet the French, while Dyneley's guns moved forward and stopped ten yards to the front of their flanks. The British 'Brown Bess' musket fired a slightly heavier ball than the French, but training alone dictated the rate of fire. Muzzle-loaded muskets required the soldier to bite open his paper cartridge containing ball and powder, then hold the ball in his mouth while pouring a little of the powder into the priming-pan and the rest down the barrel, ramming in the paper to act as wadding, and the ball after it. Although under ideal conditions in training a skilled man could load and fire five shots a minute, when firing volleys in action the rate was about three; so, when deployed in two lines, one rank would be reloading as the other fired. Before the general issue of rifles accuracy was poor so the effective range was about 100 yards, 150 at most; to fire at greater distance was usually a waste of ammunition. One of the most important decisions an infantry officer was likely to take was exactly when to shout 'Fire!'

The two most effective opponents faced each other on the north bank of the Lamato. Directly opposite Kempt's Light Brigade was the 1st *Légère*, supported on its right by the 42nd Regiment, which had fought the British in the Netherlands during the Revolutionary War. 'Never did I see a finer and more soldier-like body of men', thought Colonel Bunbury. It now became clear that Reynier had deployed his infantry in three divisions: the other light infantry regiment, the 23rd *Légère*, on his right and, in the centre, a Polish and a Swiss battalion. In front were his cavalry, 300-strong, the 9th *Chasseurs*, and his four field-guns.

In the British line of battle, the 81st and 78th Foot were in the centre, next to Kempt's light infantry and the grenadier battalion, and the 27th Foot were on the left, while the 58th Foot and some of the Swiss mercenaries were held in reserve. The weakness of the British was their left flank, which seemed vulnerable to sniping from scrub and to being turned by cavalry; the artillery was between and just in advance of the infantry divisions. A British major was impressed, remarking, 'Our troops as steady and in as good order as on the parade-ground, *vis-à-vis* the French, also in line, their arms glittering in the sun.'[17] It was nine o'clock and hot. When the range had closed to about 500 yards, Reynier, on horseback with his staff, gave the order to halt, load muskets and fix bayonets, then march on.

When Kempt's line was still more than 100 yards distant, the 1st *Légère* presented their muskets and fired. It was a volley at extreme range and when the smoke cleared the red-coated line still stood. Reynier ordered the attack, and all along the line the French drummers beat the *pas de charge*. Compère shouted, 'Ne tirez pas! Ne tirez pas! A la bayonette! A la bayonette!' (Don't fire! With the bayonet!) And Kempt ordered, 'Steady, Light Infantry! Wait for the word! Let them come close, let them come close!'[18] It was to be a test of French *élan* against British doggedness.

The British had no time to straighten their line and were still stepped in echelon, so that it would be Kempt's men who took the impact of the charge. They saw the massed bayonets sweeping towards them to the fast beat of drums. Now the months of training on Sicilian hillsides would be tested. When the French seemed hin a hundred paces, Kempt shouted, 'Fire!' and the volley crashed, its smoke hiding what it had done. Swiftly the infantry reloaded. The impetus of the French was such that they came on but not in the mass as before, and at twenty paces came a second volley, 'fired into their faces'.[19]

The French line was shattered, its leading officers – Compère among them – shot down. Those still on their feet looked about, saw the carnage and the British bayonets ahead and turned back. At this Kempt ordered the charge and his men bounded forward. Some French turned to fire what should have been their own devastating volley, but it was only scattered shooting and they ran on. Soon the British were among them, stabbing them as they ran till most of the 1st *Légère* lay strewn across the battlefield. As the British raced past Captain Dyneley, he ordered his little guns to be dismantled and loaded on to the backs of waiting horses for the move forward. A second wave of light infantry ran past him with bayonets fixed.

Fighting spread across the front. In the centre the Highlanders of the 78th loosed their volley, then the files fired independently. 'Well they did their work!' noted Ensign Joseph Anderson. The Scots were ordered to charge, but, recalled the ensign:

the French at the same moment following our example and advancing towards us at a steady charge of bayonets, the rolling of drums and endless loud cheers . . . It was not till we got within five or six paces of each other that the enemy veered, broke their ranks and gave way, turning away to a man and scampering off, most of them throwing away their arms . . . but our men got up with some of them and numbers were either bayoneted, shot or taken prisoners.[20]

The French division next to the impact of Kempt's men saw its flank gone and fell back. In the centre the Poles gave way, although the Swiss made a stand. At the far side of the battlefield the *Chasseurs*, and the 23rd *Légère* on Reynier's right, thrust at the British flank, throwing out skirmishers to enfilade the grenadiers and the 27th Foot. It seemed that, while the British had triumphed on their right, they might fail on their left and the course of the battle might be reversed. Gun-flashes had set fire to dried grass and crops, and the smoke hid the confusion of the British as the young Highlanders tried to form a square to meet a cavalry charge. The *Chasseurs* galloped through the smoke in a final, encircling sweep, into what they expected to be the frayed edges of the British flank, but ran into a hail of shot. The sudden, crunching volley had been fired by Colonel Ross's 20th Regiment of Foot, just arrived on the battlefield.

After making their feint landings off Reggio, Ross's ships had headed for Sant' Eufemia and his 550 men had landed that morning. Hearing gunfire in the east, he had at once marched his men towards the distant smoke, reached the rear of the British army and been told where the danger lay. As his men, fresh and eager, heard the rumble of cavalry hoofbeats, Ross shouted, 'You have the advantage, soldiers! The sun is in their eyes.' Then the 20th fired their devastating volley and the *Chasseurs* wheeled away, as Dyneley saw it, 'to the cheers and hisses of the whole of our troops'.[21] Then Ross's line swung right, driving back the French and enfilading Reynier's flank. It was now eleven o'clock and a decision had been reached.

Those waiting at Sant' Eufemia to defend the beachhead saw the smoke and heard the guns and the volleys but could not guess the outcome. Then a mounted British officer galloped up and Captain Boothby called out to him, 'What have you done? We are half dead with anxiety!' 'Would you had been with us', came the reply. 'Never was anything more complete. They are all but destroyed. I came to tell you that you need stay here no longer. We don't think of entrenchments now.'[22]

Boothby mounted his horse and rode forward. He could soon see the French streaming away into the hills. As he arrived on the battlefield, British sailors from the ships offshore were already removing the wounded of both sides, supervised by midshipmen riding donkeys. Compère, his arm shattered by a musket shot, was lifted on to a horse to be taken to the beach and, as he passed through resting British infantry, he shook his fist, 'cursing and swearing with the most voluble bitterness'. Sergeant Farquhar McCrae, who was fluent only in Gaelic, took pity on what Ensign Anderson described as 'gallant French soldiers weltering in their blood and groaning in agony from the most fearful wounds', and made for the river to bring them water, when one of them raised his musket and fired, hitting him in the arm. McCrae wrested the weapon from him by the muzzle and, raising the butt, 'said, with a Gaelic oath, "I'll knock your brains out!" ' But he paused, then walked to the river to bring the Frenchman water.

Other prisoners were more sanguine. One remarked that, 'They told us the English were fish that could only fight by sea.'[23] Boothby recalled, 'It was a field of battle smoking with recent carnage, peopled with prostrate warriors distorted with the death agony, harnessed for battle in gay colours, feathers and gold but stained and bathed in their own life-blood.'[24] He saw the dead of the 1st *Légère*, which had lost three-quarters of its strength, noting that 'all lay in one direction, in the attitude of headlong, desperate flight . . . this beautiful regiment . . . was almost totally destroyed.'[25] When the wounded were taken aboard the ships for treatment, it was noted that 'all the French lay on their faces, being stabbed in the back; while all the British lay on their backs, being shot in front.'[26]

It was midday, and Colonel Bunbury saw the British infantry 'resting on their arms, gasping with heat and thirst, and watching through the dust the rapid retreat of the French', who were being pursued into the hills by Kempt's light infantry. There was no water except in the muddy Lamato, so General Stuart ordered them back to the beach, where drinking water could be landed from the ships. He himself was riding to and fro, exclaiming, 'Begad, I never saw anything so glorious as this! There was nothing in Egypt to equal it! It's the finest thing I ever witnessed.'[27] That morning he had taken the offensive without any clear plan, but now he found himself the victor thanks to the professionalism of his infantry. He still lacked initiative, complaining that if he had any cavalry he could completely destroy Reynier's army as it fled east towards the Adriatic. He was wary of committing his foot-soldiers too deeply, but he did send Kempt's brigade further in pursuit and some of them followed the French as they fell back on Catanzaro, twenty-five miles away. Kempt's men were tired, footsore and lacked the numbers and ammunition to attack a defended town, although they came in sight of it and of the Adriatic. There was always the risk that

Verdier's army to the north might strike south and cut Kempt off from Sant' Eufemia, so he was ordered to retire.

At the beachhead the entrenchments had been abandoned and, as Cole's brigade — the 27th Foot and the grenadier battalion — marched down to the beach they were told that they could bathe in the sea. Having piled arms and stripped, several hundred tired men plunged into the surf. As they larked in the water, Bunbury reported:

> A staff officer came galloping in from the front, crying aloud that the enemy's cavalry were coming down! In a moment, the troops sprang to their arms and formed; and Cole's brawny brigade, rushing out of the sea and throwing their belts over their shoulders, grasped their muskets and drew up in line without attempting to assume an article of clothing. The alarm was utterly groundless; a great dust and an imperfect view of a herd of scampering buffaloes had conjured up a vision of French *chasseurs* in this noodle of an officer.[28]

In bivouacs ashore and away from the beach the British troops were uncomfortable, cooking their small ration of buffalo meat over wood fires and sleeping on the ground. Captain Boothby tried to build a bed and shelter of wheat and flax, although warned by a Sicilian that 'this generated a malaria'.[29] The marshy margins of the streams bred mosquitoes which kept them awake, although they were not thought to be the source of any infection. It was not only mosquitoes, but 'all insects of nocturnal wing, especially the large, cold, chaffy locusts, with which the country was covered . . . as big as one's thumb'. He passed a miserable night.

> My under-lip, like that of all the officers, has almost cleft in two by the effect of the sun and the night air, so that to laugh or smile brought tears into one's eyes and every time the wind dashed a locust against my face I gave myself a slap on the chops that stung my poor lip to distraction. Then it began to rain like the deuce and, soon giving weight to the wheat at top, the branches could no longer support it so down it all came, wet corn, branches and insects, all at once on my face.[30]

Captain Charles Stevens of the 20th Foot noted that 'the first night we were in bivouac, a large snake crawled over me; we were lying down amongst high grass. I felt most uncomfortable afterwards and hardly closed my eyes again.'[31] However, there were tortoises about and these sometimes supplemented the buffalo meat.

Meanwhile General Stuart rode back to Sant' Eufemia, where he saw the *Pompée* anchored close inshore, and the admiral invited the general to spend the night in the relative comfort of his flagship; Stuart gratefully accepted. The two men had not met since Smith had been appointed Viceroy of Calabria and been given command of all land forces, other than the British, and he began by again trying to soothe the general's bruised feelings. 'This appointment would have been more suitable for you,' he began, disarmingly, 'but I made no difficulty about it, thinking it a great object that *one* of us should have it and the whole powers of the commission are quite as much at your disposal as if your name had been placed on it instead of mine.'[32] Then Smith changed the subject and, 'as was his usual custom', told the story of his defence of Acre, including the moment when the continuous gunfire had suddenly stopped and 'everybody jumped up in consternation, exclaiming, "What can be the matter!"' There was no discussion of future plans ashore or at sea, and 'Sir Sidney closed the evening by taking one of the many shawls with which his cabin was hung and instructing Sir John in the art of wreathing it and putting on the turban after the fashion of the most refined Turkish ladies.'[33]

But, before going ashore next morning, the general did raise with the admiral the question of future plans. Other than the pursuit of Reynier, the obvious option was the relief of Gaeta, for which Sir Sidney was well equipped. Stuart agreed that he could take a thousand British troops to reinforce the garrison, together with ammunition and provisions. Smith readily agreed to sail north, but no specific plans for embarking and convoying the troops were made. Then Stuart went ashore and led a column inland again, climbing the hill to the stone-built village of Maida to assess the military situation and write an order of the day for his army and his despatch for London.

Some of Kempt's troops were at Maida, as were Calabrese partisans, who were 'hourly bringing in prisoners from the mountains'.[34] Dating his message to his troops, 'Plains of Maida, 6th July, 1806', he began, 'Major-General Sir Jno. Stuart finds himself incapable of expressing to the troops the sentiments excited in him by their brave and distinguished conduct in the late affair on the 4th, in which they gained so signal a triumph over a boasting and insolent Enemy . . . The troops will add another immortal wreath to the laurels of the British Army . . . Every soldier the general has the honour of addressing will have equal right with himself to make the boast hereafter that he bore a part in the Glorious Battle of Maida.'[35]

General Stuart had reason to be pleased. He estimated that the French had lost 'upwards of 2,000' in killed, wounded and prisoners – some 700 French corpses had been buried on the battlefield and later calculations show that his estimate was approximately right – against British casualties of 1 officer and 44 other ranks killed and 12 officers and 270 other ranks wounded. Reynier now risked being isolated in Lower Calabria unless he retreated north to join Verdier. This would allow the Calabrese to intensify their guerrilla attacks on the southern towns still held by the French, notably Reggio and Scilla, on the Straits of Messina. Sicily was no longer threatened with invasion and the object of Stuart's expedition had thereby been achieved. Now he could return to Sicily. He gave the order on 7 July that, while some would return by sea, most of the army was to march south, capturing French garrisons on the way to the Straits of Messina.

When news of the first British victory over Napoleonic France on the Continent reached London a few weeks later, joy was unbounded, church bells rang and balladeers, who had lain fallow since Trafalgar, again flourished their pens. One effusion ran

> And now! the raptured Muse in martial strains,
> Sounds Stuart's triumph on Calabrian plains!
> The French appalled! Bold Kempt pursues the blow,
> And deals destruction, midst the flying foe;
> With horrid crash the clashing muskets meet,
> And pierced foes lay prostrate at his feet;

In contest close, the glitt'ring bayonets shine,
Thrust follows thrust and wounds the steel enshrine;
Then countless numbers strew the carnag'd green,
And some by flight escape the blushing plain.[36]

4

Childishness, wickedness and folly

NEWS OF the victory at Maida reached Palermo on 8 July, to the joy of the Queen, who now saw the recovery of Naples as only a matter of time. But other events were now in train, including changes in the British command. The successor to General Craig, for whom Stuart was deputizing, was to be Lieutenant-General Henry Fox. Old for his age and tubby of build at fifty-one – he was likened to a Buddha – and lacking any military reputation, he was, however, to be followed by his dynamic second-in-command, Lieutenant-General Sir John Moore, and a reinforcement of four battalions.

Two ships bearing these officers were already crossing the western basin of the Mediterranean. The first was the battleship *Orion*, carrying General Fox, his jolly wife, two pretty daughters, his staff and their maids from Gibraltar to Messina, where she arrived on 22 July. They had had a swift voyage, outrunning General Moore's ship, the frigate *Chiffone*. The commanding officer of the *Orion*, Captain Edward Codrington, who had fought at Trafalgar, pointed out to the young Louisa and Caroline Fox 'the tops of the mountains, which form the distance, rising one above another from the shore! . . . nowhere better seen than when the western sun is full upon it and just beginning to sink behind the Sicilian mountains', although they were disappointed that 'Etna would not smoke for us'.[1] After disembarking at Messina, Fox met Brigadier Broderick, who was in command in the absence of General Stuart

and who had just received an ecstatic letter from the latter reporting his victory. Fox's written orders from London stated that the
defence of Sicily would continue to take priority and that British
land forces would be held there to counter any French moves
towards the Levant.

General Moore's ship, two weeks behind the *Orion*, had been
delayed off Cadiz when he had gone on board the flagship *Ocean*
to meet Lord Collingwood. Although Fox had been given both
the principal military and political appointments, Moore was
regarded by his superiors as far more important, and he had been
allowed to choose his own staff for the Mediterranean. Only one
other general in the British Army was held in such regard and that
was Major-General Sir Arthur Wellesley (the future Duke of
Wellington), who had returned to Britain from successful campaigning in India. Sir John Moore, now aged forty-five, had
fought in Corsica, the Caribbean, the Netherlands and Egypt, but
had attracted particular attention during the recent threat of a
French invasion of England. Commanding a brigade at Shorncliffe
on the coast of Kent, the main force to counter a landing in the
south-east, he had pioneered light infantry tactics, using the newly
introduced rifle. Moore cut a fine figure, with an alert face and
quick eyes, often masking his shrewd perception with easy banter.
He had, however, fallen out with Sir Sidney Smith, who had then
tried to persuade him to join an amphibious attack on the French
base at Boulogne. Moore had complained to William Pitt, the
Prime Minister, and to the Duke of York, the Commander-in-
Chief of the Army, that the scheme was hare-brained and it was
quashed. Moore and Smith, both brave and active, were otherwise
opposites: the former, the pragmatic pessimist; the latter, the over-
enthusiastic optimist.

Before leaving London, Moore had been briefed on future
strategy. The Emperor Napoleon was thought to be in Paris but
still embroiled in plans for the conquest of the Continent. Having
crushed the Austrians and Russians at Austerlitz the year before, he
was now turning his attention to Prussia and then there was the
possibility of a new campaign against a recovered Austria and
Russia. He might well move farther east, as the Ottoman Empire
and India still enticed him now that the Royal Navy had put an

end to his plans for expansion in the Caribbean and North America and the invasion of England. That was why the British were strengthening their presence in the Mediterranean. Lord Collingwood reinforced this view with his more up-to-date knowledge of that theatre.

Collingwood stressed the naval threat. There were eleven sail of the line in Cadiz ready for sea, and four more soon would be. Seven or eight were in Cartagena and another four or five in Toulon. He was sure that they would try to combine but this time it would not be for an attempt to invade England; it would be to overwhelm the British in the Mediterranean and fulfil some grand design that could only be imagined. They might strike at Sicily, or Constantinople or Alexandria.

Sir John reached Messina on 5 August, to be regaled with descriptions of the Battle of Maida. After the abortive pursuit of Reynier, he was told, most of the army had headed south on 12 July to attack the garrisons of the southern Calabrian towns, notably Reggio and Scilla, just across the straits from Messina. Captain Boothby, the engineer, had been sent forward alone on horseback to advise the British command on siege-works and, as he approached Scilla, he found that

> the road lies over bold mountains and is so intricate and devious I lost my way . . . but, having the near-sounding sea as a general guide, sometimes showing itself through the cleft of two mountain peaks and sending up the report of every gun fired on its surface multiplied by the muffled echoes of the mountains . . . The incessant sound of guns advertised me of my approach to the scene of action and soon by one of those dangerous paths whereon a horse moves with difficulty and a stumble would precipitate both horse and rider many hundred feet, I descended to the small marine town of Scilla (bounded to the south by the peninsula rock on which the besieged castle stood), and saw on its highest tower the tricolour flag flying.[2]

Reggio fell quickly, but the defences of Scilla were more formidable. The British had only been able to bring up their light field-guns, carried across country by pack-horses, and these were

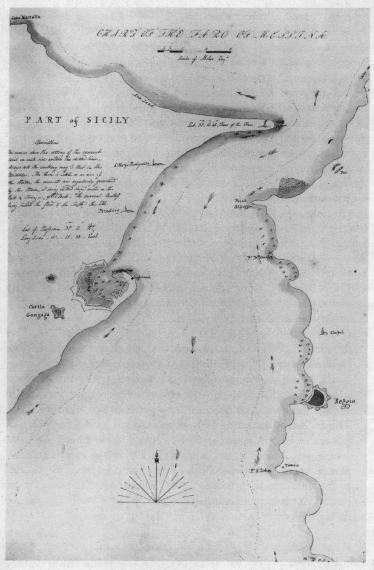

The Straits of Messina, drawn by Lieutenant William Pocock, R.N.

of little use against thick walls. Heavier weapons could be mounted in gunboats, but these could not be elevated sufficiently to hit the castle on its crag above the sea. The British had found that heavy guns could be mounted on wooden slides and sunk in pits on the Sicilian shore so as to be elevated to forty-five degrees.★ They could then fire across the straits. But since this was plunging-fire, it was unlikely to breach fortifications.

At Messina, Moore was told that Scilla had surrendered on 23 July, that Lower Calabria had now been cleared of the French and so the threat of an immediate invasion of Sicily had ended. But he also heard bad news. Five days before the fall of Scilla, the supposedly impregnable fortress of Gaeta had surrendered. The indomitable Prince of Hesse had been wounded and his second-in-command, lacking his spirit, had immediately accepted the lenient terms for surrender offered by Masséna. What had surprised all at the British headquarters in Messina was that Sir Sidney Smith had not, as he had promised, sailed directly from Sant' Eufemia to relieve the fortress, where even the presence of a ship of the line with open gun-ports might have stiffened the resolve of the defenders.

Where had Sir Sidney gone? The *Pompée* had been sighted here, there and, it seemed, everywhere but off Gaeta. He had, it emerged, sailed south to the headland town of Tropea, where the French garrison had surrendered and been embarked as prisoners. Then he had continued down the coast to Scilla, there to land ammunition and provisions for the Calabrese partisans. He put marines ashore to help with the siege of the castle and, on 11 July, had landed naval guns to be dragged on sledges to the siege-works. No masonry could stand against 24-pound shot, which pounded the walls until its stone fell in sheets. Eventually, they would batter a breach, which the commander of the waiting infantry would consider 'practicable' for an assault. The admiral had been ashore daily and then returned to Faro, the anchorage near Messina, to load more ordnance for the Calabrese, before sailing north again

---

★ This inspired the Austrians to similarly elevate their cannon during the siege of Venice in 1849 so that they could hit the centre of the city from the mainland.

on the day that Gaeta surrendered. He spent the next three weeks cruising off the towns of Amantea and Policastro, sending ammunition 'to the mountains for the Calabrian Soldiers', as it was recorded in Captain Dacres' log. On 1 August, he noted, 'Sent on shore one barrel of powder and 400 flints'; the next day, 'Sent on shore two barrels powder and two boxes musquet balls'; and, on the 3rd, a Sunday,

> Hot and sultry. Chaplain performed Divine Service, mustered by divisions. P.M. at 4, heard quick fire of musquetry on shore, supposed to be the Calabrians and French in action. Armed the launch and got the Marines ready for landing. Sent on shore 4 barrels of powder and two boxes of musquet balls.[3]

'The coming of the Admiral', Lieutenant-Colonel Bunbury considered,

> and the energy of his first proceedings soon produced a wide effect; arms and ammunition were conveyed into the mountains of Calabria; the smaller detachments of the enemy were driven from the shores; and some of the strongest points were armed and occupied by the insurgents and parties of English marines and seamen . . . the insurrection soon kindled throughout the two Calabrias.[4]

However, General Moore, who had long had doubts about Sir Sidney, thought otherwise. Colonel Bunbury's initial enthusiasm also waned and he remarked with tart realism, 'Sir Sidney was an enthusiast always panting for distinction, restlessly active, but desultory in his views; extravagantly vain; daring, quicksighted and fertile in those resources which befit a partisan leader; but he possessed no great depth of judgement, nor any fixity of purpose, save that of persuading mankind, as he was persuaded himself, that Sidney Smith was the most brilliant of chevaliers.' But he added, 'Let me not, in exposing this brave man's foibles, omit to add that he was kind-tempered, generous and as agreeable as a man can be supposed to be who is always talking of himself.'[5]

Both Nelson and Smith had enjoyed their foreign titles and now Sir Sidney had edged ahead as Viceroy of Calabria and, as he assumed, commander-in-chief of all naval and military operations there, much to the continuing irritation of General Stuart. The division of opinion was becoming crystallized. The Queen and Admiral Smith favoured immediate intervention on the mainland, while the King, Elliot and the generals were determined that the defence of Sicily should be accorded overwhelming priority over all such adventures. This was in accord with the view of Lord Collingwood, wherever he might be, and could be presumed to reflect the policy of the British government.

While direct news from London took about two months to reach Palermo, some did filter south from the Continent, mostly in Continental newspapers brought by passing ships. Early that summer it had become apparent that the Foreign Secretary, Charles James Fox, had responded to an approach from Talleyrand, Napoleon's foreign secretary. It seemed that he might be hoping that the stalemate resulting from the British victory at Trafalgar and the French victory at Austerlitz might be grounds for a peace settlement. One of the principal aims of Talleyrand's move was the acquisition of Sicily but, as Fox saw it, that island and the alliance with Russia were the twin pillars of British defence, both being vital to the prevention of another lunge into the Middle East by Napoleon. Secret negotiations began, and Fox went so far as to suggest the exchange of Sicily for Venice, Istria and the Dalmatian coast, all occupied by the French. This would block the way east even more effectively and would please the Russians, who feared the French presence in the Balkans and, indeed, still occupied Corfu. But for those commanding in the Mediterranean this remained no more than rumour. It was recognized that Venice with its Arsenale and shipyards was potentially the mainspring of any eastward move by Napoleon and this had, at least, to be contained. In July 1806 William Windham, the war minister, therefore sent a formal directive to the Admiralty: 'The King has judged it expedient for the Protection of His Subjects and for the Annoyance of His Enemies to establish the most rigorous Blockade at the entrance to the port of Venice . . . according to the usages of war.'[6]

There was enough to occupy the sharp mind of Sir John Moore in the central Mediterranean. The defence of Sicily, the key to British strategy, depended on the Royal Navy and, in its theatre of war, that was under the command of the mercurial Sir Sidney Smith. It was obvious that Smith was trying to implement the wishes of the Queen rather than the orders of Lord Collingwood and hoping to repeat the success of Lord Nelson's strategy of 1799 in supporting the mainland loyalists in recapturing southern Italy and Naples. All Sir John knew was that the admiral was at sea somewhere between the Bay of Naples and the Straits of Messina. With General Fox's agreement, he sailed north on 16 August in the frigate *Apollo* in the hope of finding him.

A week later Moore sighted the admiral's flagship, together with another ship of the line, the *Thunderer*, and two frigates with gunboats and transports in the Bay of Salerno, south of Naples. 'They seemed floating on the face of the waters without object',[7] he wrote in his diary. There was something wrong with the look of the *Pompée*, as if she had suffered damage in action, which, it transpired, was the case. Two days earlier Sir Sidney, 'coasting along as was his wont', was off the headland of Licosa, where a small anchorage in the lee of a little island was commanded by one gun mounted on a tower, like the Martello towers built along the English coast during the recent threat of invasion.

The story was told by Colonel Bunbury, who had heard it from the ship's officers:

Sir Sidney . . . looking out for brigands to receive his muskets and orders, espied a French flag on this tower of ancient days. He simply gave orders that the ship should run in and drive the enemy out of their little fortress by cannon shot; and . . . the Admiral went quietly to his cabin to write his letters. The *Pompée* drew near and opened her fire; the one gun then responded; the broadsides of the man-of-war were returned for half an hour by this solitary but unerring gun; at length the captain found it necessary to interrupt the Admiral's correspondence by informing him that Lieut. Slessor and a midshipman and several men were killed, many more wounded and the ship seriously damaged.

Sir Sidney looked surprised but gave orders that the boats should be lowered and the marines sent ashore to reduce these obstinate Frenchmen. As soon as the boats touched the beach, some thirty Corsicans ran from the tower to meet them, waving a white handkerchief and telling the officer that they had been longing to desert to the British but, as the ship fired at them instead of inviting them to surrender, they had no choice but to use their gun to the best of their ability.[8]

The flagship had suffered severely, with seven killed and thirty-two wounded, her masts damaged and more than thirty shot-holes in her sides. A further humiliation was that the marines had come upon a store of alcohol and as result, noted Captain Dacres, he ordered nine of them to be given, 'twenty-four lashes each for drunkenness and neglect of duty when on shore in sight of the Enemy.'[9]

General Moore went on board the flagship for a long talk with Admiral Smith and recorded in his diary, 'He spoke like a man who was directing a formidable force under distinguished leaders and nothing but the want of money and arms . . . had prevented him driving the French from lower Italy and placing Ferdinand on the throne of Naples.' However, Moore concluded that this was hardly the case.

The Calabrese were a people divided amongst themselves: the persons of property were unfortunately favourable to the French. Those with us, or rather with the Court, were . . . the briganti, or banditti, who were averse to all order, or civil government, and intent on plunder and murder rather than united by a love of liberty . . . Their chiefs were, most of them, low vagabonds, who had deserved, or escaped the gallows.[10]

Colonel Bunbury agreed, describing the partisans as 'the dastardly dregs of the Calabrese, led by assassins to plunder and murder every person who is decent and respectable in the country'.[11]

Moore determined to put his views in writing in letters both to the admiral and to General Fox, and, while he did so, he decided to inspect the British garrison of Capri, which was proving a valuable vantage-point for intelligence gathering, regularly receiving reports and foreign newspapers from Naples across the bay. Since Smith had captured the island in May, his marines had been withdrawn and the garrison now consisted of a battalion of the Royal Corsican Rangers commanded by Lieutenant-Colonel Hudson Lowe, who had fought at Toulon, in Corsica and in Egypt. Lying offshore were British transports with two infantry battalions embarked; they had arrived there after Maida in case they were required for coastal raiding. Moore spent a few hours ashore with Lowe, and walked with him to the ruins of the Emperor Tiberius's villa, finding the island 'delightful'[12] and easy to defend. Most of the Corsicans were on the highest part of the island, around Anacapri and Monte Solaro, protected by precipices falling sheer into the sea and down to the town of Capri, the latter passable only by the Phoenicians' steps and the rumoured goat track, Even where the cliffs were less forbidding at the far end of the island, they seemed unscaleable and above them rose thick, thorny scrub. So long as a guardship provided by the Royal Navy kept watch on the island, it must surely be impregnable, and Moore ordered the infantry in the transports to return to Messina.

He returned to find 'Sir Sidney nearly in the spot in which I had left him, floating in search of adventures for no earthly use' and gave him a written summary of his own strategic views. Again Smith launched into a lengthy *tour d'horizon* bounded by Palermo and Naples, which Moore regarded as 'much falsehood and misrepresentation'. He listened with cool detachment, determined to see for himself and make up his own mind. So, on passage to Sicily, the *Apollo* called at the Calabrian towns where, as he put it, Sir Sidney had been 'amusing himself with the idea that he was directing a campaign'.[13] He added in his diary:

I found the inhabitants frightened and disheartened, hoisting the white or republican colours as danger threatened and massacring and pillaging each other as one or other party was uppermost . . . [The *massi* partisans] were beaten and dispersed, their leaders had fled and the country must be lost unless supported by troops of the line. It was evident that the Calabrians were incapable of taking advantage of the strength of their country to protect themselves . . . It seems therefore to me to be cruel and very unbecoming the British nation to encourage this kind of insurrection.[14]

He was equally blunt in a report to General Fox, urging him to curb Sir Sidney. 'In his imagination he is directing the operation of armies,' he wrote,

> but where in reality he is only encouraging murder and rapine and keeping up amongst that unhappy people, whom we have no intention to support, a spirit of revolt which will bring upon them the more severe vengeance of the French Government. As long as Sir Sidney had money he distributed it profusely and now with as little judgement he is distributing arms, ammunition and provisions.[15]

Smith's implementation of Queen Maria Carolina's strategy had, however, contributed to British success in 1806. The initial rising of the Calabrese had helped in clearing the French from Lower Calabria and removing the threat of invasion from Sicily. French military capability had been damaged not only by defeat at Maida but also by hundreds of casualties from guerrilla warfare and from sickness: thousands of French troops had gone down with malaria and nearly a quarter of Masséna's army further north was already sick. Together the British, the Neapolitans and the Calabrese had caused the French more than 10,000 casualties in southern Italy in that year.

At this time Sir John received a letter from General Fox asking for his advice on whether or not support should be given to the Calabrese by the British troops under his command, which, since the arrival of the reinforcements, amounted to more than 13,000 men. Fox, too, had become disenchanted with Sir Sidney and after visiting the court at Palermo, where he found 'more childishness, wickedness and folly than is to be met in any other part of the world', he reported that 'Sir Sidney is there intriguing and encouraging all their extravagances. Sometimes he is . . . Viceroy of Calabria; at others to have the island of Lampedusa to hold as a fief . . . with the title of Duke.'[16]

In Palermo there was confusion. On General Stuart's departure for England to receive a knighthood, an annual pension of £1,000 and permission to use the title Count of Maida conferred on him by King Ferdinand, he had advised his successor to follow the strategy promoted by Sir Sidney and the Queen. The flaws in this were illustrated by the experience of Captain William Hoste of the *Amphion* – a favourite protégé of Nelson. After the fall of Reggio and Scilla, as the French had retreated north, Hoste had harried them along the coastal roads and tried to reassure the Calabrese that the British would support them. He reported to Admiral Smith that he had told them 'to trust your Allies and Sovereign, who will not desert you. But how long my words *alone* will have effect is quite uncertain.' As the French continued their retreat northward, he noted that 'from the *Amphion* we plainly observed the flames and the destructive ravages of the French army.'[17] It would need more than the landing of a few British infantrymen to stop that.

Worse was to come. Since Admiral Smith had failed to prevent the fall of Gaeta after the Battle of Maida, 12,000 French troops had become available for operations elsewhere. As General Reynier retreated north, falling back on General Verdier's army in Upper Calabria, they were joined by reinforcements from both Gaeta and northern Italy. There were now 16,000 French troops ready for a counter-offensive in the south, with another 30,000 waiting in the north. These would be commanded by Marshal Masséna himself, a brilliant commander who had been campaigning in Italy for a decade. Most ominously, a shadow seemed to fall across Italy from beyond the Alps; the Emperor Napoleon was looking south. Joseph, King of Naples, might be a mild man of liberal tendencies, but his ruthless brother was increasingly inciting him to act otherwise. 'Show severity, make examples!' he urged. 'In a conquered country it is not good to be humane . . . Shoot down at least a hundred rebels . . . sack five or six large villages . . . Rob without reservation, nothing is sacred after a conquest . . . Your courtiers tell you that you are loved for your kindness. Mere folly!'[18]

Joseph complied, acting through subordinates. In Naples this was through his Minister of Police, Antoine Saliceti, who arranged the deaths of those thought disloyal. In Calabria he worked through divisional commanders, who had lost men to capture and subsequent torture and execution by the partisans, and through Calabrese opposed to the return of the Bourbons and loyal to *Maestro Peppe*, as they nicknamed King Joseph. As Masséna marched south, there was no force capable of stopping him and what little there was inflamed the savagery of his reaction.

As the French turned and pushed south, capturing towns that the British had briefly occupied, the cycle of atrocity and counter-atrocity began. As the French discovered the fate of their own stragglers from Reynier's retreat, they were incensed. 'We took down one of our men, who had been hanged and stabbed', wrote one French officer. 'We found six of our gunners in a cell there, stark naked and half dead of hunger. They were being kept for a little *auto-da-fé*, which was to be held on the morrow.'[19] The French reaction was made easier because their Swiss mercenaries wore plum-coloured coats, which the Calabrese often mistook for the red of their British allies. 'The inhabitants of Cassano mistook us for the English: this had often happened', he continued. 'They came out to meet us, embrace us and congratulate us on having given those rascally Frenchmen . . . a trouncing.' The Calabrese began boasting of the French they had killed – 'I shot six of them; I stabbed ten' – each trying to out-boast the others.

> Thus we received all their confidences and they only recognized us when we fired at them point-blank. Many of them were killed. Fifty-two were taken and shot that evening in the square . . . they were despatched by their compatriots, the Calabrians, our friends, the good Calabrians of Joseph, who asked as a favour to be employed in this butchery.

A few days later, fifty-two French soldiers 'who were pillaging without thought of evil'[20] in a nearby village were killed by Calabrese in revenge. Both Moore and Smith could see the smoke of burning villages from their ships sailing south for Sicily. Moore concluded, 'We should either march our whole force into Calabria if its defence is a British object, or leave them to themselves.'[21]

Smith still believed that Calabria could be held, and pleaded with the Queen: 'He who can speak as supreme commander can accomplish master-strokes. It is this unity of plan and action that gives Bonaparte his success. Now this unity of power is vested in me. Let it remain in me and I will dare to do more than he will dare to imagine.'[22] But only General Fox could provide the forces and the munitions he required and he was not inclined to do so, maintaining, 'It is certain that, if the enemy is determined upon the repression of Calabria and sends down an immense force, we cannot prevent it.'[23] Still Smith persisted, meeting the Queen constantly and finding an ally in her chief minister, the Marquis of Circello, who had just replaced the ageing Anglo-Italian Sir John Acton. He even hoped to join an attack she proposed on Naples itself by 8,000 Sicilian troops commanded by the Prince of Hesse, now recovered from the wound suffered at Gaeta.

But Masséna was now marching overwhelming forces into Calabria, and a diversionary attack on the Adriatic coast by Russians based on Corfu had failed to materialize, so Fox realized that Smith's optimism was unfounded. Calabria could not be held and inevitably the last British footholds at Reggio and Scilla must fall. It was Moore's opinions that now carried most weight in deciding Mediterranean strategy, not only with General Fox but also with the government in London. Complaints against Sir Sidney Smith's behaviour had reached Whitehall from Sicily. Most vociferous were those from Moore himself, who declared of the admiral, 'So unprincipled is he that he is capable, for any advantage to himself, or gratification to his vanity, to betray us and then the Queen. His head is a most perverted one and his nature false without bounds.'[24] Smith's enemies and critics also included Generals Stuart and Fox and the diplomat Hugh Elliot; even the far distant Lord Collingwood felt that Sir Sidney might be better employed off Boulogne, where he could write reports of his own actions for the London newspapers.

These complaints – starting with that of General Stuart – reached Lord Grenville, the Foreign Secretary, and William Windham, the Secretary for War, both of whom had known and liked Smith, and both of whom admired his feat at Acre and his intelligence work. Both had also been devoted to his cousin, the late William Pitt. The government was, as a whole, displeased that its naval commander in the central Mediterranean should be carrying out the strategic plans of a foreign sovereign and have accepted his title and military command in preference to those of his own royal and professional masters. But they had no wish to destroy his career. He had to be reprimanded, but Grenville wrote to Windham agreeing to make 'the censure of Sir Sidney Smith as mild as possible'.[25] It would have to reprimand him for having accepted a commission from a foreign government; for having assumed command of the Calabrese insurgents at the time of the Battle of Maida, when all military command should have been vested in General Stuart; and for having acted on orders from the King of Sicily in contradiction to the wishes of the British minister at Palermo. It would be couched in bland language but, of course, it would be another matter when Sir Sidney had to contend with the displeasure of his superior naval officer, Lord Collingwood, in whose hands lay the disposal of the professional future of every naval officer in the Mediterranean.

The commander-in-chief's reproof, written on board the *Ocean*, still off Cadiz, on 22 December, was a model of oblique disapproval, making no mention of Queen Maria Carolina. He stressed that, unless the British government decided on a major attack on Naples,

> any desultory war carried on in districts is injurious to the King's cause . . . I have no doubt that at the Court there is a great deal of intrigue. The King, impatient to be restored to his throne of Naples, will always find courtly people about him to flatter him with the early accomplishment of his desire . . . But, as English officers, we have little to do with their counsels . . . When the political questions of state are arranged, the sea and land Commanders will consult together as to the policy and practicability of the warlike measures which are proposed, always keeping in view their distinct duties and original orders.[26]

He revealed his true feelings in a letter to his brother, writing, 'I am sadly off with this Sir S. Smith at Sicily; the man's head is full of strange vapours and I am convinced Lord Barham [the First Lord of the Admiralty] sent him here to be clear of a tormentor, but he annoys me more than the French, or Spanish fleet.'[27]

Smith was aware that his attempted emulation of Nelson was not appreciated by Nelson's closest friend and that he had, in effect, been dismissed. 'I thus take my leave of this service', he replied, 'with the conscious certainty that I have acted from the purest motives for the common cause.'[28] Sir Sidney was also well aware that he was saying not *adieu* but *au revoir*.

5

An eastern turn

IN NOVEMBER 1806 and again in January 1807 French agents watching Gibraltar from across the bay in Algeciras had something to report. Out of the Atlantic appeared British ships of the line, which, joined by others lying at Gibraltar, passed the straits and sailed into the Mediterranean. The first squadron flew a rear-admiral's flag but the second, which sailed east on 18 January, was led by a battleship of 100 guns wearing a flag to show that she was the flagship of Vice-Admiral Sir John Duckworth, second-in-command of the Mediterranean Fleet under Lord Collingwood.

Duckworth, who, as a boy, had fought under Admiral Hawke in Quiberon Bay in 1759, had recently commanded at Jamaica and defeated a French squadron off Santo Domingo. A thickset man of sixty-four, with an aggressive nose and a face suggesting toughness rather than originality, his presence showed that something important was afoot. But what? Such a force could hardly be bound for Toulon, where only four French sail of the line were already blockaded by the British. If it was bound for Sicily, this might mean that a major attack on Naples was indeed intended.

But neither the first squadron of three sail of the line and two frigates, under Rear-Admiral Sir Thomas Louis (one of Nelson's captains at the Battle of the Nile), nor the second of four sail of the line under Duckworth was steering for Toulon or Sicily. Instead, they called at Malta then headed east, collecting reinforcements, so

61

that the British fleet in the eastern basin of the Mediterranean included eight ships of the line.

Admiral Duckworth's voyage was in consequence of a succession of reports that had been reaching London from Paris, Berlin, Moscow, Constantinople, Alexandria and Bombay for the past six months. Napoleon had been active in exploiting his devastating victory at Austerlitz a year before. The Russians had withdrawn into their immense hinterland, and the defeat of Austria had torn a breach in the coalition that had held him in central Europe. The Austrians' loss of their territory bordering the Adriatic meant that Napoleon could now threaten the Russian position at Corfu and that opened further possibilities. As the Emperor sent General Marmont and the two corps of the newly formed Army of Dalmatia down the eastern shores of the Adriatic, there now lay nothing but mountains between his vanguard and the Ottoman Empire.

France had been enjoying improved relations with the Porte since 1802, and the rift brought about by Bonaparte's invasion of Egypt and Syria four years earlier had healed. In 1806 the able General Horace Sebastiani, who had been intriguing secretly for French interests in the Levant in the manner of Sir Sidney Smith, was sent to Constantinople as ambassador. He was surprisingly successful, particularly in souring relations between Russia and the Porte, so that by 1806 there was a virtual state of war between the two. That vast, ramshackle conglomeration of vassal states, ostensibly ruled from Constantinople, had, as Admiral Smith had forecast, become the alternative grand objective to Napoleon's dream of invading England. A move into the Ottoman Empire, whether peacefully as an ally or by force, would not only outflank the Russians and enable him to reach their southern frontiers but could also open the gates of India. That this was a long-term objective was stressed in a despatch written in the autumn of 1806 from Mysore by John Malcolm, a British administrator in India and recent envoy to the Persian court in Teheran, to Nelson's friend Lord Minto, the former Gilbert Elliot, who was about to take up the appointment of Governor-General of India. Warning that 'British India will be exposed to a danger, which it will require every measure of preventive policy to avert . . . the imminent risk [is] to the very existence of British power in India,' he reported that the Ottoman Empire was 'inundated with French officers' and their diplomats were successfully intriguing in Persia. 'The danger, though prospective, is very serious,' he concluded, 'and will require the most early and spirited measures on the part of the British Government to defeat it.'[1] When the despatch reached the desk of the war minister, William Windham, he concluded, 'The war is taking an eastern turn.'[2]

In moving south-east to brush aside the Russians on Corfu and at the Montenegrin port of Cattaro (now Kotor), Napoleon's principal military problem was lack of roads. Artillery and heavy stores would have to cross by sea from Venice and Ancona, which would only be possible with command of the Adriatic. The Emperor's dashing stepson, adopted son and son of the Empress Josephine, Eugène de Beauharnais, was now Viceroy of Italy and Prince of Venice, where he had reactivated the great Arsenale, which had lain derelict since the French occupation in 1797. By the end of 1806 five ships of the line and several frigates were being built there, destined for what would be called the Royal Italian Navy, under French command. In addition, there were, it was reported, 'seven gun-brigs well adapted for the defence of that city and now ready for sea. These vessels will become a very formidable and effectual means of annoyance to the British ships of war on that station during the calms of June and July.'[3] Venice had also become the main base for supplying the Army of Dalmatia by sea. In consequence, Collingwood detached a frigate squadron to watch developments at the head of the Adriatic, under the command of Captain Patrick Campbell. He achieved some immediate success; Collingwood noting that the best way of helping the Russians against the French was 'the activity of the frigates preventing their supplies and stopping their communication between Venice and the Eastern Coast [of the Adriatic], which I believe Campbell has done as effectually as it can be'.[4] But it was soon realized that it would take more than a few frigates to contain Napoleon's eastward expansion.

Particularly ominous were reports from the British ambassador in Constantinople about the success of the French ambassador to the court of Sultan Selim III, General Horace Sebastiani, in persuading the Sultan to close the Dardanelles to Russian shipping. This, it was feared, could lead to an alliance between the Ottoman Empire and France, which could mean French troops marching overland to the borders of Persia on the road to India. What could be done? The British strategic reserve in Sicily now amounted to more than 20,000 men, with about half that number also available from the garrisons of Malta and Gibraltar. Collingwood had been ordered to send a squadron of battleships into the eastern Mediterranean and had also written to the Russian admiral at Corfu asking him to reinforce this with four of his own sail of the line. Already Sir Sidney Smith, who had acted as commander of Turkish forces after his defence of Acre at a time when his brother had been British minister in Constantinople, had warned Windham that 'line of battle ships alone have weight in the minds of the inhabitants of the seraglio'.[5] So should this force, under Duckworth's command, be sent up the Dardanelles with a strong force of infantry to clear the forts on either shore and then occupy Constantinople if the Sultan refused a British ultimatum to surrender its fleet, expel Sebastiani and meet Russian demands for free passage to and from the Mediterranean?

British ministers in London had another fear. They knew that Napoleon still hankered after Egypt as a colony on the way to India. Might he try again? Another expedition gathered at Toulon, or Venice, might evade Collingwood's blockade if his ships were, as had happened before, blown off-station in a storm. So the case began to be made for the British to reach Egypt first or, at least, that, should the French arrive there and have to be expelled, the British army should not be enmeshed in Turkey.

The final decision was to meet both threats. The Royal Navy would go to Constantinople and the British Army would go to Egypt. At the end of November 1806 secret orders were sent to General Fox in Messina that the two operations should be co-ordinated and that he was to hold 5,000 men ready to embark for Alexandria as soon as he heard that action had been taken against Constantinople. While sending so strong a force eastward, Collingwood would have to watch his southern flank, where the North African states could never be trusted, if only to restrain their piracy and slave-raiding. This had prompted a directive from Windham's successor as war minister, Lord Castlereagh, 'to keep a particular watch upon the Barbary States . . . The appearance of one of his Majesty's Ships from time to time may have a beneficial influence.'[6]

Duckworth's orders were to sail up the Dardanelles – the gut 45 miles long and 1 to 2 miles wide connecting the Mediterranean Sea with the Sea of Marmara, the Bosphorus and the Black Sea. At Constantinople he was to present an ultimatum. If this was rejected, he was to burn the Turkish fleet in harbour and bombard the city until the Sultan complied. In effect, he was to repeat Lord Nelson's action at Copenhagen six years earlier.

Duckworth was to be joined by a second rear-admiral, Sir Sidney Smith. No officer of his rank had had such intimate experience of the Ottoman court so, although his recent behaviour had disqualified him from being given any direct role in the coming negotiations, he would be there as an adviser as well as commanding a ship of the line. Some, who knew of Smith's record in the Levant, were angered that he was not to be given more responsibility, and one was to protest, 'There was one, indeed not five days' sail from the mouth of the Dardanelles, whose ability and firmness had never been doubted and whose local experience and well-known influence with the Porte eminently fitted him for such an enterprise.'[7] But when the news of Smith's departure was announced in Messina, Sir John Moore snorted, 'He is a good riddance from Palermo and it is to be hoped that Sir John Duckworth will trust him no further than he sees him.'[8]

Admiral Duckworth's squadron joined Admiral Louis's ships off the island of Tenedos (now Bozca Ada), south of the Dardanelles on 17 February 1807. Louis had recently taken his flagship and a frigate up to Constantinople and saw that the political sky was darkening. When news of Napoleon's defeat of the Prussians at Jena on 17 October had arrived in December, the Russian ambassador to the Porte had hastily left, fearing imprisonment. Louis withdrew to Tenedos, leaving the frigate with the British ambassador at Constantinople, Charles Arbuthnot. Duckworth's force was now made up of one ship of 100 guns, one of 98, another of 80, four '74's – including the *Pompée* – and one '64', two frigates and two bomb vessels; but there was no sign of Russian reinforcements. At Tenedos he was told by Louis that Constantinople was defenceless and the forts along the Dardanelles half derelict; the passage would be easy. There was tension and excitement in the fleet. One officer noted, 'We were now given to understand that we were to pass the Dardanelles, or ancient Hellespont, and anchor before the very port of Constantinople . . . A signal was made to prepare for battles.'[9]

Duckworth awaited news from Arbuthnot. The ambassador had, in the hope of persuading the Sultan to reverse his policy, told the Porte that a British fleet was on its way to Constantinople. At first this seemed to succeed, and General Sebastiani began to lose confidence, despite which he sent an aide-de-camp to the Dardanelles to urge that the shore batteries there be strengthened. Then, on 29 January, one of Arbuthnot's agents in the capital reported that the ambassador and all British merchants in the city were about to be arrested. He acted promptly, sending a message to Captain the Hon. Thomas Capel of the frigate *Endymion* – one of Nelson's officers, who had brought the news of the Battle of the Nile to London and had fought at Trafalgar – to arrange a dinner party that night on board his ship, to which they would all be invited. After dark, when the sound of their revelry carried across the water to the city, Capel ordered the mooring cable to be cut and the ship slid silently on the current, clear of the shore batteries and into the basin of the Sea of Marmara. Sails were set, the frigate passed the forts guarding the Dardanelles and, three days later, it joined the fleet off Tenedos.

Capel told Duckworth that, in the month since Louis had made the passage of the Dardanelles, the defences had indeed been strengthened and that a Turkish squadron of one 64-gun ship, four frigates and nine smaller warships lay in a wider reach of the narrows beyond the first array of forts. Realizing that they would certainly be strengthened further and could well prevent his passage of the Dardanelles, Duckworth wrote a worried letter to Collingwood, confirming his willingness to carry out his orders but stressing the dangers. The outlook, he wrote, had 'completely altered' as the Turkish batteries were now able 'to flank every turn in our passage through the Dardanelles', and he would 'enter a sea environed with enemies without a possible resource but in ourselves', so that 'when we are to return there cannot remain a doubt but that the passage will be rendered as formidable as the efforts of the Turkish empire, directed and assisted by their allies, the French, can make it,'[10] This was more to explain any coming disaster than to bring about any change of orders, because no reply could be expected from the commander-in-chief for many weeks and Duckworth only awaited a favour-able southerly wind to sail against the current pouring through the Dardanelles from the Black Sea to the Aegean.

While waiting, Smith decided to take a hand and drafted a letter to Sultan Selim, whom he knew.

> Shall it be said that Bonaparte . . . has succeeded in obtaining the dominion of the entire Ottoman territory . . . by fallacious reasoning and by bribing your Imperial Majesty's servants to desert and betray their master . . . ? No! Let it be rather recorded that Sultan Selim the Third proved himself worthy of his ances-tors . . . by placing his interests in the keeping . . . of an ally, whom your Imperial Majesty knows to be just and merciful . . . and to be most faithfully attached to your Imperial Majesty.[11]

He sent copies to the bellicose Duckworth and the more pacific Arbuthnot, who was anxious to avoid open war, with the option that either of them could sign and forward the letter to Constantinople. It was never sent.

On 11 February Duckworth moved his fleet to a more exposed anchorage to await a wind. Three nights later flames were seen on board the *Ajax*, a 'seventy-four' commanded by Captain Henry Blackwood, another of Nelson's captains. It was an accidental fire, started in a storeroom, but it raged through the ship, out of control, burning her cables so that she drifted ashore on Tenedos. As the flames took hold, thousands of men crowded the decks and rigging of the fleet to watch. One officer in the flagship described how 'the dense, black smoke hung like a pall around the ship, whilst the fire that glowed and raged within showed every spar, shroud and rope as distinctly painted as if traced by an artist's pencil. Heated by the intenseness of the fire, the ordnance are discharged one by one . . .

like minute guns at the funeral of some deceased officer.'[12] The flames raced up the rigging, the yards canted and fell and finally the blazing masts toppled, hissing, into the sea. The *Ajax* then blew up. Of the 633 men on board, 381 were saved, including her captain. A seaman in the same ship, James Richardson, jotted in his diary: 'Awful sight. Felt rather queer, thought of things I ought to have thought of before, heart not quite so high as usual, knees rather shaky, soon better.'[13]

Richardson, an educated man, had gone to sea in a merchant ship and been impressed with his brother into the *Royal George* while ashore in Malta. At seven in the morning of the 19th the wind changed, and the admiral ordered his fleet to weigh and make sail to enter the narrows of the Dardanelles. There was awe and apprehension, those who knew something of the Classics remembering that this was the Hellespont of Homer and Hector, of Achilles and Troy, of Hero and Leander. After the loss of the *Ajax* 'the name of the ship occasioned many reflections', one captain of the marines wrote home, 'and the *Iliad* was the topic for some time; it is singular that we should lose her on the very spot where the mighty Grecian defended his own vessels so obstinately.'[14] To the seamen it just looked as if they were steering inland, as indeed they were. An hour later the leading ship was within range of the first of the Turkish forts. 'Prepare for action', noted Richardson, 'Down bulkheads and chests, made all smack smooth for a while, all bustle and confusion. All hands old Trafalgar heroes except us. Stationed at 32-pounder on the lower deck, brother on quarterdeck. Bang, bang, bang. Dead silence. Deaf as a beetle.' Richardson had heard that huge mortars in the Turkish forts could fire marble cannon-balls of 800 pounds and he added, 'Going to have a game of marbles with the Turks'. Then the forts were astern and he continued, 'Passed all the forts . . . came to anchor, 3 cheers. Glad it was all over, knees strong again. Heard there was sad havoc in the quarterdeck, sent to see after brother, all right. Dreadful sight, flocks, feathers, pillows,* man-

---

* Hammocks and bedding stowed in netting along the gunwales of the upper deck as some protection against splinters and small-arms fire.

gled human flesh all swept in a heap together to throw overboard.'[15] Three men had been killed and twenty-nine wounded.
But it was not all over.

As the bare, brown hills of Europe and Asia parted to reveal
the channel and the forts were passed, the masts of ships
anchored in a bay were sighted. This was the Turkish squadron
that Capel had seen. So, having snubbed Smith's attempt at
diplomacy, Duckworth now gave him employment and ordered
him to destroy them. While the main fleet sailed on, Smith led a
division of four ships of the line and a frigate into attack and, as
Duckworth reported, 'closed into the midst'.[16] The Turks
fought fiercely, but Smith's ships, 'anchoring within musket-shot
of the enemy's vessels and redoubt . . . opened so heavy a cannonade that in half an hour all the Turkish craft, except a corvette and a gunboat, which struck and were taken possession of,
ran ashore'.[17] Several of the Turkish ships had been boarded; cutlass against scimitar. The British had lost four killed and twenty-
six wounded. Smith then followed the fleet up the Dardanelles.

'We fought our way past Gallipoli into the Sea of Marmara and
were safe at eight o'clock for the present', one officer of the
Repulse wrote in his diary; 'Took something to eat, cracked our
jokes and laid down for a nap, but who could sleep?'[18]

Nothing, it seemed, now lay between them and Constantinople.
Duckworth had used Smith to fight, but he had disregarded him as
a diplomatist and now, to his own cost, he ignored him as a naviga-
tor, too. Having left Smith's squadron astern of the fleet,
Duckworth ordered his navigation master to lay a course directly
for Constantinople, some 120 miles to the north-east, on the far
side of the almost landlocked little sea. He soon discovered what
Smith could have told him. Unless there was a strong southerly
wind, sailing ships had to hug the western, European shore of the
Sea of Marmara because of the powerful current that swept south
from the Black Sea, funnelled through the Bosphorus and then
straight across the Sea of Marmara into the Dardanelles and the
Aegean. If ships steered into the wider stretch of the sea to the east
of the current – as Duckworth had done – they would be unable to
reach the Bosphorus and Constantinople without that southerly
wind. On 20 February, when this wind was needed, it did not blow.

That evening the sunset lit the minarets, domes and low, russet roofs of the city of Constantinople eight miles ahead. Beyond them, telescopes revealed the masts of ships lying in the Golden Horn and these they might try to burn. Duckworth could see his destination but he could not reach it across the racing current. Next morning a light breeze sprang up, enabling a frigate to work its way to within four miles of the city and send a boat ahead flying a flag of truce to deliver a letter from the admiral to the Sultan. It was a peremptory demand to accept British terms. If they were not accepted, wrote Duckworth, he 'had it in his power to destroy the capital and all the Turkish vessels' and 'the British fleet will avail itself of the first favourable wind to proceed towards Constantinople.' Realizing that the Turks would be well aware of the difficult position of the fleet on the wrong side of the race, he added, 'when orders have been given to British officers, no difficulties, no dangers, can retard their execution a single moment.'[19] A reply was demanded within half an hour of the letter having been sent ashore. This was not language to persuade the proud ruler of a vast, albeit ramshackle empire: Sir Sidney's flowery approach would have been more likely to produce the desired result.

However, the officer bearing the letter was not allowed to land and returned to the frigate. A second, even more strongly worded, letter was sent and that too was rejected. General Sebastiani was aware of the probable contents of the letters and had urged the Sultan to play for time and use it to strengthen the defences of the city and the Dardanelles and so trap the British fleet in the Sea of Marmara. Duckworth could see what was happening and, next day, wrote another letter saying, 'As it has been discovered by our glasses that the time granted the Sublime Porte to take its decision is employed in warping ships into places more susceptible of defence and constructing batteries along the coast, it is the duty of the Vice-Admiral to lose no time.'[20]

Then, at dawn on the 22nd, a south-easterly wind blew and, that afternoon, the *Royal George* hoisted the signal for the fleet to weigh anchor, clear for action and begin the bombardment of Constantinople. But even as the signal flags were run up, the halyards began to droop. The wind was dropping and soon the Sea of

Marmara was in a flat calm. The fleet anchored again. A boat was seen and 'an elderly gentleman . . . with a grave and solemn aspect and more than a common length of grizzled beard, shawled and turbaned . . . slowly ascended the *Royal George's* side.'[21] The emissary was received by the admiral and Arbuthnot who had been ill but had risen from his sick-bed. He spoke at great length of the Sultan's desire for peace, so beginning apparent negotiations, but he too was playing for time. While the old Turk talked, five Turkish battleships were warping out of the Golden Horn anchorage to bring their broadsides to bear on the seaward approaches to the city and 300 guns were being mounted along the shore. When the emissary departed for the last time on the following day, it was seen that the Turks had landed on the small island of Prota and were mounting batteries there too. Landing-parties were sent to dislodge them but ran into heavy fire, lost seven killed and nineteen wounded and retreated, their morale lowered further by reports that General Sebastiani had himself been on the island and could have been captured.

On the 22nd, the ambassador suffered a relapse and was confined to his cabin, having repeatedly warned against provoking the Sultan into war rather than trying to persuade him to dismiss General Sebastiani. Duckworth now consulted Smith, who could still see himself going ashore wearing in his hat the diamond spray Sultan Selim had given him for his defence of Acre – and such as Nelson had been given after the Battle of the Nile – and achieving success through the direct diplomacy that Arbuthnot had urged. He advised that the fleet should remain off Constantinople to blockade the city and continue to threaten it with attack. However, Duckworth feared that he would be trapped in the Sea of Marmara as the shore defences along the Dardanelles were being strengthened; this was being supervised by French artillery officers seconded from General Marmont's army on the Ottoman frontier in the Balkans. The morning of 1 March was 'dark and lowering . . . and the wind, which for several days had been light and variable, sprang up fresh from the north-east'.[22]

This could carry the fleet closer to the city, but it was also the wind needed for escape down the Dardanelles to the Aegean. Signals flew, the fleet weighed anchor and made sail, but there was a face-saving operation to be carried out: the Royal Navy must appear to be challenging the Ottoman fleet to come out and fight. So the fleet steered as close as was possible to Constantinople with guns run out. On the deck of the *Royal George* Lieutenant Abraham Crawford inspected the city through his telescope as they drew nearer. 'Constantinople,' he was to recall, 'embracing a wide sweep of its matchless bay, swells gradually upward . . . expanding as it rises from the sea, a succession of white shining houses, amid which domes and kiosks and slender minarets rear their glittering heads . . . relieved by the dark green foliage of innumerable cypress trees.' He knew exactly what was to come, and wrote afterwards that 'the threatening and bellicose attitude, which the squadron assumed and maintained throughout the day, was but a feint; for, soon after dusk, the ships' sterns were presented to the Golden Horn. Urged by a fresh northerly wind, the squadron was soon many leagues distant'[23] making for the Dardanelles.

The fleet reached Gallipoli at the northern end of the narrows and, at half-past seven on the morning of 3 March, approached the first of the forts. Duckworth tried a ruse, ordering a salute of thirteen guns to be fired in the hope that the Turks might suspect that terms for a peaceful withdrawal had been reached at Constantinople. But they were not to be fooled and, as Richardson, the seaman, put it, 'had another game at marbles'[24] over the next three hours as the fleet slowly passed the forts and batteries. From the upper deck of the flagship, the third in the line, Lieutenant Crawford saw the mortars fire 'huge stone shot' of marble and granite.

> I watched this monster-shot almost from the cannon's mouth till it struck the ship; and, so little swift was its flight that, had it come in the direction in which I stood, I should have had time to avoid it . . . The whole scene on shore resembled the bursting of some mountain's side, which . . . vomits forth in fire and smoke fragments of rock and iron, than the sharp, quick fire of a well-served battery.[25]

The flagship was hit by a marble shot of 500 pounds and an iron cannon-ball of 98 pounds, while the *Windsor Castle* was struck by a marble shot of 850 pounds and the *Active* by an 800-pound stone nearly 7 feet in circumference. Another stone shot weighing more than 500 pounds killed eleven and wounded nine in the *Repulse* and her captain of marines, Marmaduke Wybourn, noted in a letter, 'I have a piece of it to make into seals, it is granite.'[26] When the battered ships finally emerged from the smoke into the clear, peaceful water of the Aegean, they had lost 29 killed and 138 wounded.

When the fleet anchored off Tenedos to repair battle damage, Captain Wybourn wrote to his sisters:

> You will perhaps imagine I will give you a sketch of all these Classic Islands and that we are enjoying the beauties of these delightful places while laying in the very spot the Grecian fleet anchored before Troy . . . but no such thing . . . neither myself, or, I believe, anyone else, can think, or speak, of one earthly thing but our dangers and the crippled, wretched Fleet we are in – although the mischief (we hope) is passed.[27]

Then Duckworth was surprised to see the sails of an approaching fleet. It was the Russians, at last responding to repeated pleading for help both from London and from Collingwood. Their commander in the Adriatic, Admiral Siniavin, had finally sailed on 22 February with eight ships of the line, which would have doubled Duckworth's fleet, and 2,000 troops to clear the shore defences. It was, of course, too late. However, Siniavin suggested to Duckworth that they make a joint attempt on the city but Duckworth protested that the 2,000 troops were not enough to capture the defences of the Dardanelles and refused.

It could not be admitted that the attempt had failed. Duckworth did what he could to paint it boldly as 'forcing the Dardanelles', and wisely enlisted the help of that master of psychological warfare and propaganda Sir Sidney Smith, whose 'zeal and distinguished ability'[28] he praised in his despatch to Collingwood. Smith responded by writing a stirring ballad, making play with the ships' names, beginning,

> *Canopus* led the way, 'twixt neighbouring strands
> Of Hellespontus, thronged with Turkish bands,

Dreading *Repulse*, the Turks dared not assail;
The British *Standard* turned the Crescent pale . . .[29]

Ironically, Duckworth now had orders to take his fleet south to Alexandria, where the British expeditionary force had been sent in a move to pre-empt another French invasion of Egypt. This was the force that might have accompanied his fleet, cleared the Turkish defences from the Dardanelles and ensured his triumph at Constantinople.

6

A calculated risk

O N 16 March 1807, as Admiral Duckworth repaired his battered ships, the British soldiers who could have taken the
shores of the Dardanelles and delivered Constantinople to his
mercy were about to land in Egypt. The 'seventy-four' *Tigre*, once
commanded by Sir Sidney Smith and now by another of Nelson's
friends, Captain Benjamin Hallowell, anchored off a beach to the
west of Alexandria, where Bonaparte had landed his army nine
years earlier. But Hallowell was as worried as Duckworth had been
in the Sea of Marmara. Ten days before he had left Messina in a
troop convoy of forty-nine transports with 6,000 troops embarked.
On the first night at sea the ships had become scattered, and
Hallowell had arrived off the intended beachhead with only a third
of his transports and men. So small a force was surely inadequate to
capture Alexandria, but if the attempt was not made at once, surprise would have been lost. Since the victory at Maida, nothing
had succeeded.

There were other doubts about the enterprise. Many had
hoped the troops would have accompanied Duckworth to
Constantinople. Others thought they should have been held in
Sicily, where they had formed a third of the strategic reserve.
Collingwood himself said that the British had 'no business'[1]
in Egypt, but the decision had been taken by politicians and
generals.

If the expedition was to go ahead, then the obvious choice for its commander was Lieutenant-General Sir John Moore, General Fox's second-in-command, although Fox, knowing his own limitations, was reluctant to lose him. On the death of his brother Charles James Fox, the Foreign Secretary, in the previous September, he had lost his patronage, and he felt secure as military commander in the volatile Mediterranean theatre only so long as the clever, loyal Moore was at his side. Fox was nevertheless enjoying life at Messina; his jolly wife was a popular hostess and his two pretty daughters had both attracted the attentions of highly eligible officers: Colonel Bunbury, dashing, square-jawed, not yet thirty, the son of the caricaturist Henry Bunbury, and General Moore himself. So he gave the command to an officer 'everyone in the Army loved', Major-General McKenzie Fraser, described by Bunbury as 'a fine specimen of an open, generous, honourable Highland chieftain. A man of very good plain sense but one who had never studied the higher branches of politics, or of military science . . . No one deemed him qualified for a separate and difficult command.'[2] Fraser had fought with the 78th Highlanders at Maida and his open, friendly face and manner made him a leader that most were happy to follow.

Was it to be so difficult? Those who had fought at Alexandria to expel the French from Egypt in 1801 remembered it as a dilapidated city with tumbledown fortifications; dirty, smelly, plagued by flies, mosquitoes and the diseases of squalor, but an easy prize. It was known that the Ottoman Empire had only the shakiest hold on Egypt, which had been in turmoil since the British had left in 1803. Mutinous Albanian troops and the strange, fierce Mamelukes, the descendants of Circassian slaves, who had evolved into a warrior breed, vied with the Turks for power, reducing the country to anarchy. Now only Alexandria was held by the Turks.

Regular reports from Egypt had reached Messina and London from the British consul-general, the curious Major Ernest Missett, who had been left behind when the British had departed four years before, having then had to move from Cairo to Alexandria to keep in touch with the Porte's Egyptian viceroy, the Albanian Mehemet Ali. The viceroy was known to favour the French, although he had fought them in 1798, so the consul also kept in touch with the

A new theatre of war: fearing Napoleon's ambition to strike eastwards again, the British landed in Italy, defeating the French at Maida in their first victory on land in the Napoleonic Wars. Detail of an engraving after William Heath

Above left: Palermo, the capital of Sicily – the political fulcrum – below Monte Pellegrino. Painting, *c.* 1812, by Lieutenant William Pocock RN

Above: The siege of Gaeta, the Bourbons' last stronghold in mainland Italy, seen from the French lines. French engraving

Left: Messina, the British base in Sicily, with mainland Italy across the straits. Painting by William Pocock

Triumph at Maida: the British exulted in their victory at Maida, celebrated in this woodcut, published in London when the news arrived

Popular soldier: Major-General McKenzie Fraser was loved by his men but led them to disaster in Egypt. Engraving after Richard Cosway

Unpopular soldier: Major-General Sir John Stuart won the Battle of Maida but was widely regarded as incompetent. Engraving after William Wood

Rear-Admiral Sir Sidney Smith, the British naval commander off Sicily, followed Nelson in implementing the ambitions of Queen Maria Carolina. Contemporary engraving

Queen Maria Carolina saw Admiral Smith as a second Nelson and her champion in the reconquest of Naples. Painting in oils, attributed to Angelica Kauffmann

As the British saw it: Admiral Duckworth's fleet 'forcing the Dardanelles' on passage to Constantinople. Painting in oils by Thomas Whitcombe

As the French saw it: Admiral Duckworth booted out of Constantinople by Sultan Selim, urged on by General Sebastiani. Caricature published in Paris

Le Vice-Amiral Anglais Duckworth à la Porte, le 3 mars 1807.

Violent arrival: General Lamarque's French infantry storm ashore on Capri to wrest the
island from the British. French engraving

Festive arrival: the Emperor Napoleon arrives in Venice, passing beneath a triumphal arch
floating on the Grand Canal. Engraving after Giuseppe Borsato

Cavalier and king: the dashing cavalry commander Marshal Joachim Murat, who married Napoleon's sister, Caroline, and became King of Naples. Painting in oils by François Gérard

Mameluke beys, who dominated the Egyptian hinterland and seemed likely to welcome any British intervention. Missett, who had served with the cosmopolitan officers of the 9th Queen's German Regiment of Foot until invalided after an injury, was described as 'clever, vain and impatient . . . a cripple; he was unable to go forth from Alexandria and see things with his own eyes'.[3] So he wove around himself a web of spies, double agents and informants, relishing the intrigue. It was Missett who had encouraged General Fox to launch the expedition into Egypt.

General Fraser scanned Alexandria through his telescope, noting the lighthouse, the slanting masts of the Levantine merchantmen in port, the walls and citadel, the minarets and the unmistakable Pompey's Pillar, the hundred-foot column of polished red granite set up in honour of the Emperor Diocletian. To reach it, his men would have to breast the surf pounding the long, sandy shore and, after that, face an unknown number of Turkish defenders. So he was inclined to wait in the hope that the rest of the convoy would appear. Next day a boat arrived with a letter from Major Missett, urging Fraser to land at once and attack the city before Albanian troops could be summoned from Rosetta, some forty miles to the east.

That evening the landing began, the boats crashing through the surf on to the sand and spilling the soldiers waist-deep into the swirling water. After a few hundred had been put ashore, they were left to shiver on the beach in the cold night air until joined by more next morning. But the wind increased, the surf rose and the landings were stopped, leaving about a thousand men ashore. Another message from the consul urged an immediate attack, claiming that the walls were defended by only 250 Turks, and Fraser ordered his little force to march towards the city. As they came within range, cannon opened fire from redoubts and then musketry; the city gates, he could see, were shut. So, rather than risk an assault, Fraser led his men eastward, around the outer walls to prevent reinforcements reaching the city. There were enough officers with experience of the campaign of 1801 who remembered the lie of the land, so Fraser set up posts on the narrow isthmus between the sea and the two large brackish lakes across the neck of land that separated them. He then marched on a dozen miles to occupy the fort at Aboukir, overlooking the wide bay where the British had landed in

1801 and where Nelson had destroyed the French fleet three years before that. It was a wise move. On the morning of the 20th the frigate *Apollo* appeared, shepherding most of the missing transports into Aboukir Bay. Two days later Admiral Duckworth's fleet came over the horizon and, daunted by the sight, the Turkish governor of Alexandria surrendered the city.

The British marched through the gates and their task seemed to have been accomplished for, with the sea and the Royal Navy at their backs, Alexandria seemed secure. For the little army of nearly 6,000 men – British soldiers of the 31st, 35th and 78th Foot, the Royal Artillery and Engineers and the foreign mercenaries of the Chasseurs Britanniques cavalry, the Swiss and assorted European of de Roll's Regiment and the Sicilian irregulars, together with some 700 of their wives and children – the prospect was not unpleasant. Alexandria was on the sea and, once their quarters were cleaned and made habitable, there would be the minimum of risk and the principal problem might be boredom.

Then, two days later, Major Missett limped into General Fraser's headquarters with unexpected bad news. To Fraser's amazement, he announced that the city was in imminent danger of starvation. There was not enough grain to feed the inhabitants for more than ten days and the British garrison itself would survive only by eating the salt meat and fish in their ships and then relying on that being replenished. The worry was, he continued, that Alexandria was dependent on wheat and rice from Rosetta and meat and barley from Rahmanieh, farther up the Nile. So, to ensure the survival of Alexandria and its British garrison, the general would have to capture and hold both towns. Nothing like this had been mentioned in General Fraser's orders.

According to Missett, there was no time to ask the permission of General Fox to occupy these towns and large tracts of the Nile delta. It was vital to act at once, he said, because of the threats of starvation and a counter-attack by Albanians. Missett insisted that the defences of Rosetta were almost non-existent and that the Albanians were an undisciplined rabble. Indeed, it was assumed in the British Army that Ottoman troops, whether Egyptian, Turkish, Syrian or Albanian, could never stand against European volleys, whether British or French, unless trained and led by

European officers; they were likely, it was learned, to be commanded by Mehemet Ali himself. So Fraser ordered two battalions – 1,400 men of the 31st, recruited around Huntingdon, and the Chasseurs Britanniques with four small guns, commanded by Brigadier the Hon. Robert Meade of the 50th recruited in west Kent – to march. To direct operations he also sent his second-in-command, Major-General Patrick Wauchope of the 50th.

At dawn the next morning, 29 March, as the column marched through the city's gates, heading east, a few, who had fought in the Battle of Alexandria six years before, would have recognized the scenery: huge fragments of ancient masonry, heeling and sinking in drifts of sand; the wide, shallow, reed-fringed lakes; the pale yellow desert stretching to the horizon, or to the vivid green of the delta; distant views of mud-walled villages and tufted palms, quaking in the hot air; sandstorms, murky as London fog; hot, dry days and cold nights. Then there was the desert itself and, for some, more memories of 1801:

> This plain is the most miserable of any in Egypt, not a tree or even a bit of grass, all sand and scorching as a furnace. Vermin of all sorts but most fleas and ants, scorpions and beetles crawling over one in the night and getting under the clothes and no man is permitted to undress, or even take off his sword.[4]

The first night was spent under the stars, and the following evening they reached some relatively high ground overlooking Rosetta. 'All was still,' said Colonel Bunbury,

> The walls appeared to stand without defenders and the gates remained open. But no person came forth to meet the British; no information was received as to the state of affairs within the town; nothing was known of the number, or the temper, of the Albanians . . . there might be two, or two hundred, or two thousand of them. All was dark and silent and doubtful.[5]

It seemed likely that the town had been evacuated so it should be occupied quickly and fortified against counter-attack. Wauchope decided to be bold and himself led the infantry forward in three columns and, then in single file, through the open gates and into 'the narrow, gloomy and intricate lanes of Rosetta'. It was a calculated risk for, once within, the particular skills of his men – the volley-firing, the bayonet charge and the grapeshot of his guns – would be useless. Soon each soldier could only see the man ahead in the twisting alleys beneath the tall, shuttered houses. Then, when Wanchope and his men were 'thoroughly entangled and hemmed in by the lofty buildings', the ambush was sprung.

'From the house-tops and every cranny and opening in every house' came 'a storm of fire . . . Our soldiers could make no return for no enemy met their eyes. All that they could see were the quick flashes of the fire-arms and our brave men fell fast and helpless under the deathshot.'[6] Wauchope dropped dead and then Meade fell with a bullet in the head. Men were shot down trying to break into the houses for cover. The survivors fell back, dragging the wounded. Outside the walls, Turkish cavalry whirled into view, sweeping through the artillery and baggage trains and cutting down the rearguard.

Lieutenant-Colonel Bruce, the most senior officer in the town still standing, took command and ordered his drummer to beat the retreat. All who heard it ran back through the alleys and into the open, and the Chasseurs Britanniques took up a defensive position on the high ground from which they had started an hour before. They were just in time. Stopping first to kill the wounded, the Albanians rushed out through the gates to cut off stragglers only to be halted by the first volley the British were able to fire. Having beaten off the first attack, Bruce ordered an immediate retreat to Alexandria. The cost had been terrible. Four officers – including Wauchope – and 181 men had been killed and 19 officers – including Meade – and 263 men wounded. A third of the force had been lost. Two days later the survivors straggled into Alexandria.

Major Missett was unsympathetic and in his despatch to London blamed the disaster on Fraser for not having sent the force sooner, on Wauchope for rashly entering the town and on the wretched soldiers for cowardice. He enclosed other accounts calculated to discredit the British commanders. One claimed that the Albanians had abandoned the town before the attack, then returned and that the British had been sitting in coffee shops when their officers panicked and ordered a precipitate retreat. Missett told Fraser that the force he had sent had been far too small and that now he must not only make another attempt with a stronger force but also capture Damietta on the far side of the delta to prevent Ottoman reinforcements arriving from Syria. He assured him that a Mameluke army was about to take Cairo and would soon be marching north to support the British in the delta.

But General Fraser had lost heart and, as Duckworth's ships were still offshore, talked of evacuating Egypt while he still had enough salted meat to feed his men. However, Missett was persuasive and finally convinced him that when he had taken the three delta towns he would have all the provisions he could want. So on 3 April a second force of 2,500 men marched out, commanded by Brigadier William Stewart with Colonel John Oswald as his second-in-command. The column was accompanied by siege artillery dragged over the sand by Captain Hallowell's seamen and camels laden with ammunition and stores. Next day they reached Aboukir, where more heavy guns and ammunition were landed from the sea.

The vanguard of some 500 British troops commanded by Lieutenant-Colonel Patrick Macleod, who had fought at Maida with the 78th Foot and commanded them in Calabria, was ordered inland towards the village of Edko, on the shore of a wide lake, where he was joined by the main force next day. General Stewart now heard that Turkish cavalry occupied the hamlet of El Hamed, some five miles south of Rosetta, commanding an isthmus three miles wide between the Nile and Lake Edko. This would threaten the right flank of his advance on Rosetta and was the route by which enemy reinforcements could reach the town from the south. Major Macleod was ordered to take it. As he approached, the Turkish horsemen galloped towards him in a show of resistance, then wheeled away. Macleod was also told to watch for the Mamelukes, but of them there was no sign. So his Highlanders quickly fortified the hamlet, which was bordered by dry ditches, offering good defensive positions against cavalry. Then his force was relieved by 300 foreign mercenaries of de Roll's Regiment under Major Vogelsang, and Macleod rejoined the advance on Rosetta.

As Stewart reached the high ground overlooking the town on 7 April, officers scanning the defences through telescopes saw the rotting remains of the British dead still sprawled before the walls. Stewart sent skirmishers forward to clear enemy outposts and ordered working parties to bury the corpses, many of them mutilated. His infantry dug positions in the sandhills, while the gunners prepared batteries in readiness for a formal siege. Mortars and carronades opened fire first, followed on 12 April by fourteen heavy guns concentrated on one point in the walls to batter a breach. This took time, as all ammunition had to be carried by camels across seven miles of soft sand from boats coming ashore on the beaches of sea and lake. It was difficult to assess results but one ensign reported that 'the only visible effect . . . was the cutting in two and upsetting of many lofty minarets of the mosques'.[7]

For ten days the desultory bombardment continued without sign of a breach in the walls. The British had only enough troops to invest the western side of Rosetta and so were unable to prevent reinforcements reaching the defenders from the other side of the Nile. There was still no sign of the Mamelukes, who had been expected to have taken Cairo, but a growing fear of more enemy reinforcements reaching the town. The defenders made violent sorties, which were beaten back by a few dragoons; the British responded by ferrying 250 Highlanders in ships' boats across the Nile to attack Rosetta from the east, surprising an Albanian battery and turning its own guns on the town before returning the way they had come. Otherwise there seemed to be a stalemate. Stewart decided to try summoning the town to surrender, the alternative being an assault and subsequent massacre. But officers approaching under a flag of truce were fired on from loopholes in the walls and had to retreat. Finally an Arab was induced with the promise of a handsome reward to carry a letter into the town; he disappeared through the gates and was then seen being hanged on the ramparts.

On 19 April the Albanians launched their biggest sortie from Rosetta and, although this was halted by musket fire from the Sussex farm-boys of the 35th Regiment, reports reached Stewart that a strong force of Turkish cavalry had crossed the Nile to the south and was attacking El Hamed. So he ordered the light companies of the 35th and de Roll's Regiment under Captain Tarleton to reinforce Major Vogelsang there.

Tarleton marched all night, nearing El Hamed before first light and, in the lurid light of the desert dawn, sighted and attacked the Turkish cavalry in the hope of driving them back across the Nile. They were too strong and it was he who fell back to make a stand in the dry bed of a canal; although the Turks themselves left El Hamed, they did not re-cross the river. Then, rashly, he divided his force, sending one hundred men of de Roll's to enter El Hamed and marching his own company of the 35th to the west bank of the Nile, where they formed a defensive post. As the mercenaries marched towards the village, the Turkish cavalry charged. Caught in the open, the infantry tried to form a square but were cut down, a few running to El Hamed to join Major Vogelsang's post. Watching this, Tarleton sent a rider to General Stewart, pleading for reinforcement.

Stewart was in despair. After more than a fortnight of bombarding Rosetta there was no sign of its defence weakening. Having sent a substantial force to El Hamed, he was in no state to send more and so decided to raise the siege and retreat to Alexandria. First, he loaded his sick and wounded and the remaining provisions on camels and sent them west under escort of the survivors of the 78th and de Roll's regiments. It would be impossible to save the heavy artillery, so on the night of 20 April, while seven companies of the 35th held off the enemy with volleys, the big guns were spiked and buried in the sand. Next morning his remaining 2,000 men formed a large hollow oblong with the field-guns and ammunition and camel train in the centre. He then sent a rider to Colonel Macleod, ordering him to abandon El Hamed and retreat to Edko, where he would meet the main force for the retreat west.

'We had scarcely moved off', recalled Ensign Anderson of the 78th,

when our square was surrounded by thousands of Turkish cavalry and infantry, howling, screaming and galloping like savages around us, at the same time firing at us from their long muskets, We occasionally halted our square, wheeled back a section and gave them a few rounds of shot and shell from our artillery, then moved on in the same good order. This was a long and trying day and the only retreat in square I ever saw. It occupied us nearly twelve hours, from five in the morning to the same hour in the evening. The enemy with fearful shouts, followed us, firing the whole of that time . . . when they ventured sufficiently near they were sure of more volleys than one and we had the satisfaction of seeing numbers of them fall . . . But when we got to Edko, there was no appearance of Colonel Macleod.[8]

That morning El Hamed had also been attacked. Macleod had established his headquarters and most of his men on and around a hillock with outposts, each manned by up to fifty men, commanding interlocking arcs of fire. Then sentries reported a flotilla of eight craft – two square-rigged and mounting heavy guns, the rest, high-sailed feluccas – on the Nile, approaching from the south. These were Turkish reinforcements for Rosetta – said to number 6,000 – but, seeing that the British still held El Hamed, they landed. Macleod, noting the odds, lost confidence in his own dispositions and ordered his troops, including those on the river bank and in the village, to fall back and Major Vogelsang to establish his four companies and a field-gun on a sandhill more than half a mile to the rear of El Hamed. But as they hurried across the open ground 'in a hasty and disorderly manner'[9] the Turkish cavalry charged again, cutting them down and sending the survivors running for cover behind the bank of a dry canal. Albanian foot soldiers rushed the village and from there fired on the fugitives.

It was a shocking scene. 'The Bedouin Arabs have a curious mode of making prisoners', wrote Admiral Lord Collingwood, when he heard about it some weeks later.

They are well mounted, gallop in upon those they would surprise and hooking them with a hook-rope, tow them off at full speed; if they fall off they are killed by the hook. They carried off two officers of Marines and some sailors who were employed watering and a woman, who, poor body, was gone to the stream to wash her smock. The day after she was found she had lost her head; did not tow well, I suppose.[10]

Captain Colin Mackay, commanding a company of grenadiers, lost both his subalterns and half his men in hand-to-hand fighting. He himself was cut down with a sabre slash across the neck and ordered his surviving men to leave him and fight their way out. They refused, but two sergeants carried him across open ground under fire and reached the hillock, where they were told that Colonel Macleod was dead. Major Vogelsang now took command of some three hundred survivors, fighting back to back, and he decided to surrender. But the Highlanders refused, with the wounded Captain Mackay crying out 'Soldiers, never, never, while we have a round left!'[11] Soon all ammunition was gone and Vogelsang waved a white cloth, shouting, 'Cease firing! Cease firing!'[12] But the Turkish cavalry had launched their charge and galloped over the sandhill, cutting down all with a weapon in hand, rounding up the rest. 'The Turkish pasha, who commanded, then rode up and inquired, "Where is the brave man who has so long and so ably resisted me?" ' as a survivor, Lieutenant Mathieson, recalled. 'Colin Mackay, the hero of the day, was pointed out to him lying still in agony under a gun, on which Ali Pasha dismounted and, creeping near Mackay, said, "You are indeed a brave man and you deserve to wear my sword." '[13]

Mathieson continued:

The few prisoners who survived were then secured, the dead were decapitated (and, I fear, many of the wounded also) and their living comrades were forced to carry their heads in sacks to the boats and poor Colonel Macleod's conspicuous amongst the number. Most of the enemy then embarked with their prisoners and their trophies and returned in triumph to Cairo. There the heads of the dead were exhibited on poles for some weeks around the principal palaces. The survivors were committed to confinement and the officers were allowed at large on their paroles and treated well, especially Captain Mackay, who continued to receive the most marked attention from everyone.[14]

General Stewart continued his retreat, harried by Turkish cavalry, finally reaching Alexandria and the protection of General Fraser's artillery on 24 April. In the siege and on the retreat his losses had been surprisingly light: 11 men killed and 8 officers and 161 men wounded; at El Hamed, however, all 36 officers and 780 men of Colonel Macleod's force had been lost. Fraser was appalled at the sight of the exhausted survivors as he watched them march and ride on camels into the city. He had lost about a thousand men, a fifth of his entire force and now had barely four thousand left to defend the long perimeter of crumbling walls around Alexandria, which might soon have to face an assault by the Ottoman army.

Fraser was in a dilemma. Should he await starvation, then siege and the probable destruction of his entire army? His soldiers were stricken with ophthalmia and some had already lost the sight of one, or both, eyes. But what was the alternative to remaining where they were? He had been ordered to hold Alexandria and the order could only be countermanded after an exchange of despatches with General Fox in Messina, if not with the government in London, which could take weeks, and by then it might be too late. In any case, evacuation would require a large fleet of transports and warships which would also take weeks to assemble, even after being ordered to do so. Fraser had reported the first disaster at Rosetta to Fox and asked for reinforcements but there was no news of any; nor was there any news of the Mameluke allies that Major Missett had promised.

Deep in depression, Fraser confided in Missett, hinting that evacuation might be the only option. At this, the consul seemed alarmed and, to the general's amazement, said that, although there were no stores of corn in Alexandria, there was plenty of rice and, if a suitable price were offered, the Arabs might bring wheat and barley from neighbouring farmland. This proved to be the case, food stocks were quickly replenished and the fear of starvation removed.

Fraser and his staff wondered what Missett's motives had been in his warning of famine, which had brought about the disasters in the delta. Gradually a theory took shape. Alone in Cairo and then Alexandria, Missett had made friends with the Mamelukes and supported their plan to seize Egypt from the Ottoman beys. In this, he seemed to have told them, they would be supported by the British. But when General Fraser arrived with his little army, this was not part of his orders, so Missett had resorted to subterfuge to persuade him to occupy as much of Egypt as possible. He announced a critical shortage of food, insisting that salvation only lay in the occupation of the delta. When fighting began, as he expected, the Mamelukes would, he believed, join the British and, eventually, the latter would hand Egypt over to the former. But what Missett did not know in March and April was that, while marching on Cairo, the Mamelukes had been defeated by Mehemet Ali and had abandoned plans to join the British at Rosetta. Hence the calamity.

Fraser's dilemma was resolved when, on 25 May, the sails of a convoy were sighted out at sea to the north-east and this proved to be the reinforcements of two British infantry battalions – the 21st and the 62nd – and two store-ships from Malta. Now, at last, Fraser could hope to hold Alexandria, Soon afterwards, a succession of horsemen rode out of the desert and asked to see General Fraser. The first was a spare, sunburned young man in Arab dress, who announced himself as Lieutenant Mathieson and that he had been captured at El Hamed. He told the general that he had been released and sent to Alexandria with a message from Mehemet Ali, asking whether Fraser would receive an emissary with an offer of an armistice. Fraser agreed and some days later another British prisoner, Captain Delancey, arrived with an Ottoman emissary from Cairo. He proposed a settlement whereby the British should evacuate Alexandria unmolested and Mehemet Ali would release all his prisoners and grant an amnesty to Alexandrians who had helped the British. The meeting was cordial, but Fraser had to explain that he could not evacuate without orders and there would inevitably be a delay in his reply.

The British spent a hot summer in Alexandria without further fighting. Then, on 2 September, orders arrived to evacuate, the decision having been taken in July by the government in London and relayed by a special messenger, Sir Arthur Paget. On succeeding Windham at the War Office, Lord Castlereagh had read a despatch from Major Missett, urging the occupation of the Nile delta and, realizing that Fraser's force would then be overstretched and vulnerable, the war minister had sent an urgent message that no more than Alexandria itself should be held. When news of the disasters in the delta reached him, Castlereagh had decided that a campaign in Egypt was, in any case, irrelevant and could only be considered if Sicily were evacuated.

Fraser could now accept Mehemet Ali's terms, stressing the urgency of returning prisoners. The Albanian's response was, as Fraser put it, 'truly noble'[15] as he returned not only all his British prisoners but also those sold into slavery farther up the Nile. All reported that, after the horrors at El Hamed, they had been treated with relative compassion.

On 19 September the last of some 8,000 British soldiers embarked and the convoy sailed for Messina, leaving the disgraced Major Missett behind. He did not linger long because his Mameluke friends had begun to fight among themselves and seemed to have lost hope of seizing power.* After he left Egypt, he devoted himself to trying to persuade all who would listen that his advice to General Fraser had been prudent and that the defeats were the fault of the officers who had commanded in the delta.

The British were thankful to be sailing for Sicily. Few had understood why they had been in Egypt, although some thought that it had been to forestall the French, while Ensign Anderson believed that it was 'to create a diversion in favour of Russia against the Turkish army'.[16] But on arrival at Messina they heard news that made Anderson's theory irrelevant and, indeed, transformed the whole strategic scene. News took many weeks to reach Sicily from England, but European newspapers were regularly smuggled out of Naples to Capri and from there brought by dispatch vessel to Messina. Now it was learned that, on 8 July, Russia had become an ally of France. Following the defeat of the Russians at Friedland in East Prussia on 14 June, the Tsar had sued for peace, and on the 25th he had met the Emperor Napoleon on an elaborate raft moored symbolically in the River Niemen at Tilsit. The Emperor had been able to dictate his terms. Russia was to abandon the Mediterranean – notably Corfu and the Ionian Islands – and join France in an alliance against the Ottoman Empire, which, eventu-

---

* Four years later the Mamelukes were lured to a gathering at the citadel in Cairo at the apparently friendly invitation of Mehemet Ali and were massacred there.

ally, they might divide between them. If Britain continued to reject peace terms based on the return of former French possessions overseas, Russia was to help coerce the Baltic nations and Portugal to join the Continental System banning trade with the British. Prussia had already been marginalized after its defeat at Jena, and now Poland was to be divided between Russia and the Grand Duchy of Warsaw, which was to be ruled by the King of Saxony and closely tied into alliance with France. Napoleon had, it seemed, reached the summit of power, dominating the whole of Europe except Portugal, Sicily and the Ottoman Balkans.

The two great British efforts of the past months – the expedition to Egypt and Duckworth's display off Constantinople – could now be seen for the fiascos they were. When Duckworth's ships dropped anchor off Sicily and Fraser's soldiers filed ashore, the future looked as bewildering as ever it had. Lord Castlereagh acted quickly to forestall Napoleon's expected moves. Fearing that he would not only close the Baltic to British trade but was also about to seize the Danish fleet, in September Castlereagh sent Admiral Lord Gambier to Copenhagen to seize it; he bombarded the city, landed troops commanded by Major-General Sir Arthur Wellesley and removed the Danish ships to British ports. Portugal, the only maritime nation in Europe still open to the British, was invaded by France after General Junot's army marched through Spain in November. But Sir Sidney Smith had been recalled from the Mediterranean and appeared off Lisbon to rescue the royal family and the government together with its gold reserves just as Junot's cavalry was clattering into the outskirts of the capital. His critic and the other dominant British officer from the central Mediterranean, Sir John Moore, had been ordered to Gibraltar with 8,000 of the best British troops from Sicily to form a new strategic reserve and he had sailed from Messina on 25 October. Sir John left with mixed feelings: relief at being free of the entanglements of Sicilian royalty and Anglo-Sicilian intrigue; and regret at leaving a task unfinished; sadness that his demure courtship of Caroline, the seventeen-year-old daughter of General Fox, had withered, while her sister Louisa had already married Colonel Bunbury. To succeed Moore, General Stuart, Count of Maida, was sent back to Sicily. Despite his victory at Maida, he was not welcome. When he had been recalled two years earlier, Major John Hamill, an Irish officer who had been wounded at Maida, had written of General Stuart, 'I am confident that he takes with him the detestation of the whole army. As an individual, he is abhorred and, as an officer, despised.'[17] There had been another change in Sicily. Hugh Elliot had been replaced as minister to the Bourbon court by William Drummond, an experienced diplomat who had held that post before Elliot's arrival, and at once he too became enmeshed in the debate over future strategy.

While British eyes had concentrated on the coasts of Europe, a bizarre distraction was reported on the other side of the world. In 1806 the British had captured the Cape of Good Hope from the Dutch and then taken it upon themselves to cross the South Atlantic to attack the Spanish in Buenos Aires. They had failed and the following year the commanders had been replaced, although their reinforced army had captured Montevideo. It was a Pyrrhic victory because, isolated and out-manoeuvred, the British were forced to withdraw. It was yet another costly blunder.

The year 1807 ended and 1808 began with one apparent certainty: whatever his immediate intentions, Napoleon was still looking east and, with Russia now his ally, the British alone could stop him from reaching the Levant and his goal: India. Even that was not all, for the subcontinent with its limitless natural resources and vast, compliant population was also the way to, and the entrepôt for, trade with the East Indies, South-East Asia and China: all the riches of the Orient, real, potential, and imagined, that dazzled Europeans from so far.

7

The Emperor and the Queen of the Seas

THE SKY over Venice was dark and threatening at the end of November 1807. The *bora* might be about to howl out of the mountains of the north and east, or the warmer *sirocco* might blow from the south and, if heavy rain over the Austrian Alps combined with a southerly gale, an *aqua alta* might flood the city. But there was another, more disturbing, apprehension. It was ten years since General Napoleon Bonaparte had overthrown and humiliated the ancient republic of the *Serenissima*. Thereafter he had remained aloof, commanding his army on the Italian plains and bullying Austria. Those well-to-do Venetians who wished to maintain their palaces and their villas and estates in the Veneto had become pragmatic and learned to live with their conquerors, like most Italians since the fall of the Roman Empire. So they would offer a form of welcome to the Emperor Napoleon – the Corsican ogre of contemporary mythology – who was about to arrive in their city.

Venetian eyes looked north to the shores of the lagoon, where they knew he must already be. He was, in fact, being shown the huge and magnificent Villa Pisani, the grandest of the Venetian mansions on the banks of the Brenta Canal, which ran south from Padua, escorted by his stepson the dashing Eugène de Beauharnais, whom he had appointed Viceroy of Italy and Prince of Venice. Over glasses of milk and biscuits he admired the spectacularly sycophantic painting of *The Glorification of the Pisani Family* by

Tiepolo on the ceiling of the ballroom, disappointed that, as it was painted directly on to the plaster and not on canvas, it could not be removed to his palace at Fontainebleau. The Emperor was not overawed by such splendour and was, in any case, planning to buy the house and give it to his stepson.

He could not command the weather. Next morning, Sunday the 29th, broke cold, wet and windy. As a show of piety the Emperor heard Mass in the chapel of the villa, saying that he was giving thanks for his successful invasion of Portugal. Then Count Alvise Querini, the chamberlain, who had planned and would conduct the forthcoming arrival in Venice, led the imperial party, which included Marshal Berthier, the former war minister and now Napoleon's chief of staff, and the glittering Marshal Murat, the formidable cavalry commander, to Fusina on the shore of the Venetian lagoon. There they boarded five specially built barges, encrusted with gilded stucco and allegorical statuary. The Emperor, muffled in a heavy coat reaching his ankles and wearing heavy boots, immediately retired into a little domed pavilion crowned with the imperial eagle, carpeted and furnished in oriental style and swagged with brocade curtains. At half-past two the twelve oarsmen began to row out on to the tossing water while the Emperor pontificated on the decadence of Venice and its corrupt aristocracy which, he said, had brought about its downfall. It was getting dark as the procession approached the ancient port of departure from Europe for the East, the Emperor now afloat on the same salt water that bore the ships of the Royal Navy and broke on the shores of the Levant.

As the domes and *campanili* of Venice materialized through driving rain and freezing fog, the thump of saluting guns was heard and the flotilla entered the north-western mouth of the Grand Canal that wound through Venice. Querini suggested that the Emperor go outside to seat himself on a gilded throne shaped like a scallop-shell but he refused, although he emerged from shelter as the barge drew up to a floating pavilion, where a reception had been prepared. As they drew alongside, the mayor and patriarch of Venice came on board and began speeches of welcome, to be cut short by Napoleon with a gesture with his left hand as his right held his cocked hat to his head in the blustering wind. Now the keys – one gold, one silver – of the Serenissima were presented to him on a velvet cushion as a symbol of abasement by two turbaned moors, for the Venetians had heard of his liking for exotic attendants.

Ahead, lit by oil lamps and torches, was an extraordinary sight. Spanning the Grand Canal, loomed a huge triumphal arch, seemingly of stone but in fact of wood, canvas and gilded stucco, designed by Gianantonio Selva, the architect of the new Fenice opera house. Flanked by tall columns crowned with imperial eagles, it floated between the churches of Santa Lucia* and San Simeone Piccolo, standing as high as the churches themselves. The chilled Emperor urged haste and his barge passed under the arch, followed by a fleet of other barges and gondolas, past palaces hung with French *tricolore* flags, flapping damply in the wind, towards the Rialto bridge. Crowded balconies and windows were hung with rugs and flags, and within the arcade of the Fondeca dei Turchi, the former mansion of the Turkish merchants, a band was playing the *Marseillaise*. The Emperor, mindful of symbolism, remarked, 'We owe it to Turkey if the haughty Queen of the Seas is now compelled to implore our indulgence.'[1] Finally the barge slid alongside the Istrian marble steps at the Piazzetta di San Marco, beside the white colonnades and pink façade of the Doge's Palace. Huge crowds had gathered, for Venetians enjoyed a festival and had come to prefer French rule to Austrian, to which they had been subjected from 1797 to 1805. Mindful of this, the authorities had distributed posters warning restaurants, wine shops and gondoliers not to put up their prices for the occasion. Venice might be ready for a carnival but the Emperor, after five hours on the water, was cold, wet, tired and irritable. In the Piazza, beneath sopping French banners hanging from the ceremonial flagstaffs and writhing in the wind, there waited another welcoming delegation with an invitation to a formal dinner that evening and to hear a Te Deum at the basilica next morning. But the Emperor simply acknowledged the bows and salutes and walked across the great Piazza to the doors of the newly defined Palazzo Reale on the south side. He climbed the stairs, announced that he would attend

---

* Now replaced by the Santa Lucia railway station.

no more formal engagements that day, waived his daily medical consultation and his supper, climbed into a hot bath, then wrapped himself in a towelling dressing gown. He had finally occupied Venice in person.

Originally Napoleon had planned to stay there for three days but now he decided to remain for at least a week; not, it was rumoured, only for sightseeing. There was only one member of his staff, a confidant named Clerici, who was privy to the other whispered motive: an assignation. On his way to Venice the Emperor had stopped at Milan, and at La Scala opera house was said to have met a beautiful young woman, the Countess Nahir de Lusignan.★ They had, in fact, met nine years ealier, in Egypt, at a party by the Pyramids when she, brought up in Alexandria, the daughter of a French father and an Indian mother, had been eighteen. Now she was to be described as 'a thoroughbred . . . a harmony of curves'[2] and she had again caught his eye. He had asked her to follow him to Venice incognito and charged Clerici with making arrangements in secret, stressing that on no account must they be known to his sister Elisa, who was accompanying him. He was told that Nahir had already arrived to stay at the Palazzo Sandi and would meet him at the Fenice opera house on Tuesday evening. So, content, Napoleon went to bed and put on the spectacles, which he never wore in public, to read a book of Venetian history to gather controversial talking points for the following day.

On Monday the sun shone on his procession to the Basilica of San Marco for the Te Deum and the singing of an anthem, 'God Save the Emperor and Our King Napoleon'. Looking up, Napoleon saw in the gallery against the gold mosaic vaulting, Nahir gazing down, having disobeyed his order to avoid appearing in public. Afterwards, he was asked to leave by a side door for fear that the huge and exuberant crowd in the Piazza might try, as was their wont with visiting celebrities, to hoist him on to their shoulders. Once outside, he looked up to see whether the removal of

---

★ The story of Nahir de Lusignan relies on a single known source and has been questioned by some historians. But it rings true and so has been included.

the famous bronze horses had diminished the magnificence of the façade, decided that it had not and decreed that the basilica should become the cathedral of Venice in place of the remote church of San Pietro di Castello. He was also shown the great campanile and it was explained that Galileo had demonstrated his telescope at the top. At the far end of the Piazza, which he declared to be the finest drawing-room in Europe, he inspected the building of the extension – including a grand staircase and a ballroom – to the Palazzo Reale following the demolition of the church of San Geminiano. 'It was an old, tired church', said his guide, the architect Selva, to which he replied tartly, 'You are a good architect but you are also good at destroying.'[3]

Napoleon became aware of the colossal damage inflicted on Venice by his administrators during the past decade. In the early days of French occupation the Arsenale had been wrecked and already thirty-four monasteries and convents and eighteen churches had been, or were being, closed.* Some of the churches were given other uses – one as a prison, another as a tavern – but at least a dozen were demolished, including some of high architectural and artistic splendour.

During the coming week he constantly produced ideas for practical, sometimes grandiose, municipal improvements, based loosely on his plans for Paris. Street lighting should be better. A new piazza, twice the size of San Marco, should be laid out by Selva on the island of Giudecca for military parades. There must be a new cemetery, so two islands should be combined into one for the purpose and be known as San Michele. He visited the wide, new Via Eugenia† built over a former canal and, beside it, the new Giardini Pubblici, which were being laid out where the French had ordered the demolition of three churches, a seminary, two convents, a hospice for sailors and many old houses, initially to provide sites for shore batteries. A smaller garden was being planted between the Palazzo Reale and the mouth of the Grand Canal in place of

---

* This was only a beginning and these were to be followed by another 25 monastic foundations, 15 more churches and 385 *scuole*, the local charitable and social institutions.

† Now the Via Garibaldi.

the ancient state granary, which had been demolished, to provide a view from the palace windows. He suggested that the island of San Giorgio should become a free port, to encourage trade. The Scuola di San Marco should be converted into a hospital. The state archives should be housed together in an old building by the church of the Frari. He ordered that a cultural academy be founded as the *Instituto Veneto Scienze, Lettere e Arti*.

At the Arsenale, at the launch of two corvettes, he announced plans for the expansion of naval shipbuilding in order to sweep the British from the Adriatic; and he ordered that the workers be given an extra eight days' pay. Told that ships of the line had difficulty in making a passage from the Arsenale to the open sea, he decided that a deep channel was to be dredged from the dockyard to the Malamocco entrance to the lagoon. Shown a ruinous stretch of the great *murazzo* sea-wall protecting the lagoon from the Adriatic, he offered funds for its restoration. A chain of fortresses was to be constructed, or, where they already existed, strengthened, to guard the northern shores of the Lagoon; the largest of these – gigantic, with moats and bastions in the style of Vauban – to be at Marghera, north-west of Venice on the mainland. He announced that the debts of the city would be met by the Kingdom of Italy while quietly asking his financial adviser to devise means of taxing the Venetians so that they would think it for their own benefit rather than that of his campaign in Spain.

There was time for sightseeing and it was at a hectic pace, with meals being bolted in ten minutes. He was taken out to the island of Torcello, where he walked to the cathedral and the ruins that marked the original Venetian settlement, to Burano and to Murano, where he watched glass-blowing and bought identical mirrors and goblets as '*souvenirs de Venise*'[4] for the Empress Josephine and other women in his life. At the Marciano Library he searched unsuccessfully for evidence that the Bonapartes were descended from the ancient Roman family of Bona Pars, but still gave money for new acquisitions. He enjoyed displaying his own recently acquired knowledge, telling his hosts that the marble lions outside the gates of the Arsenale had originated in Athens. But, while there, he asked to see the ancient state barge, the *Bucintoro*, only to be told that it had been burned by the French on their arrival a decade earlier. He enjoyed, or pretended to enjoy, entertainment in his honour: singing in the torchlit Piazza below his windows, after which he invited the choir inside for mulled wine; acrobatic dockyard workers performing their traditional 'human pyramid' gymnastic display; opera at La Fenice, where his bodyguards sat among the orchestra in case one of the musicians might be a British assassin. He watched a lamplit regatta on the Grand Canal from the Palazzo Balbi and the illumination of the Piazza di San Marco by 4,000 torches and 1,000 candles, which ended at midnight when a sudden downpour extinguished them, prompting Napoleon to say with relief that it was God's way of closing the festivities. Next day, the city was flooded by an *aqua alta* and Napoleon was surprised to see the Venetians wading to work, knee-deep but with little concern.

His social round had included a reception for the Venetian aristocracy, whose names had been recorded in the Golden Book, which the invading French had ceremonially burned. He had been briefed on current talking points and was at his most charming, discussing French fashions and the theatre, mentioning that the Venetian comedian and playwright Carlo Goldoni had also been popular in Paris. Then, it was whispered, he left Eugène to preside and was guided by Clerici to a small drawing-room, where Nahir awaited him and he greeted her with, 'What a surprise to see you!'[5] He lingered so long, that when Querini knocked on the door to announce that a celebrated soprano was about to sing in the music-room, he glared 'with the eyes of a basilisk'.[6] However, his sister's suspicions had been aroused and he told her that he had been detained by an urgent conference about his plans in Spain. His next meeting with Nahir was more discreet, it was said, and, telling his sister that he had to attend another important conference about the war, he met her after dark in the Campo San Giobbe, which was so chill that after an hour she had caught cold and retired to bed with a temperature. Tonsillitis was suspected, so she missed their meeting next day, the third anniversary of his coronation, sinking him in gloom despite a letter of congratulation from Josephine. Nahir was well enough the next night to watch a grand ball at La Fenice from a box, but the day after the doctor ordered her to bed with bronchitis.

The world beyond the lagoon was pressing upon him. There was a meeting about the future of Spain with Marshal Murat, whom he ordered to take command of its planned occupation with a promise of an eventual throne. Then a letter arrived from Talleyrand stressing the urgent need for his presence in Paris. It was time to leave. On Sunday he reluctantly heard Mass, seated on a throne in the church of the Redentore, followed by a hot drink in the refectory afterwards. Next day farewells were to be made, one to a Jewish delegation wishing to thank the French for having removed the gates to the Ghetto. He had given bronze busts of himself to the Arsenale and the Marciano Library but decided against the erection of a large statue of himself outside the Doge's Palace as it might be defaced and ridiculed. There was a formal meeting with Venetian worthies in the Grand Council Chamber there, where the Republic had been signed away ten years earlier, and he congratulated those who had made the visit so spectacular, including Selva and the sculptor Canova. A final reception for the aristocracy had been arranged but, although realizing his absence would offend them, he ordered Eugène to preside. On Monday 7 December Napoleon's grand plan for Venice was announced publicly. The official architect was to be Selva, and his projects would include the driving of wide new streets through the maze of alleys and canals, the extension of the great Riva degli Schiavoni waterfront promenade and several more public parks and gardens. Venetian reaction was mixed; many were said to feel that 'Venice seemed no longer ours.'[7]★

The Emperor departed next day by the barge in which he had arrived and thence by coach to Passariano, where he wanted to wait in the hope that Nahir might join him. But she remained ill in bed for another week.† Then another urgent summons arrived from Talleyrand and he again took to the road, leaving the exhausted Querini hopeful that he would never return.

★ Plans that were implemented included the enlarged Palazzo Reale and its garden on the site of the state granary, the extension of the Riva, the Giardini Pubblici, the cemetery of San Michele and the mainland fortresses, but the huge piazza on Giudecca was never realized.

† She is said to have returned to Alexandria, where she married a British diplomat, leaving another Napoleonic legend in Venice.

As Napoleon had intended, news of his visit to Venice quickly spread throughout Europe and newspaper reports were smuggled from Naples to the British on Capri, who rushed it to Sicily and to the naval and military commanders-in-chief. The presence of Marshals Berthier and Murat was noted and it seemed all too probable that, just as he had personally taken command at Boulogne during his planned invasion of England four years earlier, now Napoleon was preparing to strike south-east from his Venetian base. At the end of 1807 Lord Collingwood was in the *Ocean* off Corfu, which was still held by the French and regarded as a strategic stepping-stone to the Balkans and Constantinople. 'From the great preparations fleets and armies are making in the Adriatic and Bonaparte's arrival in Venice, I have little doubt of their destination being this place', he wrote, adding characteristically, 'I am rather disappointed to have heard nothing of them.'[8] As was his wont, the Emperor was keeping his enemies guessing.

8

This island of despair

ON 6 September 1808 the pageantry in Venice of the preceeding autumn was echoed in a Neapolitan pantomime. The new King of Naples was arriving at the Palazzo Reale and the crowds, agog to see the latest performer in the royal puppet show, were not disappointed. King Joachim I outdid their most extravagant expectations. A British officer described his

> good-humoured smile on his broad and manly countenance. His figure is fine and he had large blue eyes and immense whiskers and mustachios. His dress was a light blue frock coat with two silver epaulettes, a cocked hat garnished with feathers and an immense plume waving above all. His long, coal-black hair hung in ringlets over his fine, broad, athletic shoulders.[1]

French officers might have smiled at the latest incarnation of Marshal Murat, Grand Admiral, Duke of Berg and Cleves and a prince since he had married the Emperor Napoleon's sister.

It was this marriage that had sealed his success. In the beginning his only advantages had been his looks and his courage. An innkeeper's son from central France, Murat had shied away from his father's ambition for him to become a priest and, just before the Revolution, he had enlisted in the cavalry as a trooper. After five years he was commissioned and had commanded the guns that gave General Bonaparte his 'whiff of grapeshot' that put down the

Vendemaire royalist rising in Paris in 1795. As a cavalry officer he
had shown flair and dash in the campaigns in Italy and Egypt and
supported Bonaparte in the Brumaire *coup d'état* that made him
First Consul in 1799, to be rewarded by the command of the
Consular Guard. Then he met the youngest of his patron's three
sisters, Caroline Bonaparte.

In 1800, aged eighteen, Caroline had her family's classical looks,
a surprisingly fair complexion and memorable dark eyes, which
seemed to show sense and artistic sensibility. But she was defenceless against the overpowering attraction of General Murat, the *beau
sabreur* of the cavalry, the hero of innumerable battles and a notorious seducer. Murat was theatrically handsome, with charming
manners, and had learned to speak Italian with a fashionable
Tuscan accent. This was a veneer of cultivation, masking any
impression that he might also be an impetuous braggart. The
couple were soon married and General Murat was on his way to a
glittering future. Yet he earned his glory. In June that year he
fought brilliantly against the Austrians at Marengo and remained
on active service in Italy; in 1804 he was made a marshal and a year
later, following his brother-in-law's coronation, a prince. At
Austerlitz he had commanded the cavalry and he distinguished
himself in battle against the Prussians at Jena and the Russians at
Eylau. Then, after accompanying his imperial brother-in-law to
Venice, he had been sent to Spain early in 1808 as the Emperor's
viceroy. In May it was he who suppressed the uprising in Madrid
with a savagery recorded in paintings and etchings by Goya. Now
he was King of Naples in place of his brother-in-law Joseph, who
had been given the throne of Spain. A final touch to his transfor-
mation was the formal changing of his name to Gioachimo
Napoleone to perpetuate the new dynasty and the proclamation in
the imperial decree that from 1 August he would be 'Joachim
Napoléon par la grâce de Dieu et par la constitution de l'État, Roi
des Deux Siciles, Grand Amiral de l'Empire'. Behind his back he
was still 'Murat'.

Queen Caroline joined him in Naples on 25 September and at
once set about arranging their court in the four great palaces: the
Palazzo Reale on the city's waterfront; Capodimonte on a hill
to the north; Portici, beneath Vesuvius; and, the grandest of all,

Caserta, the vast imitation of Versailles, sixteen miles inland. To her husband, military affairs were of far more interest than civil and he quickly collected five French generals to command his army. But he also confirmed the Corsican friend of the Emperor's, Saliceti, as chief of police and his equivalent of the dreadful Fouché in Paris. Murat and his generals did not have far to look for an enemy. From the windows of three of his palaces he could see across the bay to the heights of Capri, where, from the tower of the Castiglione, flew the British flag. This was intolerable.

It was two years since Sir Sidney Smith had seized Capri. Soon after the victory at Maida, Sir John Moore had visited the island and, considering it secure so long as the Navy patrolled the bay, sent away the British troops, believing that a garrison of Mediterranean mercenaries would be sufficient for defence. These were the Royal Corsican Rangers, led by cosmopolitan officers – British, Italian, German and Swiss – and detachments of artillery-men and engineers. The commanding officer, Lieutenant-Colonel Hudson Lowe, another veteran of Maida, had had plenty of time to prepare defences. The town of Capri and its two harbours, the Marina Grande to the east and the Marina Piccola to the west, their fortifications based on Castle Hill, were under his direct command. Another 300 Corsicans were under Captain Richard Church, an energetic young Anglo-Irishman, small, wiry, with a determined chin and an 'agreeable and easy'[2] manner, who had fought with Colonel Kempt's light infantry at Maida. They were stationed on the high plateau of Anacapri, their defence based on the fortified summit of Monte Solaro. The Anacapri plateau seemed impregnable: to the west were precipices, dropping more than 1,000 feet to the sea; to the south another cliff, dividing it from the central saddle, passable only by the Phoenician Steps;★ Captain Church told a friend, 'Now fancy me leading a high-spirited Arab horse up these steps, which I have done!'[3] Much of the coast to the east and north was of jagged rocks and low cliffs, giving on to steep slopes of thick, thorny scrub and seemingly

---

★ Captain Church thought there were 650, but other estimates varied between 381 and 553.

impassable. Colonel Lowe improved on the natural defences, repairing the castle, building strongpoints and walls and scalping their surroundings of trees and brush that might offer cover, while the only two level fields on the island were commandeered as parade-grounds. Such was the island's apparent strength that the British sometimes spoke of it as 'Little Gibraltar'.[4]

The officers of the garrison at first enjoyed themselves on Capri. Lowe established his headquarters in a large house, the Palazzo Inglese, below the town and above the Marina Grande, commanding views of the Phoenician Steps and the signal station at their top and of distant Naples. They had just enough work to avoid boredom, inspecting their commands and reading the agents' reports and newspapers brought by fishermen, who also peddled groceries, soap and candles. The officers' messes were small but convivial, and there were always naval officers from the frigates and brigs offshore to be entertained. Colonel Lowe prepared regular shopping lists to be taken ashore, one ordering 'four dozen champagne; three dozen burgundy of three years old; three dozen burgundy of four years old; six dozen of the best wines, such as Frontignan, and any others that may be held in good estimation'.[5] At Anacapri, Captain Church wrote, 'We daily receive from Naples itself, Sorrento and Castellamare supplies of all sorts, particularly fresh butter and veal from Sorrento. We receive also gazettes from Paris, Naples, Florence, Milan, London and Amsterdam almost every day and always send the news to General Fox at Messina, perhaps a month before any account arrives to him from England.'[6] The Paris newspapers often reached Capri in little more than a fortnight and the latest maps of Italy could be ordered from Naples as required.

Captain Church passed his time riding about his command, three and a half miles by two miles of olive groves, vineyards, fig trees, surrounded by scrub and crags, siting new outposts and signal stations and encouraging his men. For recreation he played racquets with his officers, but they were few and their company gradually became stale. They could live well – local wine, fruit and fish combined well with imports from the mainland – but at dinner he complained, 'ennui becomes a guest for there is *no* society . . . Were there any English society in Capri it would be a delightful residence for the country is more beautiful than any I ever saw.'[7] This beauty – the romantic, dramatic scenery with its shades of green against the blue sea and the panorama of the Bay of Naples and Vesuvius beyond – and the balmy climate began to lull even the most energetic. Finally boredom wore them down, and he wrote, 'Nothing could prevent us from sinking under the pressure of ennui, so dreadfully experienced in this island of despair, but the soldiers' idea of a post of honour.'[8]

On 16 September 1808, ten days after Marshal Murat's arrival in Naples, Captain Church's Corsicans were relieved at Anacapri by the new arrived Royal Regiment of Malta, under the popular, easy-going Major John Hamill, yet another veteran of Maida and a friend of Colonel Lowe. They were 700-strong but inexperienced and lacked the martial vigour of those they replaced. Church led his men and his horse down the Phoenician Steps to Capri, where he joined Lowe's command. Even so, he was restive, writing, 'There is no chance of our being attacked' by the enemy he called 'the infernal Murat . . . At present we have two regiments here: I kept the place for two years with one!'[9] Capri seemed secure with a garrison of some 1,800 men.

From the windows of the Palazzo Reale in Naples telescopes were constantly trained on the island, also noting the movements of the guardship. This was usually a frigate, which circled the island, patrolled across the bay towards Ischia and visited the small island of Ponza, which was also held by the British. To the new King Joachim, Capri was more than a symbol of British power; it was an insult to himself, and he was determined that his first act as monarch should be its recapture. His staff had good reason to feel confident in the reports on the defenders' dispositions on the island. Colonel Lowe's principal intelligence agent, who moved between Capri and Naples, was a Corsican named Antonio Suzzarelli, who claimed to have been a lawyer and a former British officer. Murat's chief of police, Saliceti, whom he had inherited from King Joseph, arrested Suzzarelli and offered to spare his life on condition he change sides. So the Corsican became a double agent, reporting to both Saliceti and Lowe, although not all the details he peddled were accurate, intentionally or unintentionally, for Murat was told that only 600 men defended the island. The

King was aware of the Emperor's advice that an island should either be held very strongly or left undefended and, when he had last seen his brother-in-law, he had been given permission to attack Capri – Napoleon told him that its capture would make the British fear for Sicily. Murat would not command himself because that would risk humiliation, so he ordered one of his French commanders, General Maximilien Lamarque, to prepare an attack.

The problem, as he saw it, was not the island's defenders, whom he expected to be few and of low morale, but getting ashore. Both Caprese harbours would be covered by guns, so the landings would probably have to be on the rugged shore below Anacapri. Here, he was told, was a small inlet, offering a little shelter; but this, too, was rock-bound and any lodgement would involve climbing steep, rough, scrubby heights, which could be defended with ease. But there, and on the rocks to either side of the inlet, the landing would have to be made. There were two principal risks. The first was from the British frigate patrolling off the island; even if she were blown off-station by a gale, the seas might prevent any landing. The assault could only be launched across smooth water and then the frigate might well be becalmed and, once immobilized, herself attacked by oared gunboats each mounting a gun as heavy, or heavier, than any of hers.

Then there was the problem of climbing the low cliffs. This was to be overcome by using scaling-ladders and Colonel Maceroni, an aide-de-camp to Murat, described an original ruse: in Naples 'to prevent information being previously sent to Capri, instead of making ladders for the purpose, several hundred of these, which served for lighting the street lamps, were suddenly collected.'[10] For his assault force Lamarque chose 4,000 of his best French and Neapolitan troops. They were to be escorted by a 44-gun frigate, a corvette and some thirty gunboats, and would embark at Naples and Salerno, to the south of the Sorrento peninsula, in some forty transports. They sailed at eleven o'clock on the night of 3 October.

On Capri, Colonel Lowe heard the first warnings on the same day. That morning two boats had arrived from Massa on the Sorrento peninsula with the usual intelligence reports and newspapers and also with verbal warnings that the French were preparing to attack the island. Later in the day it was reported that 'an enemy boat'[11] had been sighted rowing along the north coast of the island, obviously on reconnaissance. Colonel Lowe ordered his troops to stand-to and alerted the guard-boats that patrolled off-shore. He then climbed the Phoenician Steps and saw Major Hamill at Anacapri, ordering him to double his pickets and keep the signal station at the top of the cliff manned and alert.

At dawn the next day the sun rose on a calm, unruffled sea with a slight swell and wind enough to carry the invaders to Capri. There was no sign of any British frigate, for the current guard-ship, the 32-gun *Ambuscade*, had not returned from a visit to Palermo. The gunboats of one of Lamarque's divisions closed the Marina Grande and opened fire, while another, having sailed from Salerno and appeared around the tip of the Sorrento peninsula three miles away, made for the Marina Piccola and also began to bombard. Both attacks were feints, for the assault was to be upon the rocky shore below Anacapri.

Colonel Lowe's few guns commanding the two harbours returned fire and the cannonade continued throughout the morning as the French approached, then withdrew. No landings were attempted until about midday, when the French boats pulled away to the north and clustered below the rocks of Anacapri. Worried about the Maltese on the plateau, Lowe ordered Church to hurry up the Phoenician Steps with three companies of his Corsicans and put himself under the command of Major Hamill. But as Church was marching across the plateau towards Anacapri, the French landed. Their leading boats nosed into the rocky inlet and, as they lifted on the swell, the first soldiers leapt ashore. The lamp-lighters' ladders were tossed to them and they began to scale the low cliffs. A hundred men, led by Colonel Livron, scrambled ashore and reached the scrub above the bare rock. There was no opposition, indeed no sight of defenders, and 400 more French infantry followed. Nearly twenty miles away, Murat – King Joachim – had been watching the distant smoke and flashes from the tall windows of the Palazzo Reale, but he was not accustomed to being a spectator and his excitement was so intense that he called for horses and rode towards the Sorrento peninsula to watch the battle at closer quarters.

Now the first Maltese appeared among the trees, overlooking

the climbing French, and shooting began. Once aware of the lodgement, Major Hamill ordered his men to the heights, where they formed a loose crescent high above the inlet. Yet when Church and his Corsicans reached them at two o'clock, he saw they were scattered and he filled one wide gap, driving back a French assault that threatened to pass through it to attack Anacapri itself. Indeed, he seemed to have beaten the enemy back along the whole of the front, for they withdrew down the slopes to keep up spasmodic shooting from behind rocks. That evening more boats were seen approaching the inlet, prompting the hope that the French were about to withdraw. In fact, reinforcements were being landed together with light field-guns. At eight o'clock, as the moon rose, the French attacked again. In three columns they swarmed up the slopes and through the scrub, broke through the Maltese and, with drums beating, made for Anacapri. As they burst into the little town, the Maltese took refuge in their barracks, while Major Hamill, sword in hand, was trying to rally them. Outside his headquarters he was confronted by a French sergeant, who called on him to surrender. Hamill refused and the sergeant killed him with his bayonet.

The Maltese and the Corsicans were in full retreat. Some Maltese escaped down the Phoenician Steps and Church sent two of his three companies after them to join the defenders of Capri town. With one company of Corsicans, Church was then climbing towards the redoubt on the summit of Monte Solaro, when, after firing on one French column, he ran into another and, shouting to them in French that they were compatriots, passed through them safely. Reaching the redoubt on the highest point on the island, Church found several hundred Maltese. Realizing that defence would be hopeless, he decided to rejoin Colonel Lowe at Capri but, hurrying downhill towards the Phoenician Steps, he found that the French had arrived there first. Then he remembered from his months at Anacapri a secret, steep and dangerous track down the cliffs, involving the descent of a sheer rock face of more than 150 feet. In the darkness, Church found the top of the track and began to lead his men down it. One Corsican slipped and fell to his death but the others reached the bottom and before sunrise were within the defences of Capri town.

Anacapri was lost and the Royal Regiment of Malta almost all captured, or killed. But Lowe remained confident. The French could only reach the town by descending the Phoenician Steps, or by landing from the sea, and he was confident in his Corsican and British defenders. As soon as the landings had been reported, he had sent fast despatch boats through the surrounding enemy flotillas to Messina and to Ponza, calling for urgent reinforcement. Once the Royal Navy and British infantry arrived, the French would be cut off from the mainland and their defeat would be certain.

When the despatch boat reached Messina, General Stuart acted quickly. Six hundred British troops were hurriedly embarked and, together with a store-ship loaded with artillery and ammunition, sailed escorted by a frigate. Meanwhile, as the sun rose on the day after the landings, the British manning the defences of Capri saw the French looking down at them from the rim of the precipice above. A French officer then descended the Phoenician Steps under a white flag of truce and delivered to Colonel Lowe a summons to surrender. The whole of Anacapri and its garrison had been captured, Lamarque had written to Lowe, continuing, 'I hold the dominant positions and, when my artillery is placed, I shall wipe out Capri, when there will be no use for discussion. At present, I can treat you with less severity. I call upon you to surrender.'[12] But Lowe, realizing that naval support must soon arrive and that time was on his side, rejected the summons: 'Your propositions of rigour, or favour, on such an occasion, must be alike indifferent to an officer whose conduct will never be influenced by any other considerations than those of his duty.'[13]

Expecting an attack from Anacapri, Lowe had strengthened his northern defences facing the cliffs, knocking loopholes in the walls of houses and having artillery dragged forward, including a 36-pounder cannon and a heavy carronade to fire grapeshot. Later that morning the French bombardment began, with flashes and smoke along the crest of the cliffs of Anacapri and the whirr of shot that fell short of the town. Then infantry were sighted filing down the Phoenician Steps and the British guns fired to such effect that the French only dared to descend in ones and twos and at a run, but the French gunboats were sighted rounding a headland and opened fire on the Marina Grande. The siege of Capri had begun and could be raised only by the Royal Navy and replenishment, for Lowe's guns had fired most of their ammunition.

Next day, sails were sighted on the northern horizon. It was the Sicilian squadron of two frigates, two corvettes and more than a dozen gunboats from Ponza. Rescue, it seemed, was at hand. The Sicilians opened fire at long range and the French flotillas hauled away towards the mainland, leaving their troops marooned. Then the wind dropped, and the Sicilian commander began to fear the oared gunboats that might return to attack him and turned back for Ponza. However, on the 9th the *Ambuscade* and another frigate, the *Mercury*, finally appeared offshore and landed their marines. The French flotilla had not tried to return and Lamarque was now marooned on Capri: the tables had been turned.

Lowe's surviving force of some 700 men was desperately short of ammunition, awaiting the troop and ordnance convoy from Messina. But the weather changed, a storm blew and the convoy was scattered. One troopship reached the island and managed to land some 200 infantry, including detachments of the 58th Foot and mercenaries of de Watteville's Regiment. The store-ship loaded with artillery, powder and shot ploughed through heavy seas and was almost in sight of Capri when the officer in charge became so prostrated with seasickness that he ordered the captain to turn back for Messina.

Not knowing this, General Lamarque feared that it would be he who would have to surrender. But a relief convoy had set out from the mainland, escorted by thirty oared gunboats; sighting them, Captain Durban launched the *Ambuscade's* boats, himself following in the frigate to engage the French. As he opened fire, the wind dropped and he too became fearful of his ship's vulnerability to the gunboats, and recalled the boats to tow his ship out to sea. So more than fifty French supply boats reached the island to land men and ammunition. Lamarque now had some 3,000 troops ashore, including grenadiers and light infantry, and all the supplies they required.

Although the British were outnumbered, the outcome depended, as ever, on command of the sea, and that depended on the weather.

Wind broke the calm that had forced the *Ambuscade* to withdraw, and the British relief convoy made another attempt to reach the island, only for another storm to blow, isolating the French as much as the British. Lowe had lost half his command at Anacapri – two British officers has been killed there and the Maltese prisoners had already been shipped to Naples – and sixteen Corsicans had been killed; some thirty had been wounded. Colonel Lowe began to despair of relief, as had General Lamarque.

By the 15th the French guns had been manhandled down the Phoenician Steps at night and were firing on the town at point-blank range. Breaches were being beaten through the walls and, inspecting the damage, Colonel Lowe's aide-de-camp was shot dead by a sniper while Captain Church, who was leading sharp-shooters against the enemy batteries, was wounded in the head by a shell splinter. The British were sometimes able to get a boat away from the cove at Tragara, near where the pinnacles of Faraglioni rocks stand in the sea, and Church was evacuated from there. Both the British frigates were again sighted on the far side of the Bay of Naples towards Ischia and French supplies were still being landed below Anacapri.

Next day Lamarque sent another summons to Lowe, claiming that a practicable breach had been made and that the town could be subjected to the brutal customs of war, 'You see now that all resistance is useless', he wrote. 'Spare the inhabitants of Capri from the horror of a general assault. You have made a defence worthy of your courage and ability.'[14] Lowe assessed his situation. His ammunition and all essential supplies were almost exhausted and that morning he had received a message from Captain Durban, admitting that because of wind and sea conditions – either a flat calm, or a storm, it seemed – his two frigates were unable to prevent the French from reaching the island. Lowe decided to negotiate terms for surrender.

The two commanders met. At first Lamarque demanded that the entire garrison should become prisoners of war, with the exception of Lowe himself and half-a-dozen officers, who would be returned to Sicily. Lowe was told that Murat, who had been frustrated by the two-week campaign and had threatened to take direct command himself, would allow no more lenient conditions.

Lowe rejected the offer. Then, on the following day, three British Army officers landed from a boat to report that relief was indeed on its way. It was a gamble. Should Lowe continue resistance in this expectation and risk a massacre in Capri town, or should he continue negotiations, hoping for better terms? But it was again stormy and there was no sight of British ships. Lowe offered to surrender the island on condition that the entire garrison could return to Sicily. This time Lamarque accepted. On the day after the surrender, the relief ships arrived. One transport with 130 artillerymen and their guns was offshore and another was near by, while three battalions of infantry were in ships shortly due. They were too late by twenty-four hours.

To the French the capture of Capri seemed as much of a triumph as had the victory at Maida to the British. In fact, only about two score of the original garrison had been British and the value of Capri to either side was marginal, but the island's fall was as symbolic as its British occupation and the effect on the morale of both sides was powerful. Ironically, one of Captain Church's intelligence reports, which had recently reached Palermo, suggested that Capri might have become an important base for offensive operations by the British. 'Italy is like a barrel of gunpowder and only wants a match to blow it all up,' he had written, 'That match is an English army of 20,000 men under Moore.'[15]

The triumphant Murat was soon marching his armies back into Calabria to attack Sicily. The first signs on the far side of the straits had already been noted in Messina, General Moore writing to a colonel on the mainland, 'Some people of rather suspicious description have been seen about the mountains ... They are dressed and armed like the masses [*massi*] of Calabria, among them are Frenchmen, who have spy glasses and are said to have been sketching.' Apprehension mounted at the headquarters in Messina and at the court at Palermo.

9

To arms!

AT THE beginning of 1809 a ship reached Sicily from the Atlantic with shocking news. Sir John Moore was dead, killed in action at Corunna in Spain. Not only was the loss of the most inspiring and effective commander in the British Army the cause for grief, but the circumstances of his death brought on an urgent reappraisal of British strategy against Napoleon.

The riots provoked by Murat in May 1808, when he arrived in Madrid to depose King Carlos IV and put Joseph Bonaparte on his throne, had lit the fuse of resistance throughout Spain. To take advantage of this, the British had sent an expeditionary force of 15,000 men under the 39-year-old Lieutenant-General Sir Arthur Wellesley to Portugal, where, in August, he defeated the French under General Junot. However, two more senior British generals were authorized to negotiate with the French, and they agreed under what became known as the Convention of Cintra to allow Junot to evacuate his army intact. When the British government heard this, there was outrage and all three generals were recalled to London, leaving Lieutenant-General Sir John Moore in command. As expected, he decided to take the offensive and marched into Spain.

Seeing the Spanish troubles as an unnecessary diversion in his rear, when he should be concentrating on the domination of central Europe, Napoleon took command himself and reinforced his army in Spain to a strength of more than 300,000, a quarter of a million of them fighting troops, including the Imperial Guard. He himself had entered Madrid in December 1808. Moore meanwhile was heading north-east towards an isolated French corps at Burgos when Napoleon ordered another corps under Marshal Ney to attack the British rear and cut them off from Portugal. Moore had had no option but to fall back in a fighting retreat through snow and across freezing mountains to the sea at Corunna, where he fought a final rearguard action in the hope that the Royal Navy would rescue the survivors of his little army.

The ships appeared on 14 January 1809, and embarkation began at once. Two days later Moore was in the thick of the fighting in the hills above the town and under heavy fire. Near him, a shot tore the leg off a soldier, who rolled on the ground, screaming. Seeing fear in the eyes of those around him, Moore told them, 'This is nothing my lads. Keep your ranks. Take that man away. My good fellow, don't make such a noise. We must bear these things better.'[1] Then he himself was shown how they should be borne when a roundshot shattered his shoulder, hurling him from his horse. It was a mortal wound and Sir John told the surgeon, 'You can be of no service to me. Go to the wounded soldiers to whom you may be useful.'[2] He was carried into the town and died that night. He was buried, wrapped in his cloak, on the ramparts of Corunna. Early on the 18th, the last of 27,000 British troops had sailed for England. The story that filtered through to Sicily was tragic but also inspiring.

Napoleon, confident that he now dominated Spain, returned to Paris with his Imperial Guard on hearing reports that Austria, subsidized by the British government, was mobilizing and intent on challenging France again, so King Joseph was left in Madrid with a large French army. The British were now confined to Portugal but there was a new threat in Spain. Although the Spanish regular army was incapable of facing the French, bands of irregulars, the guerrillas, were being organized throughout the country to harass them. At first the British tended to dismiss the partisans, as they had the Calabrese, and indeed the atrocities the Spanish inflicted on captured Frenchmen were as shocking as the reprisals these brought upon themselves. But gradually it was recognized that these wild men were the only force resisting the invaders, and the British began to look at irregulars through new eyes.

At the beginning of 1809 there was a revision of British strategy in the Mediterranean. The debate was over the choice of the next theatre of war: which of two peninsulas should it be, the Iberian or the Italian? When Wellesley had beaten Junot in Portugal and Moore had marched deep into Spain, Iberia had been favoured. That peninsula was within reach of British sea-power based on British ports; the population was hostile to the French; it lay just across the Pyrenees from France itself. Then, when Moore's army was driven out to sea and Napoleon himself commanded in Madrid, the British looked again at Italy. But the Calabrese partisans had been unable to stand up to French troops and, when they harassed them, this had brought such savage reprisals upon themselves that the gentlemanly instincts of British officers were repelled.

So should the British attempt to repeat their success at Maida, but this time remain on the Italian mainland? This was an immediate problem for Lord Amherst, who in March 1809 had replaced William Drummond as British minister at Palermo. Against the background of the unstable, untrustworthy Bourbon court and the problem of how to ensure a return for British subsidies in the form of effective Sicilian military contribution under British command, both soldiers and diplomats favoured the harnessing of the Sicilian government to a tight rein; they were restrained only by the caution of George Canning, the Foreign Secretary, in London. Although Sicily remained under threat of French attack, was this the moment to take offensive action in Italy, albeit not the invasion of Calabria and march on Naples favoured by the King and Queen?

The other Italian states were restive under French domination. A Neapolitan named Biancamano had made contact with the British, claiming that Naples was ready to rise against the French, while British intelligence agents had received encouraging reports from *patriotti* leaders in Venice and Bologna. There were hopes that Pope Pius VII might prove an ally. The Papal States were dominated by the French but had not been annexed, and in the summer of 1808 Collingwood had authorized an attempt to rescue the Pope from the Vatican, sending a frigate to land agents who would, he hoped, carry him to Sicily. The propaganda value would have been immense for, as William Windham had said, 'The Pope's name is of more power than his sword.'[3] Agents reached the Vatican but the Pope refused to leave, on the grounds that this would give Napoleon a pretext for annexation. He was still thought by some to be a potential ally but Collingwood was sceptical, writing of the real, or imagined, Italian *risorgimento*, 'I fear there are no leaders, nor any one common or durable bond, which could ensure to us the united and continued aid of the Tuscans, Romans, Neapolitans and Piedmontese.'[4] He continued, 'There is no stuff to work on there – the people are licentious, the nobles are unprincipled.' There was only one hope for a successful rising in Italy, concluded the admiral: 'It is a superior army alone that can effect a change, or maintain it.'[5] Thus the British strategic reserve, diminished as it was, was still to hand in Sicily, within easy reach of all Italy. Farther north lay Austria, which could also be helped and, beyond, the German states allied to the French and, distantly, France itself. All offered tempting options but only one peninsular campaign could be attempted.

Eyes were on Austria at the beginning of 1809. Seeing the French increasingly involved in Spain and consequently weakened in the German states, the Austrian commander-in-chief, Field Marshal the Archduke Karl, saw a chance to regain lost territories, draw Prussia into an alliance and take revenge for Ulm and Austerlitz. Mobilization and planning began in January. The army was to be split in three: the largest part preparing to strike into Germany; another, the Army of Inner Austria, under the young Archduke Johann, to be deployed along the Inn valley, running westward through the Tyrol; the smallest part to wait near Cracow. It was a huge force of nearly 300,000 fighting troops with the same number in reserve or manning communications and depots and they faced only the 60,000 French troops remaining in the German states. Napoleon, aware of this, determined to take command himself and concentrate on defeating the Austrian thrust into the central German states. But he did not expect the war to begin until May.

As the final plans were completed in Vienna, there arrived in the gilded salons of Archduke Johann's headquarters a striking visitor, who was announced as Captain Andreas Hofer, a mountain-man of the Tyrolese militia, who looked very different from the smart, white-uniformed officers of the Austrian Empire. Aged forty-seven, he was

of Herculean make . . . stooped considerably, having been accustomed from his youth to carry heavy burthens over the mountains . . . his voice was soft and pleasing – his countenance, though not generally animated, was expressive of great good humour, particularly when he smiled . . . He wore the dress of his country . . . a large black hat with a broad brim, adorned with black ribbons and a black, curling feather – a short green coat, red waistcoat over which were green braces . . . short black breeches with red or black stockings . . . But that which was most remarkable in the appearance of Hofer was his long, black beard, which reached to his girdle.[6]

Hofer lived at Sandhof between the villages of St Marten and St Leonhard in the Passeiertal, a remote alpine valley south of Innsbruck and the Brenner Pass. He was an innkeeper, wine-grower and cattle-dealer and had fought against the French as a sharpshooter until the peace of 1805 when he had been promoted to captain. Passionately patriotic and fervently religious, he had come to beg the Archduke to join forces with his militia and partisans to liberate the Tyrol. After Austerlitz, Napoleon had decreed that the Tyrol and the neighbouring province of Vorarlberg, with a population of 700,000, be ceded to Bavaria in recognition of the support that state had given to France in the campaign. The Tyrolese, proud of their traditions, hated the Bavarians. Archduke Johann, listening to Hofer, was impressed by his zeal and offered his support. Together they would throw the Bavarians back over the mountains into Bavaria. Captain Hofer returned to make ready in the high Tyrolese valleys and the remote villages, silent but for the sound of running water, cow bells and church bells. There, with beer and wine to hand, he held councils of war in the deep-eaved mountain inns, and sent orders from village to village by mountain paths. He was constantly on the move, signing his messages, 'Andreas Hofer, from where I am'; replies were addressed to 'Andreas Hofer, wherever he may be'.[7]

The Passeiertal, like all alpine valleys, lived with the contrasts of deep winters, stifled by snow and ice, and smiling summers, when the meadows had changed from white to emerald, wild flowers bloomed and the land seemed to flow with milk and honey. The Tyrolese, like the Calabrese, were easily roused. They lived harsh, physical, elemental lives amid dangers and stresses for which simple explanations were sought. They were religious and their priests presented them with the only understandable framework for their existence. Thus, however crude their little wooden houses might be, their churches, with the shiny gilding of their altars, pulpits and organs and the swirling effusion of golden gesso and white plasterwork, seemed as extravagant as imperial palaces. Natural environment, hopes and fears, endeavour and pride merged into simple patriotism which could be activated by such a leader as Andreas Hofer. When his word came, action followed. Firearms were taken down from cottage walls, powder dried by the hearths, billhooks and pitchforks sharpened. The final signal was awaited.

This was far from the sea which the British commanded, let alone the armies with which they might intervene. But the captain of any ship of the Royal Navy on reconnaissance in the Adriatic, cruising off the *murazzo* sheltering the Venetian lagoon, would have seen on a cold, clear day, beyond the domes and towers of Venice, the jagged, white ramparts of the Alps, 50 miles to the north, stretching across the horizon. Some 125 miles from the coast and at least a week's march, there lay, beyond the flat fields of the Veneto, the Brenner Pass leading north into the Tyrol with Austria and all central Europe beyond. It was also apparent that across this tremendous terrain ran the road from France eastward to Constantinople and India.

Hofer's secret was well kept, and neither the Bavarian commanders nor the French, who stiffened their ranks, were aware of the coming storm. The uprising was not only to be in the Tyrol but throughout the alpine provinces, and Archduke Johann set up his headquarters far to the south-east, at Graz. From there he sent out a proclamation beginning, 'To arms, Tyroleans! to arms! The hour of deliverance is at hand.'[8] A division of the Austrian army with seven battalions of infantry, but few cavalry, under General Chastelar, together with militia battalions from Carinthia and Styria, were to support the Tyrolese, 5,000 of whom were commanded by Hofer himself. The rising was to start on the night of 8 April 1809, sprung by a curious signal: before dawn on the 9th, sacks of sawdust would be emptied into the River Inn to flow down through Innsbruck and the villages of the Inntal. The leaders of the revolt would know what this meant.

The Bavarians and French – some of the latter on route marches from Italy to Germany – were taken by surprise. At three o'clock in the morning of the 9th, 'the stillness of the night was broken by the heavy tread of the advancing troops and the rattling of ammunition wagons and great guns'[9] as Chastelar's army marched west into the Tyrol. Then sawdust swirled down the river, the message was passed through the valleys '*S'ist zeit!*' ('It's time!')[10] and 'the village bells rang as they passed and men, women and children of all ages flocked in crowds to greet and cheer them. Mothers brought their children to look at them, and blind old men were led out of their cottages that they might hear and bless their gallant countrymen. All endeavoured to get near that they might shake hands with them, touch their clothes or even kiss their horses.'[11] Then, 'in a few hours, to the joy of the Tyrolese, the thunder of distant guns and the tumultuous din of alarm bells resounded through the valleys.'[12]

Bavarian garrisons were quickly overwhelmed, and a column of French infantry on the march from Mantua to Augsburg was surprised and captured. Alerted by echoing gunfire, the surviving Bavarians and French regrouped and got ready to counter-attack. But they were not prepared for the skill and ferocity of the Tyrolese peasantry. On the 10th, nearly 1,000 Bavarians had surrounded a detachment of Hofer's men,

but the Tyrolese sharpshooters, who were sheltered by rocks, made dreadful havoc amongst them and the artillerymen were several times shot away from their guns. At length the Tyrolese made a desperate charge, armed with spears, pitchforks and any implement of offence they could collect, rushed upon the Bavarians like a torrent; while others, who were stationed on the heights, hurled huge masses of rocks and trees upon those beneath.'[13]

After losing a third of their number, the Bavarians surrendered.

The key to the Tyrol was Innsbruck, in its flat-floored valley between parallel walls of mountains, and it was held by the Bavarians. Not only was it the capital, but it stood at the junction of communications: the ways north-east through the pass at Kuftstein towards Munich and east to Vienna, west into Switzerland and south across the Brenner Pass into Italy. The mountains to the south of the city – rather than those to the north, which the Tyrol shared with Bavaria – were Hofer's stronghold. Between those heights and the capital, the strategic key was a wooded spur called Berg Isel, standing above the abbey and village of Wilten, which lay three miles south of Innsbruck and the River Inn and overlooked the highway running east and west.

The Austrian regulars were marching towards Innsbruck from the east, and the Bavarian garrison of Innsbruck prepared for their attack. But on the night of 10 April they were shocked to see the mountainsides to the south flickering with lights, and at dawn they understood the reason as 15,000 Tyrolese swept down Berg Isel towards the town. Wilten was overrun, devout partisans pausing to kneel beneath the gilded tracery of the nave to finger a rosary before rejoining the charge. The Bavarians tried to fell trees as road blocks, but there was not time. The Tyrolese raced towards the city, through the triumphal arch built for the Empress Maria Theresa, into the wide Maria-Theresien-strasse past palaces and churches, around the column commemorating another expulsion of the Bavarians and into the heavy, stone arcades of the old quarter. Some Bavarians climbed high in the tall, leaning houses to shoot from windows, but were picked off by sharpshooters. Mounted Bavarian officers tried to rally their men but were shot from their horses, or cornered by men with pitchforks and forced to dismount and surrender; some tried to escape across the two bridges over the Inn and others jumped into the river to swim to safety, only to be swept away in the pale green torrent swollen by the spring thaw. By eleven o'clock that morning Innsbruck had fallen to the Tyrolese.

Some Bavarians fled along the valley. One group, led by a Count Erbach, took refuge in a convent, slamming the massive doors behind them, but these were burst open by fifty Tyrolese using a huge fir tree as a battering ram, and all inside were captured. Meanwhile the victors celebrated, a triumphal arch lit by candles was set up and the imperial eagle was taken from the monument to the Emperor Maximilian in the Hofkirche and paraded through the streets, to shouts of 'Long live the Emperor!' The revellers had finally fallen asleep when, at three o'clock in the morning, they were woken by bells ringing in alarm. A relief column of French and Bavarians had quietly occupied the deserted Berg Isel and were advancing on the town. The commander of the Bavarian advance guard rode through the new triumphal arch and was shot dead from his saddle. Street fighting spread through the town. It lasted three days, the Tyrolese applying their skills in stalking and sharpshooting and driving their enemies back to Berg Isel. There, too, they were at the mercy of marksmen, and on the morning of 13 April the French and Bavarians surrendered.

Then news arrived at Innsbruck that on 10 April, the day they had first encamped on Berg Isel, the huge Austrian armies had begun to roll westward. The main force was marching into Germany on an axis running midway between Munich and Nuremberg, heading for Stuttgart and the Rhine. The Tyrolese knew of the imminent arrival of Archduke Johann's corps, but there were also twin thrusts further south: one from south-east Austria, across the River Piave into Italy; the other even farther south, towards Treviso and threatening Venice. Soon they should be in sight of the sea and, perhaps, the sails of the Royal Navy.

In the alpine provinces the rising spread. While Austrian regulars, supported by the Tyrolese, occupied Salzburg and began to threaten Bavaria and even alarm Munich itself, Hofer and the main body of irregulars struck south, taking Bozen (Bolzano) and Trent (Trento). On the shores of Lake Garda, Italian guerrillas appeared, then others rose to meet Archduke Johann's southern columns in the Veneto, took Verona, Belluno and Bassano, bringing the insurrection to within forty miles of Venice and the sea. If a British expeditionary force landed on this coast, it would be two days' march from their new allies. Fears of French reaction – remembering General Bonaparte's rapid marches across the north Italian plain a dozen years before – were countered by reports of French troops being withdrawn from Italy for service in central Europe and Spain. Reports also spread through Italy to Austria that a British army, of at least twice the strength of the force that had fought at Maida, was embarking at Messina. A British landing at the head of the Adriatic and a junction with the Austrians north of Venice could prove decisive.

Then Napoleon launched his counter-offensive. On 24 April he first met the Austrians, head-on just north of the Danube at Aspern. Archduke Karl and his lumbering columns were, after some initial success, outmanoeuvred and outfought by the Emperor and his field commanders, Masséna and Lannes. The Austrians fell back and, to save Vienna from the horrors of siege and street fighting, abandoned their capital on 13 May, pulling back beyond the Danube. There they rallied and halted the French, but failed to follow with a counter-attack.

In the Tyrol and northern Italy the Austrian regulars received orders from Archduke Johann to withdraw to join Archduke Karl's main armies and began to march east, away from the sound of the guns. The Tyrolese were enraged at the sight, and drunken peasants dragged General Chastelar from his horse and beat him with cudgels. The Bavarians were close behind, now numbering 18,000 regulars and 1,700 cavalry supported by 30 guns. They began to take revenge on the Tyrol, burning villages and killing prisoners and civilians. Finally, on 19 May, Innsbruck fell. The rising, its leadership now riven by disagreement, seemed to be falling apart but Hofer and his Tyrolese took to the mountains, their patriotic passion undimmed. Instead of Austrian regular officers, they relied on their own leaders, such as two strongly built Capuchin monks, who,

> although they never carried arms, were always seen in the thickest of the fight, dealing tremendous blows on the heads of their adversaries with stout wooden crucifixes . . . They also busied themselves in making amulets, or charms, which were to render

them invulnerable, but these lost much of their effect when several hundred of the peasants had been killed, who were known to have worn them.[14].

The Tyrolese fought on in the hope of relief that could now come only from the British.

10

An abyss of misfortune

IN JUNE 1809 General Sir John Stuart, Count of Maida, watched with pride as his army embarked from Messina and Milazzo for the second time. 'It was a great armada,' wrote Colonel Bunbury. 'Innumerable vessels of all descriptions, convoyed by three ships of the line and some frigates and brigs of war, covered the blue sea from the Lipari Islands to the coast of Calabria.'[1] Its destination was secret, but there had been much speculation. For weeks news of Austria's declaration of war and the rising in the Tyrol had been arriving, together with reports of unrest throughout Italy. Murat had been withdrawing his troops from Calabria and the options open to Stuart were exciting.

As early as March the British had been told of Austrian plans by the Count de la Tour, a general in the imperial army, who had arrived to solicit British support, asking particularly that their ships land an Austrian force between Venice and Rimini to support the Archduke Johann's thrust across the Veneto. Also, noted Bunbury, he had said that 'Austria was in correspondence with the *patriotti* of Italy and she professed her readiness to afford them her aid not only in expelling the French but in setting up a constitutional and independent kingdom!'[2] Murat, it was believed, still commanded some 30,000 troops in southern Italy — fewer than half of them French — but there were several divisions available to him around Rome and in the north. To support the Austrians and the popular risings in Italy that Captain Church had forecast and in the Tyrol, a British expeditionary force would be needed.

In assessing the possibilities, Bunbury stressed the importance of co-ordination with Austrian plans but, he added, 'it was less easy to decide as to place than as to time, hampered as we were by the necessity of keeping a sure hold on Sicily. The Austrians naturally desired that we should come as near to their army as possible.'[3] The risk of leaving Sicily unguarded was an argument against landing at the head of the Adriatic, so the west coast of Italy, within easier reach of the Sicilian base, seemed preferable. But it needed to be a substantial operation, and when General Stuart had suggested a diversionary landing on the island of Ischia across the Bay of Naples from Capri, Lord Collingwood had dismissed the idea, saying that 'he could not see that such an expedition could answer any useful purpose.'[4]

Instead, the admiral proposed a major landing on the coast of Tuscany between Naples and Rome, which would threaten both, so removing any threat to Sicily, and prevent Murat from marching against the Austrians in the north, while the British would be free to reinforce their allies by land or sea. A march north by the British towards the Alps would surely relieve the Archduke Johann and the hard-pressed Tyrolese. Meanwhile, he had sent a frigate squadron commanded by Nelson's protégé Captain William Hoste – and later by the equally effective and popular Captain Jahleel Brenton – to harass the French in the Adriatic, and, if possible, support the Austrians ashore; also to keep an eye on the French garrison of Corfu and potentially hostile Russian warships laid up in Trieste. While capturing enemy merchant ships and attacking their coastal forts, they found that they were unable to help the Austrians, even when reinforced by two ships of the line under Commodore William Hargood, because their ally was cut off from the sea by the French. That had to be a task for an army and Hargood suggested a surprise attack on Venice using 4,000 Austrian troops; there was, of course, a British army available, too.

At the beginning of June, General Stuart had ordered his army to assemble and embark. This came as a relief to his command, which had become accustomed to grand ceremonial parades, described as 'General Stuart's hobby – but an abominable annoyance to the troops'[5] for this was in earnest. It was, as reported, more than double the size of his force at Maida, numbering nearly 13,000 men. Half were British infantry and there were 1,000 mounted dragoons and 400 artillerymen; the foreign element consisted of nearly 5,000 Germans, Swiss, Neapolitans and Calabrese. The army seemed confident in itself, but not in its commanding officer. During the preceding weeks his staff and then his subordinate commanders had noticed his increasing indecision. 'Our General', Bunbury had noted, 'could not make up his mind as to what he would attempt, or how, or where he would try his fortune . . . He dawdled and fretted in his office; issued no orders, nor even looked at the troops. The spirit of discontent, and even of contempt . . . became every day more general and more mischievous in the army.'[6] News of Napoleon's successes in Bavaria arrived:

Then we were roused from our sulky languor . . . by the French accounts of their victories . . . These events gave a new and a more dangerous turn to the spirit by which very many of our officers, including some of the highest rank, were infected. They had persuaded themselves already that Sir J. Stuart was incompetent for the command of an army on active service; and now they decided amongst themselves that it would be madness to go forth on an expedition.[7]

But on 11 June go forth they did. 'The fleet which issued forth from the anchorage of Milazzo made a splendid show,' wrote Bunbury.

In outward seeming we might have vied with the proudest armaments which carried the standards of England to fields of glory. But our General had done with fields of glory . . . If it was Sir John Stuart's desire only to make a grand display, the weather certainly favoured him to the utmost. Day after day, we floated on the still blue sea with scarcely a breeze to help us on our way.[8]

To all but those privy to Stuart's final plan, their destination remained unknown. It did not seem to be the Adriatic, after all, but it might be a return to the Bay of Sant' Eufemia so as to isolate the French garrisons still holding Reggio and Scilla in the south of Calabria; it might be the landing in Tuscany that Collingwood had suggested; or it could be to attack Naples itself. At sea they were joined by another convoy, carrying 6,000 Sicilian troops of uncertain value and, as the armada slowly passed the brown hills of Calabria, these were detached to make a feint landing at Policastro and then to follow the main force. Then the jagged outline of the Sorrento peninsula appeared ahead and they passed Capri, but it would obviously be folly to attempt to recapture the island, now defended by seasoned French soldiers. A landing had to be made soon, if only because the cavalry and artillery horses were suffering severely from heat in the cramped transports. The fleet did not turn east towards Naples but, led by three ships of the line, continued to sail across the mouth of the great bay. Finally, thirteen days out from Milazzo, signal flags flew up the halyards of the flagship, the 80-gun *Canopus*, and the fleet swung towards the green island of Ischia off the northern promontory of the Bay of Naples. A signal gun was fired, more signals flew and 200 anchors splashed into the clear water. Sir John Stuart was to have his own way after all.

Scanning the shore, earthworks and batteries were sighted; the landing was ordered for first light next morning. In darkness the infantry clambered into ships' boats because the expedition had no specialized landing craft, neither the flatboats, which had been in service for half a century, nor the barges fitted with ramps that had been designed by Sir Sidney Smith five years before. There was some confusion and at dawn the boats were still rocking nearly three miles from shore. Finally, under cover of the warships' gunfire, they pulled for the rocky coast and the soldiers scrambled ashore. There was little resistance and next day Ischia capitulated – although an ancient castle on the far side of the island held out for a few days; nearby, the small island of Procida was also taken.

This had been watched from the mainland by Murat – now King Joachim – and he ordered immediate reaction. When the assembly of the British expedition had first been reported, he had deployed his army in echelon down the length of his kingdom, so that any two corps could concentrate quickly to meet any threat and some 15,000 men could be ready for the defence of Naples itself. The sight of the huge British fleet off Ischia had, 'served to throw Naples into hot water', as Bunbury put it.

> The swarming populace . . . were in a ferment and were kept down only by the severest vigilance and rigour. The principal palaces in the city were closed by barricades and defended by strong posts of soldiery and through the streets patrols were pacing their rounds day and night. King Joachim called in his troops from every distant quarter though flashes of insurrection were gleaming in several of his provinces.[9]

He himself hurried to the coast opposite Ischia and ordered a counter-attack by gunboats based at Gaeta to the north. When the British destroyed them in a close-range boat action, it seemed that an assault on Naples was imminent.

This is what the British divisional commanders and ships' captains expected, particularly after the arrival on Ischia of two Italians, who introduced themselves as representatives of the *patriotti* and offered to help take the city. But General Stuart refused to meet them and ordered Bunbury to interview them and report to him. 'We are sent to ask what are the intentions of the British General in bringing his army to the Bay of Naples', they told the colonel. 'If it be simply to drive the French out of the country, we will aid him to the utmost of our power and our power is great. We wish to get rid of the French and to make our country independent. But if you come with the view of replacing Ferdinand and his Queen on the throne of Naples, we will to a man take arms with the French and fight against you.' Knowing General Stuart disliked and distrusted the King and Queen, Bunbury reported this with optimism, but to his dismay the general 'declined to make any reply whatever'.[10] The delegation departed and the opportunity was lost.

But General Stuart had had no intention of landing at Naples, only to give the impression that he might do so in the hope that Murat would withdraw forces from Calabria and the north, so relieving the threats to both Sicily and Austria. Bunbury tried to change the general's mind, suggesting other objectives: 'I pressed

Sir John Stuart to attack either Civita Vecchia, or Leghorn, or at least to try what might be the effect of a demonstration on the northern coast of Italy. But the General would not stir.'[11] The need for action became acute when news arrived that on 6 July the French had suddenly invaded the Vatican, arrested the Pope, who they feared might become a focal point of resistance, and carried him away to the north. The Italians were outraged. 'If, instead of eating grapes at Ischia,' Bunbury snorted, 'we had struck in at that moment on the coasts of Rome, or Tuscany, the landing of a British army might have been productive of a serious influence on the results of the general war.'[12]

Three excuses for inaction now appeared. First, Stuart heard from Sicily that a British attempt to take Scilla had failed, and so he ordered two brigades of infantry and a cavalry regiment to return to Messina. Then a despatch reached him from Lord Collingwood, warning that twelve French sail of the line and seven frigates now lay at Toulon and, if his own blockading squadron were blown off-station by a northerly gale, they might break out and attack Stuart's ships. At the same time he heard that, on 6 July, Napoleon had defeated the Archduke Karl at Wagram, outside Vienna, with both sides losing about 40,000 men, so nothing he could do would help the Austrians now. He ordered his army to re-embark and on 26 July the armada sailed for Sicily.

Far to the north-east, the crew of a British frigate cruising off Venice in a northerly wind would have heard the distant thud of gunfire from the plains of the Veneto and the foothills of the Alps that June, the sound of the French pursuing Archduke Johann's army towards its homeland. On 10 July Austria sued for peace, an armistice was agreed two days later and, as negotiations began, they abandoned the Tyrolese to fight alone.

This they did. Until now Hofer had been regarded as leader of the Tyrolese in the South Tyrol, particularly in his native Passeiertal, the valley south-west of the Brenner Pass, but such was his popularity that he was now elected commander-in-chief. A more effective choice might have been Josef Speckbacher from the Inntal, another Tyrolese commander, a cunning mountain fighter and masterly tactician. 'A tall, athletic man with black eyes and hair, stooped considerably, and had generally an expression of dejection and melancholy in his countenance',[13] he lacked Hofer's charisma. Yet Hofer was to take overall command, despite his reputation for 'passing the principal part of his time at the alehouse', which endeared him to the peasantry. He lacked the guile of a successful guerrilla, and had become lax in matters of security. Seated in a mountain tavern with a bottle before him, he would write and despatch orders by courier 'without considering the danger they ran of falling into the hands of the enemy'. One typical order ran:

Dear Brethren of the Upper Inntal – For God, the Emperor and our dear native country. Tomorrow, early in the morning, is fixed for the attack. With the help of our Holy Mother, we will seize and destroy the Bavarians and we confide ourselves to the beloved Jesus. Come to our assistance but, if you fancy yourselves wiser than Divine Providence, we will do without you – Andreas Hofer.[14]

The Tyrolese were amateurs in war and their leaders were often chosen for such popularity, such as the crucifix-wielding Capuchin monk Rothbart ('Redbeard') Haspinger, or for their skill with hunting rifles, usually made by Tyrolese gunsmiths. Continuing the fight with renewed vigour, their most successful tactic was still the ambush, with fearsome refinements. 'One extraordinary method of destruction used by the Tyrolese', wrote a contemporary, was when they 'felled several enormous larch trees, upon which they piled large masses of rock and heaps of rubbish; the whole being supported by strong cords by means of which they were suspended over the edge of a precipice. During the action, the Tyrolese decoyed a body of the enemy's troops, by appearing to retreat, immediately under the spot.'[15] Then a shout was heard, 'Stefan, shall I chop it off yet?' and the reply from across the gorge, 'Not yet!' 'The troops below continued their march. Then another shout: "Hans, for the most Holy Trinity!" and the reply, "In the name of the Holy Trinity, cut all loose above!" Then, in an instant the ropes were cut and the whole structure came thundering down on the heads of the unfortunate troops beneath. Few had time to escape; the principal part of them were instantly crushed to death; a death-like stillness succeeded to the

tremendous noise of the falling avalanche, which was alone interrupted by the dreadful shrieks of those who were perishing in the
ruins. For a moment the firing ceased on both sides.'[16]

News of the ambushes by avalanche spread across Europe, and in
Britain caught the popular imagination. The *Gentleman's Magazine*
publishing a bloodthirsty ballad dedicated to the Tyrolese, who

> Cleave the marble, delve the mine,
> Bid the oak and mountain pine
> Hang in dreadful jeopardy

as the invaders approach 'drunk with slaughter, gorg'd with spoil'
to meet their fate.

> Entering now the close defile,
> Franks and recreant Germans toil,
> Ploughing deep the stony soil,
> Rock their huge artillery . . .
>
> Now for vengeance shout amain;
> Loose the oaks, the pines unchain,
> Let the marble masses rain,
> Whelm the hordes of slavery.
>
> Bid the thundering ruin rush,
> Men and steeds and cannon crush,
> Drink, O Earth, the sanguine gush,
> Drink the life-blood copiously,
>
> Wild the tumult, dire the cry
> Soon shall thousands silent lie;
> While freemen from their ramparts high
> Laud their god with psalmody . . .[17]

Ambushes were not always sprung in narrow defiles. Speckbacher caught a Bavarian column as it marched confidently beside
a river. Woods rose steeply from the other side of the track, which
he suddenly blocked by felling a tree to halt the wagons. His rifle-
men opened fire from the forest, giving the Bavarians the choice

of being shot where they stood or drowning in the swift river. Elsewhere, bales of straw were hidden beneath wooden bridges and set alight as the enemy were about to cross.

Meanwhile the French had been reinforced and the experienced Marshal François Lefebvre, who had commanded a corps of the *Grande Armée* and the infantry of the Imperial Guard and had been newly created Duke of Danzig, was appointed to their command. He and the Bavarian generals determined to root out the Tyrolese in their strongholds and at the beginning of August, Lefebvre led a strong column from Innsbruck, over the Brenner Pass into the South Tyrol. In the valleys the Tyrolese fell upon them with ferocity:

> The peasants tore the dragoons from their horses and killed them with the butt ends of their muskets. Lefebvre himself escaped with the greatest difficulty . . . having lost his hat and sword . . . The whole division was dispersed over the mountains, having deserted their guns, ammunition and baggage wagons . . . Lefebvre, after having collected a few of his followers, retreated in haste to Innsbruck, disguised as a common trooper.[18]

The Bavarians attempted a counter-attack but were so harassed by snipers on the mountainsides above the road that they retreated out of range to the village of Dullenfeld. There some 300 Tyrolese, 'armed with clubs, pikes and scythes and shouting as they advanced', stormed the village and the terrified Bavarians surrendered, having lost 250 men killed and 900 captured, together with 200 horses. It was not only the mountain men they faced. A Saxon officer, commanding Bavarians, reported an attack by 'Tyrolese . . . in immense numbers and among them boys and girls of ten and twelve years of age', who, after firing, 'flung their rifles aside and rushed upon our bayonets with only their clenched fists. Nothing could withstand their impetuosity. They darted at our feet, threw or pulled us down, strangled us, wrenched the arms from our hands; and, like enraged lions, killed all that did not cry for quarter!' The officer then saw 'a man full eighty years of age posted against the side of a rock and sending death among our ranks at every shot. Upon the Bavarians descending from behind to make him prisoner, he shouted aloud, "Hurrah!", struck the first man to the ground and with the ejaculation, "In God's name!" precipitated himself with him into the abyss below.' When the officer and his surviving men surrendered, he continued, 'the Tyrolese, as if moved by one impulse, fell upon their knees and poured forth the emotion of their hearts in prayer under the canopy of Heaven . . . I joined in the devotion and never in my life did I pray more fervently.'[19]

The fighting became uglier, as the Bavarians took revenge with reprisals, shooting or hanging all Tyrolese found to be carrying such arms as home-made spiked clubs, or sharpened farmyard implements, even killing the old and the young they found in captured villages. The effect was predictable, swelling the numbers of the Tyrolese guerrillas and heightening their patriotic rage. The climax was not long in coming. Marshal Lefebvre had concluded that he could not face the Tyrolese in the mountains and that their principal objective must be Innsbruck. He therefore decided to fight them on the plain between the city and the mountains. The morale of his army was low after the ambushes and assaults but, if they could be drawn up in formal array with their artillery and the cavalry on their flanks, they could use the advantages of regular troops over irregulars: drill movements combined with volley-firing and long-range roundshot and short-range grapeshot from their field-guns. His pickets had reported that the Tyrolese were coming down from the southern mountains and had taken possession of their old stronghold of Berg Isel above Wilten. So on 11 August, Lefebvre deployed his entire force of 16,000 French and Bavarians supported by 40 guns across the flat valley floor to the south of Innsbruck and facing Berg Isel.

Hofer himself commanded the Tyrolese and volunteers from Vorarlberg and Carinthia, who numbered nearly 20,000, including a few hundred Austrian regulars who had deserted and joined them. These he deployed across the wooded hills and high meadows above Innsbruck with his centre on Berg Isel and his flanking divisions ready to descend into the valley east and west of Innsbruck to cut the city's communications. He had, true to character, set up his headquarters in a tavern and gave his orders.

Aware of the superiority of the enemy's firepower, Hofer hoped that they would attack so that his men could use the slopes of Berg Isel to launch their terrifying downhill charges. Speckbacher was to command his right flank, which would extend eastward down the valley, ready to advance towards the Inn, threatening Lefebvre's flank and even barring his retreat. That night the monk Haspinger woke Hofer to join him in prayer and then accompany him on an inspection of the waiting Tyrolese as the sun rose.

Berg Isel was well chosen as the battlefield. The lowest of a jumble of wooded foothills above Innsbruck, it was the closest to the city, and from its summit the Tyrolese could look down on the two churches at Wilten, before which the French artillery was deployed, beyond to the triumphal arch leading to the wide Maria-Theresien-strasse running to the heart of the city, the Hofburg palace, the Hofkirche and the cathedral. Their objective could be seen, tantalizingly close. The slopes were steep, often precipitous, and this would give impetus to a downhill charge by men bred in mountains which trained infantry, however skilled at parade-ground evolutions, dreaded having to face.

The opposing armies were in startling contrast. In the valley were the ranks of regular soldiers in blue uniforms with red facings and white cross-belts, white breeches and black gaiters; the infantry wearing black shackoes, the cavalry plumed or crested helmets. On the hill were the Tyrolese in their wide-brimmed black hats, red, green or buff jackets, black breeches and white stockings. Hofer – recognizable from afar by his bulk, black beard and his broad leather belt bearing the initials 'A.H.' – stood at the summit by his standard-bearers, drummers and staff, including Haspinger in his brown habit and an Austrian officer still wearing the white uniform of the imperial army. Away to his right stood Speckbacher, also recognizable with his high-bridged nose, fierce black moustache and intense eyes, seeming taller than usual with a high-crowned, feathered hat, but also wearing the remnants of his militia uniform and carrying the long, straight-bladed sword of an Austrian officer.

Early that Sunday morning many of the Bavarian officers – but not the atheistic French – were attending Mass in the white and gold Rococo splendour of the great church at Wilten below Berg Isel when they heard the first shots and their own bugles sounding the alarm. Hurrying out, they were told that the Tyrolese, occupying the heights above, seemed about to attack. At once they drew up their main force and Lefebvre ordered an advance.

The French guns opened fire but, seeing that Hofer did not seem to be advancing, the general decided to force the issue and ordered the Bavarians to clear Berg Isel. It was a mistake. As the infantry with their heavy muskets and dismounted cavalrymen in steel helmets and breastplates began to trudge uphill, the climb became increasingly laborious. Then their officers were shot by marksmen. Hofer ordered his men to charge. In packs hundreds-strong they raced downhill, the sharpshooters pausing to fire then running on behind the men with pikes and pitchforks. Here and there the Bavarians rallied, their backs to the slippery slopes, only to be swept downhill. It was too much for them, for they had faced this before; they turned and ran. As they came tumbling down the hillsides, those still drawn up below wavered. Lefebvre ordered the retreat. Trying to keep his main force intact, he decided to withdraw up the Inntal to safety in Salzburg. Fighting through Speckbacher's men on Hofer's right flank, who were trying to block the road but lacked the advantage of mountainsides, he finally broke free. For the Tyrolese it was total victory. The Bavarians admitted to the loss of 5,000 men, and 1,700 of their wounded were left behind. The Tyrolese claimed that they themselves had lost only 32 killed and 132 wounded. But Hofer, remembering the chaos when his men had stormed into Innsbruck four months earlier, ordered them to withdraw to the high ground above the valley and they crowded into village inns to celebrate.

On 15 August Andreas Hofer made his triumphant entry into Innsbruck. But the city was again in chaos, with crowds breaking into houses where the enemy had been billeted and looting. This was the first significant sign of indiscipline among the Tyrolese, and Hofer ordered all booty to be returned and heavy fines to be imposed on those who did not comply. He then ordered a service of thanksgiving to be held in the cathedral and took up residence in the lofty white and gold halls of the Hofburg palace. Proclaiming himself Imperial Commandant of the Tyrol, he set up 'a sort of court'. This, it was said, 'when we consider his origin, his character and his manners must appear in the highest degree ridiculous'.[20] Certainly it seemed incongruous in the splendiferous halls of the Hofburg – the throne room, the ballroom with its giant gilded chandeliers and the frescoed ceiling glorifying the Empress Maria Theresa, the succession of white, gold, blue and rose salons, each with its tall porcelain stove – all beneath the gaze of huge primped and coiffed Habsburg portraits of the past century. Yet around Hofer were not only the sinewy, sun-burned elders of the mountain villages but also squires from their little castles, country lawyers, doctors, tradesmen and former army officers. These were men capable of governing.

As ruler of the Tyrol, Hofer was faced with unaccustomed administrative duties. He announced new legislation and taxes but always in the name of the Emperor Franz, who had abandoned him, although he did issue a new coinage, embossed with the initials 'A.H.' instead of the gaunt features of the defeated monarch. There were pressing problems, particularly in the South Tyrol, where rivalries had arisen between villagers and guerrillas from other parts of the province, and were quelled only when he travelled there himself. 'Dear brothers in arms, recollect yourselves', he proclaimed. 'Against whom do we fight – against friends or foes? . . . Dear countrymen, the whole world is astonished at our deeds. The name of the Tyrolese is already immortalized . . . Who at this moment would wish to disturb our tranquility?'[21]

This immediate problem was controlled, but there was a greater worry. The Tyrol stood alone, except for Britain, against Napoleon's Europe, and a counter-offensive was clearly imminent. So, on Hofer's orders, two of his staff, Müller and Schenacher, were 'despatched as deputies from the Tyrol to England to implore the assistance of the British government', as a contemporary put it, continuing, 'In their present distress, it was perfectly natural that they should have recourse to a nation, in which suffering and sorrow of every kind are sure to find protection and relief.'[22] The two men reached London on 25 October, attracting attention in their black hats, embroidered jackets, leather breeches and white stockings, and 'they were received . . . by men of all ranks with the greatest kindness and hospitality.'[23] Their arrival coincided with that of the news of the Treaty of Schönbrunn, which had been signed on 14 October between Napoleon and the Emperor Franz and under which the latter was again humiliated. Austria would have to rejoin the Continental System's embargo on British trade, pay France a huge indemnity and confirm its former cession of the Tyrol to Bavaria.

The mission was too late. Not only had the British given up hope of helping Austria, which to them included the Tyrol, and to which they had paid huge subsidies before the disaster at Wagram; they had shot their bolt elsewhere too. In August an expeditionary force of 40,000 men had been landed at the mouth of the Scheldt not only in the hope of capturing the port of Antwerp as a future gateway to the Continent but also to inspire a German revolt against Napoleonic rule. Neither objective had been achieved and less than two months later, after losing 4,000 men to a form of malaria known as Walcheren fever, they were evacuated. This was so close to home that the British, who had been fed with forecasts of victory, were shocked. The *Gentleman's Magazine* published a mournful ballad:

> Ah! Wretched spot, by Nature's hand unblessed,
> Where fell Disease high rears her spotted crest,
> Where horrid fogs eternally prevail,
> And fatal damps from poisonous floods exhale,
> Where blasts pestiferous taint the sullen air
> And spread around contagion and despair . . .
> Oh! God! what horror and what grief to tell
> The dreadful fate of those we lov'd so well,
> Of Fathers, Brothers, Sons, our Country's boast!
> Unnumber'd, dying on a foreign coast.[24]

The debate over the strategic significance of the two peninsulas had been resolved. In London the Cabinet, guided by Lord Castlereagh as Minister for War, before his resignation following the Walcheren disaster, had increasingly looked to Spain as a more effective option than Italy. Indeed, a British army of the same size as that sent to the Scheldt was already in Iberia. Spain was far closer to its British bases, and the same squadrons that blockaded Brest and Rochefort could watch the Atlantic ports of Portugal and Spain. The Iberian war had taught the British the value of indigenous forces, notably Spanish guerrillas and disciplined Portuguese infantry. Although they could see the value of Hofer's irregulars, the moment of decision had passed. It was to be Iberia, not Italy.

In London the two Tyrolese were received by Earl Bathurst, the Foreign Secretary, and Lord Liverpool, the new Secretary for War, who expressed sympathy but could offer no military assistance and no more than token financial aid. After listening to their pleading, the former framed his reply in writing: 'Under circumstances so unpromising, His Majesty cannot take upon himself to urge the people of Tyrol and Vorarlberg to continue their resistance against an invasion by the combined armies of Bavaria and France.'[25] A token sum of £30,000 would be granted and paid through a Viennese bank but this, he added, 'should not be seen as pressure for them to continue resistance one hour longer than they would otherwise be inclined to do if such supplies were not afforded. It is not by pecuniary aid from without that a contest of this description ought to be encouraged, or can be upheld.'[26] The Tyrolese departed.

The British had decided that Spain would now be accorded priority over all else. Lord Liverpool ordained that all moves to sustain the Ottoman Empire – including the proposed capture of the Ionian Islands from the French – should be suspended, and what British land forces remained in the Mediterranean and could be spared from the defence of the bases in Sicily and Malta should be shipped to Catalonia. Napoleon might one day resume his plans for a march eastward but, for the time being, he was fully occupied in central Europe and the Iberian peninsula.

So there was a hollow ring to celebrations in Innsbruck that October. Just before the Emperor Franz signed the Peace of Schönbrunn, he had sent Hofer a gold medal and chain as a badge of office and officially appointed him commander-in-chief. He was formally invested with this at the monument to the Emperor Maximilian among the twenty-eight life-size bronze statues of Tyrolean heroes around it in the Hofkirche at Innsbruck, and the occasion was celebrated with drinking and feasting. But it was already known that the counter-offensive was under way, with the

French advancing from Italy towards the Brenner Pass and the Bavarians from Salzburg. Speckbacher was defeated after defending a pass inside the Tyrol against the Bavarians, losing more than 300 men. It was clear that no help would come from any quarter. As the Bavarians advanced along the Inn valley towards Innsbruck, they took their revenge and one report spoke of '17 villages . . .in ruins . . . and whole espaliers of dead peasants . . . seen hanging'.[27] The heart seemed to have gone out of the Tyrolese. Napoleon, sensing this, ordered his stepson Eugène de Beauharnais, now Prince Eugène Napoléon, Viceroy of Italy, to declare an amnesty. He issued a proclamation in October, declaring, 'Tyroleans! . . . Peace prevails everywhere except among you – you only do not enjoy its benefits.'[28] All those who laid down their arms and returned home would be pardoned. Hofer, now in the Brenner Pass, received an invitation from the French general to come to Innsbruck for negotiations and 'had the audacity to reply . . . *that he would come but accompanied by 10,000 sharpshooters*'.[29] But the Tyrolese, who had been away from their farms during the harvest and wanted to return to their alpine villages before they were isolated by snow, began to drift home. Hearing of this, even Hofer began to despair and briefly considered giving himself up to the French. But he did not.

At the end of October Hofer evacuated Innsbruck and withdrew to his old stronghold of Berg Isel. This time the Bavarians did not attack immediately but settled into the city, proclaiming the peace that had been signed at Schönbrunn, which agreed that the Tyrol was again ruled by themselves. Then they did attack in overwhelming strength; this time they prevailed and the Tyrolese streamed away towards the mountain passes. Hofer tried to rally his men but early in November, after some fighting, Bavarians had taken the Brenner Pass. The end was in sight and Hofer sent a delegation of two Tyrolese deputies, Major Seiberer and a priest, Father Donay, who had in effect become a courtier to Prince Eugène at the Hofburg, to seek an amnesty. They were successful, and Hofer issued another proclamation on 8 November, which showed how his spirit had flagged. 'Entirely abandoned by Austria, we are precipitating ourselves into an abyss of misfortune', he declared.

I can no longer command you . . . A power of a superior order guides the steps of Napoleon; it is the immutable decree of Divine providence which decides victories and the condition of states. It would be madness to strive against the course of a torrent . . . The greatness of soul of Napoleon assures us of our pardon and of an oblivion for the past.[30]

Speckbacher and a dozen other leaders escaped to Austria and Haspinger to Switzerland, but Hofer retreated to his own valley of Passeiertal and there he recovered his spirits. The valley seemed impregnable. Deep and sheltered by steep wooded hills rising to snowy peaks more than 10,000 feet high, it was self-sufficient. Running 10 miles between Meran (Merano) and St Leonhard, it was almost inaccessible from the north, the direction from which attack surely must come. The road from Innsbruck crossed the Brenner Pass, then followed the narrow, twisting trail of the Jaufen Pass, reaching nearly 7,000 feet and blocked by snow for half the year. From the south, the road ran along the valley floor from Meran, but that route involved a march of several days down from the Brenner to Bozen and north-west from there, when an invader could be watched and attacked from the heights. This sense of security had given the people of Passeiertal self-confidence.

On 15 November Hofer issued another proclamation, reversing his most recent. Protesting that he had been persuaded to abandon the cause 'by men whom I considered friends to my country but who, as I now find, are its enemies and traitors' – he presumably meant Seiberer and Donay–

All the Passeyr [sic] Valley is again in open insurrection . . . Were we to surrender to the enemy, we should soon see all the youths of the Tyrol dragged away from their homes, our churches and convents destroyed, divine worship abolished and ourselves overwhelmed with eternal misery. Fight, therefore, in defence of your native country. I shall fight with you and for you as a father for his children.[31]

A last stand was made in that valley. A Franco-Bavarian attack was repulsed, but again the Tyrolese were offered an amnesty. Most of Hofer's subordinate commanders decided to submit. They urged Hofer to escape over the mountains but he refused, and at the end of November he and his family seemed to disappear into the snows. A few of his followers knew that his destination was a remote hut, high in the mountains above St Marten, in the Passeiertal. It was isolated in deep snow, but during the next month an agent managed to reach him with a message from the Emperor Franz, urging him to escape to Vienna. He shook his head and even refused to conceal his identity by cutting off his great beard, which had turned grey.

The Bavarians now concentrated on subduing and occupying the villages. They made their mastery plain by clearing the churchyards of the freshly carved wooden memorials to village men killed in the fighting, sometimes digging up their bodies and reburying them in the unconsecrated ground beneath roads. The French, on instructions from Prince Eugène and the Emperor himself, regarded Hofer as the embodiment of Tyrolese resistance, and made his capture their priority, putting a price on his head and despatching a strong force of infantry to hunt him. There were no clues to his hiding place until Father Donay turned traitor and managed to discover the whereabouts of the hut. The 44th Regiment – 1,400 men, commanded by a Captain Renouard – was ordered to arrest Hofer, and at midnight on 19 January 1810 they struggled up the mountainside over ice and through snow, while another 2,000 French soldiers waited in the valley to throw out cordons where necessary. At five o'clock next morning, 'Hofer and his family were made prisoners. It was dark when the French approached the hut, but as soon as he heard the officer enquire for him, he came intrepidly forward and submitted to be bound.'[32] He was taken in chains across the border into Italy and a court martial was convened at Mantua. Inevitably he was found guilty of rebellion against the state, but there were differences over his sentence, with two members of the court voting for leniency. Then a message arrived from Milan, said to be from the Viceroy and conveying the wishes of the Emperor. Hofer was thereupon condemned to death, the sentence to be carried out within twenty-four hours. At eleven o'clock on the morning of 20 February 1810 Andreas Hofer was led in chains through the Cerese Gate of Mantua to where the firing squad was drawn up before the town walls. Refusing a blindfold, or to kneel, he gave money to the corporal in charge with the order, 'Shoot straight.'[33] Then he himself gave the order to fire.

11

Echoes of Trafalgar

THE DEATH of Andreas Hofer and the collapse of the alpine rebellion seemed to lower the curtain on a theatre of war. All was not well in Palermo either, despite the British according high priority to the defence of Sicily. Now that the peninsular campaign against France was being fought in Spain and not Italy, 'the disappointment and the rage of the Queen were excessive', as Bunbury put it; 'With Sir John Stuart she had been on very bad terms since his return from Ischia.'[1] However, a month after the execution of Andreas Hofer, he noted, 'There suddenly appeared a remarkable change in the tone and in the spirits of Queen Caroline. Ever since the Peace of Vienna [the Treaty of Schönbrunn], she had been depressed and seemingly desperate.' But soon afterwards news arrived from Vienna that the Emperor Napoleon had married Princess Marie-Louise, who was not only the daughter of his former enemy the Emperor Franz but also of Bourbon blood and, indeed, a great-niece of Maria Carolina herself. So, as she saw it, she was no longer facing a ruthless Corsican dictator but fellow royalty, related by marriage, to whom she sent her congratulations on his wedding. As confidential letters reached her from Vienna and Naples, wrote Bunbury, 'The Queen came forth as if inspired with new hopes . . . There arose the strongest suspicion that Her Majesty had opened, through the Austrians, a secret communication with Napoleon.'[2] Confirmation of this followed when a letter from the Queen to Napoleon – innocuous in itself – was intercepted by the British on its way to the Emperor's headquarters in Spain.

What, if anything, Murat knew of this was not clear, but the Queen became increasingly dismissive of British military plans in Sicily and the belief grew that she was hoping for a British withdrawal. No imagination was required to suspect that she now hoped for an alliance with France in return for the restoration of Naples and southern Italy to her husband. There was a risk that British strategy in the Mediterranean might implode.

The Iberian peninsula might now be the focus of British military effort but some, including Lord Collingwood, still looked east. Under the Treaty of Schönbrunn, Austria had not only agreed to cede the Tyrol and Salzburg to Bavaria and vast tracts of territory to Russia, including the Grand Duchy of Warsaw; it had also ceded all its seaboard on the Adriatic – Trieste, Istria, Fiume (now Rijeka), Croatia, indeed, all the Dalmatian coast – to France and this had now become the Emperor's Illyrian Provinces. Looking eastward from his naval base at Venice, Napoleon could congratulate himself on having leapt half-way to Constantinople.

Then, on 21 October 1809, four years to the day since the Battle of Trafalgar, another French fleet broke out of Toulon. Again a gale had forced the British blockading squadron to run for shelter, this time in the great natural harbour of Mahon in Minorca – now the Royal Navy's principal base for the western basin of the Mediterranean – and again their enemy's destination was unknown. Lord Collingwood sailed north from Minorca with sixteen sail of the line but he knew the French had had seventeen in Toulon, together with many lesser warships and transports. They could be making for Sicily, or even Greece, which was ruled by the Ottoman Empire, and the admiral was, of course, aware that Napoleon still hankered after eastward conquest by way of the Balkans. Moving an army would obviously be easier by sea than through the highlands of Croatia and the mountains of Montenegro, so Collingwood had immediately despatched a frigate squadron to the Adriatic to intercept any troop convoys sailing from Venice or Ancona towards the Dalmatian coast; the danger was also that the French might attempt to bypass that route and land directly on the coast of Greece.

The other possible destination for the convoy was Barcelona, to deliver reinforcements to the hard-pressed French armies in Spain. Then, on the 24th, a frigate was sighted running before the wind and signalling that the main French fleet was in sight. Collingwood was sickly, worn by war and sea-keeping, seeming older than his sixty years, but he was roused by the news; he later wrote to his wife, 'Every soul was in raptures; I expected their whole fleet and that we should have had a dashing business.'[3] It was not, after all, the whole enemy fleet but a large convoy of twenty transports, escorted by three sail of the line and three frigates. They were steering west, and that probably meant Barcelona. Collingwood had not only planned to meet such a move but had told the Admiralty about it a month before.

From his flagship, the *Ville de Paris* – once captured from the French – he co-ordinated the interception, dividing his fleet into three divisions and ordering a chase. Collingwood himself saw the enemy from his quarterdeck but it fell to one of his subordinates, Admiral Martin, to come up with the three French battleships and drive them ashore, where they were burned by their crews. Some of the transports were caught and destroyed at sea, but most escaped into Rosas Bay, on the frontier between France and Spain, and lay under the guns of the castle. Collingwood surveyed the anchored ships and sent a squadron in to burn them. Out of the entire French convoy and escort only one frigate escaped by running for Marseilles. It was not a victory on a Nelsonic scale, but it was a demonstration of the skill expected of his closest friend.

It was Collingwood's last battle. Aware of his failing health, he had been hoping for what he called 'one little finishing touch – a grand termination'.[4] Frustration had become acute when news reached the Mediterranean that, in April that year, Admiral Lord Gambier had failed to achieve the first great victory since Trafalgar over a strong French squadron in the Aix Roads, off Rochefort. Although Captain Lord Cochrane had burst through a defensive boom with fireships and the enemy had cut their cables and drifted ashore, helpless, the cautious admiral had failed to follow through and half the enemy ships had escaped. Collingwood had longed for such an opportunity, for he was aware that the British at home regarded the Mediterranean as a remote theatre of war. The realities of war must seem remote to them, too: 'When they read in a newspaper of the destruction of 28,000 or 30,000 men, the impression is lightly felt at Charing Cross', he wrote, but it would be different if they could see 'the inhabitants flying from their town in flames . . .women and children running from death and, when they come to the Po or the Pavia find the bridges broken down . . . scenes like that.'[5]

More than a year earlier, he had had to ask the Admiralty for permission to return home to 'recover my shaken body'[6] but this had been refused. The government realised that he was now the only British officer in the Mediterranean with a full and balanced grasp of the changing strategic scene and so he could not be spared. Also, the Admiralty was worried that the Duke of Clarence – the King's son and an enthusiastic but unreliable naval officer, who had with difficulty been kept ashore throughout the war – was insisting that he succeed Collingwood to the command. After five years' absence, the latter longed to see his wife, Sarah, and their two daughters, but his sense of duty was so strong that he had refused to resign his command on grounds of health. So he immersed himself in the duties of command, assessing intelligence reports, keeping in touch with the army commanders and politicians and reporting his views to the Admiralty. His one link with his family, apart from letters, was his dog Bounce, which had been taught to dance by one of his daughters. But that August, Bounce fell overboard in the night and his master was stricken. He confided in his sister: 'He is a great loss to me. I have few comforts but he was one, for he loved me.'[7]

Collingwood returned to Minorca. He was low in spirits and lower in health, telling his sister that 'the physician has much difficulty in determining on the nature of my complaint, which is in my stomach, and they say entirely the consequence of the sedentary life I must have', but he was recommended to take up riding. He was probably suffering from cancer and, aware that his condition was deteriorating, gave an ominous order: enough lead was to be brought on board to make a coffin so that his body could be taken to England for burial. At the end of the year he heard that his old friend Sir Alexander Ball, the Governor of Malta and once one of Nelson's captains and 'Band of Brothers', had died and, aware of his own approaching death, he told a friend, 'I often wish I was peaceably settled in heaven.'[8] On 22 February 1810 Collingwood at last wrote to the Admiralty, resigning his command. On 6 March he sailed from Mahon in his flagship and, as they cleared the harbour, he said, 'I may yet live to meet the French once more.' Next day, as the *Ville de Paris* lifted to the swell, he was asked if the ship's movement disturbed him. 'I am now in a state in which nothing in this world can disturb me more,' he replied, 'I am dying.'[9] He spoke about his family and bade his officers farewell. Then, as the ship's surgeon wrote later, 'In no part of his Lordship's brilliant life did his character appear with greater lustre than when he was approaching his end. It was dignified in the extreme.'[10] He died at six o'clock that evening. His body was wrapped in lead, as he had ordered, and shipped to England to lie in state at Greenwich Naval Hospital, where Nelson's body had lain four years before, and was then taken to the crypt of St Paul's Cathedral to lie beside his friend.

The Nelson connection did not die with Collingwood. Many, perhaps most, of the captains in the Mediterranean had served under Nelson's command and one in particular had been almost as close to him as Collingwood, although of a younger generation. This was Captain William Hoste. Like his mentor, the son of a Norfolk parson – albeit a very different and more worldly and extravagant one than the shy Edmund Nelson – William had been taken to sea in 1793 at the age of twelve, when Captain Nelson had been recalled to duty after five years of unemployment. He was a keen, lively boy and Nelson was soon writing to his father that 'he highly deserves everything I can do to make him happy.'[11] He was with Nelson for the disastrous attack on Tenerife in 1797 and at the battles of Cape St Vincent and the Nile, after which he was given command of the brig that took news of the victory at Naples and thence to London. As captain of the frigate *Amphion* he had been sent on a diplomatic mission to Algiers in October 1805 and, to his dismay, had missed Trafalgar. He had been mourning his patron and hero ever since and trying to emulate him.

Since Trafalgar, Hoste had been serving in the Mediterranean under Collingwood, operating off the coasts of Spain, France and Italy, where he had been supporting the landing that had led to victory at Maida. Like all frigate captains, he had envied the exploits of the most dashing of them all, the flamboyant Lord Cochrane, who was ravaging the coasts of France and Spain, capturing forts, cutting roads and seizing merchant ships, the latter to considerable gain in prize-money. Hoste was inspired by him, too, and now he was to have his chance. In June 1808 he was ordered to the Adriatic. He was delighted because, as he put it, 'I have at last got on good ground for *pewterising*' – 'pewter' being the naval slang for prize-money – and I trust . . . to be able to give my good father a lift over the stones.'[12] However much Hoste could earn – a captain now collected a quarter of the value of enemy ships and cargoes he captured – most would go to finance the political ambitions of his father, Dixon Hoste, who was spending vast sums on electioneering on behalf of the Whigs in Norfolk to ingratiate himself with his patron, the great landowner and agriculturalist Thomas Coke and in the hope of an eventual bishopric.

The Adriatic was a self-contained theatre of war. After passing the Straits of Otranto – the 45 miles between south-eastern Italy and Corfu – it ran some 500 miles north-west to Venice, a deep, often stormy, trough about 100 miles in width. To the west lay the hills and plains of Italy and the port of Ancona; to the east, the Dalmatian and Ionian islands and mountains. Across the Adriatic lay the principal trade and military supply routes to the Balkans and to the gates of Constantinople; most carried in small, sturdy *trabaccoli* of some 70 tons, which often sailed in convoy and could hide among the myriad islands of the Dalmatian coast. There the principal ports were: to the south, Cattaro (now Kotor) at the head of a long, deep, steep-sided fjord; Ragusa (now Dubrovnik), the ancient, trading city-state; then Fiume, to the east of the mountainous Istrian peninsula; and to the west of that, Trieste. Finally, of course, came Venice. Here Hoste would be in command, except when a more senior frigate captain joined him, or when a ship of the line was thought necessary to watch the Arsenale at Venice, where warships were again being built.

For his own base Hoste chose the island of Lissa (now Vis), the most westerly of the islands, some 30 miles off Spalato (Split). Like so many ports of the eastern Adriatic, it had once been Venetian, as was shown by a campanile decorated with the Lion of St Mark.

The hilly island, rising to a 2,000-foot peak, had two deep-water harbours, one of which offered good anchorage off the town of Lissa and the potential for a naval base.★ Soon Hoste became familiar both with the maze of islands to the east and the fierce winds: the *bora*, which howled from the mountains of the north-east; the *fugo*, blowing from the south-west in spring and autumn; and the warm *mistral* from the west in summer. Storms brought the risk of being 'pooped' when a huge wave crashed on the stern of a ship and forced it underwater beyond recovery. Even a sturdy 'seventy-four', the *Repulse*, narrowly escaped this. 'A tremendous sea struck the stern and made all stagger through the ship', recalled an officer.

> The galley fire was put out by it and everything displaced everywhere; the men said the ship trembled for ten minutes fore and aft and everyone thought a thunderbolt had struck us. In the wardroom [in the ship's stern] the wave burst in all our windows, window-frames, woodwork, etc., and rushing into . . . every place at once, filled us all with consternation and we really thought we were going down, the crash was so great, which with the loud thunder, and all confusion, that no one had the power to get away till washed into a heap together: tables, chairs, musical instruments, backgammon boxes, etc., all swimming about, the water above our knees before it got vent, when it rushed impetuously out between decks and half drowned all the sailors. Had any small vessel been struck by such a mountain of a wave, it would have been sunk in an instant.[13]

The Adriatic tried any seaman to his limits.

Captain Hoste was a cheerful, robust, handsome young man with an open, friendly face, uncomplicated and unsophisticated and almost as popular as Nelson once had been. His ship's company chose to serve under him and, as his reputation in England grew, Norfolk friends asked him to take their sons to sea with him

---

★ Vis again became a British base during the Second World War, when small warships, fighter aircraft and commandos operated from there in support of the Yugoslav partisans, whose leader, Marshal Tito, set up his headquarters on the island.

as volunteers to qualify as midshipmen. Like other captains who became familiar with the rocks of Ushant, the currents of the Straits of Gibraltar and the wind off Toulon, Hoste seemed at ease in the Adriatic. Indeed, this familiarity had been symbolized by a strange event on 8 November 1808, when the *Amphion* was cruising off Trieste.

Early that morning Hoste had ordered away the frigate's yawl under the command of Lieutenant George Jones to search inshore for possible prizes. Cruising along the mountainous coast to the east of the port, they had sighted a small boat and, as they drew near, they were hailed in English. It was an escaped British naval officer. Taking him aboard, Jones was amazed to recognize a friend he had not seen since they had been midshipmen in the *Amphion* six years earlier. Donat Henchy O'Brien had later been shipwrecked on the coast of Brittany and taken prisoner, only to escape, be recaptured and sent to the fortress of Bitche★ in the hills of Lorraine, north of Strasburg. He had escaped again in September 1808 and, as he put it, as 'a sort of Nebuchadnezzar wandering in the fields and forests' for many weeks, he had reached Trieste. There he had paid a boatman to take him out to a British frigate that could be seen on the horizon, only to find that it was his old ship.

No sooner had the friends been reunited than they sighted two coasters under sail and, scenting prize-money, gave chase. But their quarry was armed and a fight began at point-blank range. Although O'Brien was wounded, he was still the tough enthusiast that Jones remembered, and he later recalled, 'Who can conceive my pride and elation when I thus found myself participating in the glories of my profession . . . a ship's cutlass and a black musket were good substitutes for my chains and padlock.'[14] Hoste welcomed him on board the *Amphion* and later appointed him his third lieutenant.

Hoste mastered the Adriatic. Singly, or in company with one or two other frigates, the *Amphion* swept up the enemy's coastal trade from Venice to the Straits of Otranto: 13 *trabaccoli* seized from under the guns of Pesaro, 36 prizes taken on one cruise and 29 on

---

★ Equivalent to Colditz Castle in the Second World War.

another. The French seemed helpless to prevent it. In Ancona, Hoste sighted a French frigate and a brig and,· as he wrote to his father, 'I saw my friends lying in Ancona, to whom I sent a friendly invitation in the name of *Amphion* and her crew requesting they would come out and try their strength for the honour of their flag; but I might have spared myself the trouble for all my efforts to rouse one spark of national honour failed and there they remain.'[15]

But a spark had been roused in the Emperor himself. Determined to drive the British from the Adriatic to secure the flank of a future movement into the Balkans, he asked his Minister of Marine, Admiral Decrès, to recommend an exceptional officer for the task. He chose Captain Bernard Dubourdieu. Most senior French commanders had begun their careers in the old royalist navy and survived the Revolution but, at thirty-seven, Dubourdieu was as much a product of those years as Napoleon himself. Intelligent, aggressive and physically hard, his dark, expressive eyes and his tight mouth expressed his zeal. The son of a cooper, he had joined the navy as a seaman at the beginning of the Revolution and, once commissioned, showed his mettle in command. As a captain, he had fought and won a duel with a British frigate, for which he had been awarded the *Légion d'honneur*, and he had twice been taken prisoner in action. He was therefore ordered to travel overland from Toulon to Milan, where he would place himself under the command of the Viceroy of Italy. From there he would go to Venice and discuss the building of ships of the line at the Arsenale and the Malamocco shipyard. Then he would assume command of a squadron consisting of five frigates – three French and two Venetian – which would outnumber Hoste's command.

In the spring of 1810 the British squadron consisted of four frigates: the *Amphion* and *Cerberus* of 32 guns, the *Active* of 38 and the little *Volage* of 22. On Hoste's first cruise as commodore of this force he took, or destroyed, forty-six enemy merchantmen, which, he said, 'will bring us a little pewter', and even attacked convoys sheltering under the cover of shore batteries. Coastal raids became almost as commonplace as the cutting-out of shipping, and the marines became accustomed to skirmishing through the umbrella pines and grassy savannahs of the Italian coast and the scrub, thorn and rosemary bushes of the rocky Croatian shore. At Grado, near Venice, he sent his marines and seamen ashore to clear the French from the town in hand-to-hand fighting, while his boats captured twenty merchant ships and burned another eleven, returning to Lissa with his prizes for brief relaxation. 'We have established a cricket club at this wretched place', he noted, 'and, when we do get anchored for a few hours, it passes away an hour very well.'[16]

Cruising and cricket were interrupted at the end of September, when it was learned that the French ships at Ancona had arrived off Chioggia, at the south-western mouth of the Venetian lagoon, there to meet reinforcements, and that the full squadron had sailed under the command of Commodore Dubourdieu. Hoste at once made for Ancona with only the *Amphion* and *Active* and, on arrival, found the enemy already in the port. This time their reaction was very different and, through his telescope, he saw their frigates warping out of the harbour and making sail. This time they wanted to fight. Dubourdieu commanded a formidable force: his own heavy frigate, *La Favorite*, and two others of 44 guns, one French, *Uranie*, and one Venetian, *Corona*; two Venetian frigates of 32 guns, *Bellona* and *Carolina*, and two 16-gun French brigs, *Jena* and *Mercure*. As he cleared the coast, Dubourdieu split his force into two divisions, each taking a different tack so as to intercept Hoste's two ships on whichever course they took. Now it was the turn of the British to refuse action and Hoste, realizing how hopelessly outnumbered he would be, ordered his ships to go about and run to the north-east and Lissa for reinforcement. Dubourdieu followed in pursuit but the wind was freshening and the sea rising and, after an hour, he bore away and disappeared from sight in a gale. Arriving at Port St George, as the British called the island's main harbour, Hoste found the *Cerberus* and the 18-gun brig *Acorn* at anchor and ordered them to follow him back to Ancona, ready for action. But the gale had blown itself out, there was little wind and, after lying becalmed for three days, the hills of Italy finally appeared on the horizon. Telescopes were trained on Ancona and soon it was clear that there were no frigates in the harbour. Dubourdieu had gone: but where? Hoste decided that his most likely destination was Corfu, from which any attack on Sicily was likely to be mounted. So he steered south-east, tacking into a strong head wind. But there was no sight of the enemy and, like Nelson before him, he had no idea where to look for his enemy in the Adriatic or, indeed, the Mediterranean itself.

Dubourdieu had anticipated Hoste's reasoning and realized that the British base at Lissa would now be empty and virtually undefended. So he had embarked a battalion of infantry at Ancona to carry out a plan of his own. A few days later Hoste did return to Lissa and, as its bare hills rose out of the sea, he trained his telescope on Port St George and saw a shocking sight. The anchorage and foreshore were littered with wrecked, burned-out ships: Dubourdieu had been there while he was away. Without entering the harbour, Hoste laid course for Ancona, crowding sail. But when they arrived, he could see the enemy squadron safely moored under the guns of the forts and batteries. They were too late. He returned to Port St George

There he was told what had happened. On the fifth anniversary of Trafalgar and the first of Collingwood's last battle, Dubourdieu, cruising close to Lissa, heard from a passing fisherman that the British had been sighted, steering south. The next morning he led three of his frigates into Port St George, flying the British flag. The British warships were absent, but privateers and merchantmen lay there at his mercy and he later claimed to have captured thirty and burned sixty-four although Hoste was to report that he had captured only three and burned five. 'It was a bitter drug of disappointment and none felt it more keenly than our gallant captain', wrote O'Brien. 'I dined with him that day and saw the big drop trickle down his manly cheek. Never was there a more gloomy, melancholy dinner-party than this.'[17]

Hoste sailed again in search of the enemy, but a gale blew out of the night and the *Amphion* collided with the *Volage* in the wild darkness; repairs were necessary and his ship would have to make for Malta. There, aware that Dubourdieu's success was being trumpeted across Europe, Hoste tried to forget his humiliation, writing home, 'We are all gaiety in this place and nothing but masquerades and balls . . . one would suppose that Tarantula had made cruel devastation amongst the fair ladies for dancing is the order of the day and night, too.' He even despaired of achieving any ambition: 'I begin to think that I could be happy enough in dear old Norfolk without going further in search of honour, or riches. I hope to have a lick at the partridges next season.'[18]

At Malta, Hoste heard that, while he had been sparring with Dubourdieu in the Adriatic, Sicily had been under direct threat. In the summer of 1810 Murat had decided to invade the island. This was on instructions from Napoleon, who also saw this as a feint to draw British troops away from Spain. In Sicily, General Stuart was under pressure to send to Spain at least four British battalions from his army of about 16,000, half of whom were foreign. In Sicilian waters there were about a dozen British frigates, but these would be no match for the French fleet in Toulon, now numbering thirteen sail of the line and eight frigates. So, throughout that hot summer, a French army 15,000 strong, together with 10,000 Neapolitans and Corsicans, marched south under the command of Murat's chief of staff, General Paul Grenier. Pushing through Calabria and extinguishing resistance with the usual savage reprisals, the French established themselves on the Straits of Messina with 500 landing craft and 100 gunboats assembled along the coast. By late summer the army was ready to cross.

In mid-September a strong southerly gale blew, driving the British frigates from their stations off Messina. Then the wind dropped and there was a flat calm, ideal for rowing the two miles from Calabria to Sicily. On the 17th Grenier gave the order to embark but then, as a breeze sprang up and the return of the British frigates was feared, he cancelled it. The last order did not, however, reach a Neapolitan and Corsican division and this did make the crossing, landing only to find themselves alone and facing two battalions of British and German infantry. While the French army watched from across the straits and heard the musketry, the invaders tried to re-embark and some managed to escape, leaving 800 behind, including 40 officers. General Grenier lost heart and then even Murat himself realized, when he heard, that the moment of opportunity had passed. The invaders struck camp and began to withdraw: that particular threat to Sicily was over.

When his ship's storm damage had been repaired, Hoste was

ordered back to the Adriatic by the new Commander-in-Chief, Admiral Sir Charles Cotton, whom he described as 'very civil but . . . not, like my Lord Collingwood, *in my way*.'[19] He was no longer senior officer there because a ship of the line had been sent to watch for any large, newly built warships emerging from the Arsenale at Venice. But he did command his own squadron of four frigates – *Amphion*, *Active*, *Cerberus* and *Volage* – and, once assembled off Lissa, decided to take them across to Ancona for another attempt to taunt the French into action. The night before, leaving the lee of Lissa, the ships rode under easy sail, the *Active* some way ahead and to windward, when at three o'clock in the morning of 13 March, Hoste heard the report of a distant gun and then a second, followed by a blue flare in the darkness ahead. This was the signal for enemy in sight and he answered it with a blue light, making sail to join the *Active*, which had made the signal.

It was getting light when Hoste sighted the frigate, and he saw something else too. Faintly at first in the dim light were tall shapes, which slowly separated into ships. Then as the sun rose, he saw, six miles ahead, the strongest squadron he had ever seen in the Adriatic, rippling towards him across the wide sweep of water and the islands and mountains of the Dalmatian coast. It was Dubourdieu, come to offer battle. With him were six frigates – the French *La Favorite*, the *Flore* and *Danae*, all of more than 1,000 tons, each mounting 44 guns, and the Venetian *Corona*, also of 44 guns, and *Bellona* and *Carolina* of 32 – together with a corvette, a brig and four smaller ships. A quick calculation showed that Dubourdieu faced the four British frigates with their 124 guns and 900 men with his own 276 guns and nearly 2,000 men.

Commodore Dubourdieu was at last confident of victory. A month earlier he had received an order from the Emperor himself to take Lissa again, and this time to occupy and hold it against the returning British. For this purpose he had embarked 500 troops and six heavy guns with which to defend Port St George against counter-attack. He was confident in the qualities of his three French frigates and their crews but not of his Venetian ships; one of them, the *Corona*, newly completed at the Arsenale in Venice and commanded by the volatile Venetian Captain Pasqualigo, was as yet untried in action. Dubourdieu knew of his opponent's naval education by Lord Nelson and had studied Nelsonian tactics, particularly those at Trafalgar, and was determined to make use of them himself. Realizing that Hoste, with only four ships, would probably fight in line of battle, he decided to attack in two columns, as had Nelson at Trafalgar, to break the line apart and fight a close action in which his superior firepower would tell in the first impact. But, realizing that British gun drill was unrivalled in speed and effectiveness, he planned to follow this with the tactics of the French officer who had caused Nelson's death, Captain Jean-Jacques Lucas, whose ship's company had been trained in sniping and boarding; so this he would also do. Overwhelming gunfire, followed by boarding, should decide the battle.

Hoste, too, remembered Nelson. With practised ease and speed his ships cleared for action and ran out their guns. There was something more to be done. Although Hoste had, to his abiding anguish, missed Trafalgar, he, of course, knew of his mentor's famous signal 'England expects . . .' and some such inspiration was now required. But William Hoste was not an imaginative man and no ringing phrase came to mind. Nevertheless, one thought was in his mind and, on impulse, he ordered that to be spelled out in signal flags and hoisted. Up the halyards flew sixteen brightly coloured flags, and on the upper decks of the three ships astern they read his words: 'Remember Nelson'.[20] Captain Phipps Hornby of the little *Volage* said, 'Never again so long as I live shall I see so glorious a moment.'[21]

James Bealy, the quartermaster of the *Amphion*, was to write in a ballad,

> Then now, my boys, brave Hoste did say,
> We conquer, or, like Nelson die![22]

while a seaman in the *Volage* wrote,

> Our commodore, bold Captain Hoste, a signal did display
> 'Remember Nelson!' was the word, here is a glorious day;
> At that we mann'd the rigging and gave three hearty cheers,
> 'To sink, or die!' was each man's cry, or bang the proud
> Monseers . . .[23]

It was nine o'clock. Captain Hoste had ordered his ships to close into a tight line, the bowsprit of each frigate astern of the *Amphion*, almost touching the taffrail of the ship ahead. The British sailed slowly under only topsails and topgallants, steering north-west a mile off the rocks of Lissa as the enemy approached at right angles in two columns, just as Nelson had at Trafalgar. Not a shot had been fired, but Lieutenant O'Brien, standing on the upper deck of the *Amphion*, noticed that the quartermaster was covered in blood. He had cut his leg while sliding down a stay after making sail, and O'Brien ordered him down to the surgeon. 'It's not worth while, sir, to go down for this', the man replied. 'Perhaps I may soon have something more to complain of and then make one job of it.'[24] Then Hoste shouted to O'Brien, 'Try a single shot from one of the main-deck guns at Dubourdieu's ship!'[25] The report and the smoke and a waterspout just ahead of *La Favorite*, opened the action. The next order to fire would be for a broadside, double-shotted.

Half a mile away Dubourdieu was also buoyant, telling his officers on the quarterdeck of *La Favorite*, 'This is the happiest day of our lives.'[26] He was leading the windward column to break the British line between the *Amphion* and the *Active* but, as the flame and smoke of the first broadside burst from the British ships, he saw that this could not be done; the British line was drawn together too tightly. So he chose another Nelsonian tactic, remembered from the Battle of the Nile: he would steer immediately ahead of the *Amphion*, put about and run down her far side so that the British would be attacked from port and starboard. Now they were a few hundred yards apart and the British were not, as usual, firing into the hulls of their enemy but at his masts and rigging, which began to splinter, sag and crash to the decks. Dubourdieu saw that his ship could not respond to the manoeuvre he planned, so he changed tactics again: now he would run alongside the *Amphion* and board her. Shouting orders to muster boarders with cutlasses, pikes and pistols, he ran forward with drawn sword to lead them on to the British deck himself.

In Hoste's ship only one gun on the starboard side had remained silent: a bronze howitzer loaded with 750 musket balls. As the bows of *La Favorite* surged towards them, they could see

Dubourdieu and his boarders crowding the forecastle ready to spring. The howitzer was aimed. Hoste gave the order to fire. When the smoke blew back, they could see the wreckage and the corpses, including that of the brave Dubourdieu. Hoste ordered the helm to be put hard over and the whole British line went about, reversing course, as *La Favorite* surged past the stern of the *Amphion*. But the second ship in the enemy line, the *Flore*, followed her and O'Brien, commanding the main-deck guns, saw that they were about to be raked from stern to stem by a broadside and shouted to his men to lie flat between the guns. It was just in time. The broadside crashed through the stern windows of Hoste's cabin and 'the enemy's shot rattled along the decks without doing injury to the men,'[27] as O'Brien said later.

But the *Flore* was still under control and she bore up on the starboard side of the *Amphion* while the third ship in the enemy line, the *Bellona*, ran alongside to port. Hoste ordered all sails to be set and the ship leapt ahead and out of the trap. Then he put his helm hard over again, sweeping across the bows of the *Flore* and down her lee side so that she shielded him from the fire of the *Bellona* and he shattered her with a broadside. The frigate was a wreck and a surviving officer on deck shouted that she surrendered. Then the *Bellona*, trying to aid the *Flore*, neared the *Amphion* and she too was raked from bow to stern and surrendered.

Now the fighting had become the mêlée that Nelson had always sought, giving British gun drill the advantage. The French and Venetians fought hard but, one by one, their decks heaped with dead and wounded in the wreckage of collapsed spars, rigging and sails, they struck their colours. *La Favorite* had drifted on to the rocks of Lissa, where she was set on fire by her crew. Three ships escaped: the *Flore*, when her captain, after having surrendered, realized that the British had had so many ships' boats smashed in the action that they could not send across a prize crew, suddenly hoisted his colours again and made sail, and the *Danae* and *Carolina*.

Hoste decided that the *Bellona* must be boarded before she, too, might hoist her colours again and escape. All but one of the *Amphion's* boats had been smashed or splintered by shot and, in any case, could not have been launched because the yards and tackle had been shot away, but one surviving boat was manhandled over the side to be pulled across to the prizes. In command was O'Brien, taking the place of Lieutenant David Dunn, whose face had been flayed by an explosion on deck. Boarding the *Bellona* with two armed seamen, he was appalled by the sight. 'It would be difficult to describe the horrors, which now presented themselves', he reported. 'The carnage was dreadful – the dead and dying lying about in every direction; the agonies of the latter were most lamentable and piercing.' The ship's surgeon, 'a Herculean man, with an apron and his shirt sleeves tucked up,'[28] was examining the wounded, indicating which were beyond his help and should be thrown over the side with the corpses. The captain, he was told, was lying mortally wounded in his cabin and he was led below to see him along the main deck, reduced to a shambles by double-shotted broadsides. One entire gun crew lay dead, while 'at another gun, the skull of one poor creature was actually lodged in the beam above where he stood.'[29] Then he met the dying captain, whose stomach had been cut open but who managed to take O'Brien's hand in both of his and thank him for anything he could do for his surviving crew.

A north-easterly *bora* now threatened and, before the gale struck, O'Brien ordered that his prize should be put into the best possible state to ride it. Finding two prisoners who spoke some English, he himself took command and 'the sprung and shattered spars from aloft were sent down; the sails, which stood in need thereof, unbent and replaced; and the decks shovelled and cleared from the heaps of gore and ordure with which they had been encumbered'.[30] He could see that the action was not yet over, for the *Active* was still fighting the Venetian *Corona*. Captain Pasqualigo, who claimed to be descended from a Doge, continued to fight his shattered ship for two hours until his mainmast caught fire and he too surrendered. At half-past two *La Favorite*, still burning on the rocks of Lissa, blew up and the sea fell silent. The Battle of Lissa had ended, leaving a panorama of broken, smoking, drifting ships, the sails of the three fugitives now far distant.

It had been a hard and gallant fight. The French and Venetians had lost one frigate destroyed and two captured, while three had escaped. Their loss in men was never known but the *Bellona* had

had some 150 men killed, or badly wounded, and the *Corona* about 200. The British had lost no ships, but the *Amphion* and *Volage* had been badly damaged and the squadron had lost 50 killed, with another 132 wounded, the heaviest loss being in Hoste's ship. As off Cape Trafalgar, a storm followed the battle, but the British were able to retire to the shelter of Port St George.

The exhausted British crews were triumphant and the quarter-master of the *Amphion* was already beginning to compose his ballad, concluding,

> At length and from his ouzy bed,
> Old Father Neptune rose his head;
> And viewing Lissa as he spoke,
> Who's this has made such fire and smoke?
>
> I'm so pleased, by Styx I swear,
> Old England still shall be my care;
> In Spain, let Mars decide the day,
> Hoste and his squadron shall rule the sea!
> Fol de riddle lol dol, etc,[31]

Congratulations began to arrive, first from Captain Eyre of the *Magnificent*, the battleship that arrived to hunt the fugitives from the battle while the victors' ships were repaired. Then followed more echoes of Trafalgar when Rear-Admiral Charles Boyles, also a Norfolkman, wrote to Hoste from Palermo that his victory would 'make our county of dumplings and dripping rejoice to think they have, still preserved for its protection, a brilliant spark from the shrine of our immortal countryman, Lord Nelson'. Lord Radstock, whose son the Hon. William Waldegrave was a first-class volunteer and a future officer in the *Amphion*, wrote, 'When I look at you as the truly worthy *élève* of my incomparable and ever-lamented friend the late Lord Nelson, I contemplate the giant steps with which you have pursued him in the path of Glory.'[32] Hoste was overwhelmed, and wrote to his mother, 'You might have knocked me down with a feather and I certainly did not exactly know whether I wore my own hair or a wig.'[33]

The *Amphion* and the captured *Bellona* reached Malta on 31

March to a tumultuous welcome and a round of routs, receptions and lavish praise. There, among those to meet those he called the 'triumphant sons of truest blue', was Lord Byron, who had arrived from Greece and was to take passage in the *Volage* to England. He wrote of them thus in his poem 'Farewell to Malta':

> While either Adriatic shore,
> And fallen chiefs and fleets no more,
> And nightly smiles and daily dinners,
> Proclaim you war and woman's winners.

Byron was not the only poet to put the victory into verse, for he too had heard the sailors' ballads and, writing home, offered 'a mouthful of saltwater poetry by a Tar on the late Lissa Victory', quoting one extolling Captain Hoste, which ended:

> If I had an edication
> I'd sing your praise more large,
> But I'm only a common foremast Jack
> On board of the *Volage!*[34]

12

Nature pauses and sheds a tear

THE ADRIATIC could be seen either as a backwater or as the way
to victory in Europe. Although the alpine risings had seemed
to end with the death of Andreas Hofer, sparks of revolt were still
alive in the mountains, and in August 1810, two more Tyrolese
emissaries arrived in London via the Baltic. Described in their
letter of introduction as 'most conspicuous Heroes of the
Mountains',[1] they were named Marberger and Nessing and
they brought exciting proposals. In essence, these were that there
were more than 170,000 Tyrolese, Vorarlbergers, Venetians and
Dalmatians ready to rise against the French, but they would need
military and financial aid. The specific military requirement was
that a British expeditionary force of 15,000 men should be landed
at the head of the Adriatic with strong naval support. It was suggested that the base for an advance through the Veneto into the
Tyrol should be at Venice itself and would be welcomed by the
Venetians if there were to be 'a plan for the restoration and
acknowledgement by England of the Republic of Venice',[2] the
resurrection of the Serenissima herself. The Prime Minister,
Spencer Perceval, a lawyer and former Chancellor of the
Exchequer, who had succeeded the Duke of Portland in the preceding year, was known to be worried by the cost of the campaign in Spain, so he might be persuaded that this lesser operation
in the Adriatic would be more effective.

But the balance of British strategic thinking had swung west from Italy to Iberia – Napoleon was still embroiled in kneading central Europe into the mould of his empire – and the major effort was in Spain and Portugal. After General Moore's death and the evacuation of his army from Corunna in 1809, the French had seemed omnipotent, but three months later Lieutenant-General Sir Arthur Wellesley had arrived in Lisbon and had succeeded in driving them out of Portugal. Napoleon had again defeated the Austrians at Wagram that year and imposed humiliating terms on them but Wellesley – now created Viscount Wellington – had advanced into Spain and again defeated the French at Talavera. They had counter-attacked and forced him back to the defences he had built across the Lisbon peninsula as the Lines of Torres Vedras, and there had been talk of withdrawing from Portugal altogether. But Wellington now had 60,000 British and Portuguese troops under command and planned a counter-offensive early in 1811. This had begun in March, when Hoste was winning his victory off Lissa and, as Wellington advanced and fought a series of bloody battles, Masséna's and Soult's armies fell back, harried by Spanish guerril-las. As winter approached, Wellington again retreated into Portugal, ready to resume the offensive at the beginning of 1812.

With all eyes on the Peninsula, as Iberia was now known, and Wellesley's naval support, the Adriatic might have seemed a sur-prising appointment for one of the most vigorous junior admirals in the Royal Navy and another of Nelson's 'Band of Brothers'. This was Rear-Admiral Thomas Fremantle, who had fought beside the great man at Tenerife and Copenhagen. A tough, intel-ligent officer with rakish tendencies when young, Fremantle had, in 1797, married Betsey Wynne, of an expatriate English family, at Sir William Hamilton's embassy in Naples and she had been with him in his ship when he had led the assault with Nelson at Tenerife and he had been wounded. In 1810 he had been pro-moted to flag rank and sent to join Vice-Admiral Sir Charles Cotton, Collingwood's successor, in the Mediterranean, where he operated from Minorca in the western basin off the Spanish coast and within striking distance of Toulon. In August 1811 he had been ordered to Palermo before making for the Adriatic.

If Queen Maria Carolina had expected another reincarnation

of Nelson, she was disappointed. Fremantle was a hard man in attitude and looks: round head, tight mouth and a shock of dark hair, just turning grey. He spoke Italian, knew the Bourbon court from his time in Naples and was not open to blandishment, while aware that the court at Palermo had 'almost ruined, indeed for a time did ruin, the character of Nelson and paralysed all the energy and zeal which distinguished him in every other situation'.[3] Indeed his first reaction was that 'nothing can equal the insolence and despotism of the Queen.'[4] In this view, Fremantle found an ally in Lieutenant-General Lord William Bentinck, who had been sent out to replace both General Stuart and the minister at Palermo, Lord Amherst, at the end of 1810. Son of the Duke of Portland, Bentinck was, at the age of thirty-six, experienced in soldiering and diplomacy. As liaison officer with the Russian and Austrian armies, he had already seen action in Italy, Flanders, Egypt and Spain. He had commanded a brigade at Corunna so effectively that he had been offered, but had refused, appointments as second-in-command to Wellington and then as Minister for War in London. His time in Italy – he had been present at the defeat of the Austrians by the French at Marengo in 1800 – had inspired a love of the country and a dream of its liberation and even unification. Surprisingly liberal in outlook and unconventional in strategic thought, he was, however, shy and lacking in the social airs that counted for much in Palermo.

On arrival, Bentinck had found his political options so limited that he had immediately returned to London to ask for wider powers, particularly that of withholding the substantial British subsidy to Sicily, as a means of applying political pressure. Both he and Fremantle knew that overriding priority was being given to the Peninsular campaign but, viewing Mediterranean strategy from their present vantage-point, they still favoured the easterly option combined with mass risings throughout Italy and revolts in the mountains of Austria, Switzerland, the Veneto and Illyria, as Dalmatia was now known. They had heard that the latest Tyrolese mission to London had failed and that the alpine rising, planned for November 1810, had been cancelled. Marberger and Nessing had returned to Austria, the former to be assassinated in Vienna 'by some persons, who did not think it worth while to rob him'.[5] Even so, they believed that this was the moment to strike. Not only had Napoleon withdrawn many of his best troops from this theatre to fight in Spain, but there were persistent reports of the massing of a vast army for a possible invasion of Russia; the road to Constantinople could also run across the plains of Russia, it was realized. So Bentinck prepared. He bullied the Queen, who was again suspected of secret negotiations with the French for a conditional return to Naples, by withholding the subsidies in the hope of imposing political reform and more effective defence of the island. He had at his disposal a potential striking-force of some 10,000 men, which could be used to support a rising in Italy, and he continued to encourage such plans. One was that the Archduke Franz d'Este, a brother-in-law to the Emperor of Austria, should be given sovereignty over the Ionian Islands off the west coast of Greece and become the focus for dissent and then revolt in a wide arc from the Swiss and Italian alps into the Balkans and including, of course, the wounded but still restive Tyrol. The moment to rise would be if, and when, Napoleon invaded Russia.

The case for Bentinck's favoured strategy had been strengthened when, in September, 1811, the frigate *Pomone* was diverted to Sardinia to collect an urgent report from a British agent in Cagliari. This was thought so important that it had to be rushed straight to London, so, under full sail, the frigate arrived in the Channel in October. But her captain decided to take the short cut to Portsmouth via the narrow Needles channel to the Solent, and the ship was wrecked in a storm on the chalk pinnacles. Her crew were saved and so was the agent's despatch, which the captain managed to rush to London within two days, so that it arrived on the 11th. The report was that an estimated 1 million Italians were ready to rise against the French and would seize Naples, This, however, was dependent on financial and military aid from the British. The government caught the excitement and offered an initial payment of £100,000.

Bentinck now felt that he had a clear run and a free hand. At the beginning of 1812 King Ferdinand, bored by his continual nagging, decided to withdraw to the hunting field from such royal duties as he had performed, but without actually abdicating.

He appointed his heir, Prince Francesco, as 'vicar-general', leaving him in Palermo as his regent – yet still subject to his own distant authority. He, to much surprise, ordained that his first task would be to set up a new, parliamentary constitution based on the British. Bentinck would next have to rid Sicily of the Queen and that might prove more difficult but, even so, he now felt able to concentrate on supporting those he believed ready to rise against the French in Italy and the Balkans.

Admiral Fremantle's part in this would be to open a way by sea to support the insurgents. Hoste had cleared the enemy from the Adriatic – although there were the new ships now building at Venice to be watched – and its shores were still held by the French. Much of Marmont's Army of Dalmatia had been withdrawn to fight in Spain, and the marshal had himself relieved Masséna there. However, the French still maintained garrisons in Corfu and the succession of coastal fortress–cities, supposedly impregnable, that guarded Napoleon's potential line of march towards Constantinople. The most southerly of these was Cattaro, at the head of a deep fjord winding through the mountains of Montenegro; then Ragusa, once another, smaller, Venice in trading with the Levant; Fiume, at the head of the gulf to the east of the Istrian peninsula; Trieste, formerly the mercantile entrepôt for the Austrian Empire; and finally, of course, Venice. To the east and south of the Dalmatian coast was a strange, mountainous hinterland ruled by warlords who nominally owed allegiance to the Ottoman Empire and might become allies against the French. In the spring of 1812 a report of fighting in Montenegro reached Bentinck and Fremantle from Lieutenant-Colonel George Robertson, who commanded the 700-strong British garrison on Lissa. 'The Montenegrins and the French have had an action in which the latter have suffered much', he wrote. 'Many of their wounded have been brought to Ragusa; the action took place near the Bocca di Cattaro. The Montenegrins have about 20,000 men in arms and the French about 4,000.' But he concluded with worrying news: 'The Montenegrins have a Russian General, three Colonels and many other officers with them.'[6] The Russians had fought on both sides during the war and themselves had designs on the Ottoman

Empire, so were they about to pre-empt British hopes of taking the eastern shore of the Adriatic from the French? There might still be time for the British to assert themselves and Bentinck consulted Fremantle, afterwards writing, 'I am happy we so perfectly coincide in opinion as to the policy of giving every aid in our power to the insurgents in Dalmatia.'[7]

The admiral had just been given a sharp reminder that his task might be more dangerous than anticipated. Fremantle, cruising off the Venetian lagoon, reported to his commander-in-chief:

> From every information I can get from vessels coming from Venice and by fishermen, I understand that three sail of the line and one frigate are put in the water in the Arsenal . . . they cannot be seen from the mastheads of this ship for houses and public buildings . . . The different accounts say that there are from three to five sail of the line building and in different states of forwardness, that one is launched and another is laid down and that there are altogether eight ships building at Venice.[8]

It was also reported that three ships of the line had just been launched at the Malamocco shipyard, on one of the long spits of land that separated the Lagoon from the open sea. From there they could be eased over the sand-bar and out of the Chioggia entrance by the use of flotation camels, such as had to be used at Amsterdam and St Petersburg. Two were to be manned by the French, the *Rivoli*, of 80 guns, and the *Mont-St Bernardo*, and another 'seventy-four', the *Regenitore*, by the Venetians and commanded by Captain Pasqualigo, who had fought so bravely at Lissa. Two other ships of the line were also nearing completion and eight others were on the stocks. These ships alone would require the presence of more than frigates. Fremantle's own flagship, the *Milford*, a new 'seventy-four', was with him at Palermo but he had sent another, the *Victorious*, of 80 guns, commanded by Captain John Talbot, to cruise off Venice in case the *Rivoli* came out, and she arrived on 16 February 1812, in fog. Unknown to Talbot, the *Rivoli*, under the command of Commodore Jean-Baptiste Barre, had left the Lagoon the day before in company with three brigs, bound for the Istrian port of Pola (now Pula).

It was five days before visibility cleared enough for Talbot to see the distant towers of Venice and try to count the masts of ships in the lagoon. At half-past two on the afternoon of the 21st, sailing east, he sighted a brig and, half an hour later, a large warship accompanied by two more brigs also steering east. Crowding sail, Talbot gave chase, soon seeing that his quarry was an 80-gun battleship, like his own. Duels between ships of the line were rare, except in the context of a major action, so anticipation ran high that night as the *Victorious* closed with the *Rivoli*. Barre shortened sail, clewing up his mainsails. He was ready to give battle.

The two big ships were well matched. In armament they were almost equal, though the *Rivoli* had a slight advantage, and, although the British seamen were experienced and the French ship's company had not had time to work up, the latter had 300 more men, including a draft of 60 from the frigate *Flore*, which had escaped from Hoste's clutches at Lissa after having struck her colours. In the grey light of early morning both ships opened fire at point-blank range. For hours they loosed broadsides into each other until both were disabled, the mizzen mast of the *Rivoli* crashing over the side and the top-masts and rigging of the *Victorious* shot away. Beyond the smoke and flame of the duel the brigs had been fighting; one of the French ships had blown up and the others made off. So the British brig joined the *Victorious*, tacking across the bows of the *Rivoli* and raking her.

After nearly four hours' fighting, for half of which time the French ship had been out of control, and with half her company killed or wounded, Commodore Barre surrendered. Captain Talbot, who had himself lost 126 men, recognized the opponent's courage, reporting to Fremantle, 'I had to deal with a most gallant and brave man and in the manoeuvring of his ship a most experienced and skilful officer.'[9] When the news reached Vice-Admiral Sir Edward Pellew, who had just succeeded Cotton as Commander-in-Chief, he congratulated Talbot on a 'very brilliant action'[10] and ordered both ships to Malta for repair. Talbot was knighted and the *Rivoli* commissioned into the Royal Navy.

Admiral Fremantle decided that two of the three ships of the line under his command – currently the 'seventy-fours' *Milford*,

Eagle and *Achille* – should cruise off Venice to watch for the other enemy battleships to emerge from the lagoon, while the third should be based at Lissa. He arrived there in June 1812 in his flagship, the *Milford*, and set about inspecting his main base. Since Hoste had left, the island had changed. In April it had been formally annexed by the British and Colonel Robertson appointed Governor, and it now commanded a garrison of 1,300 men: a quarter British, a quarter Swiss mercenaries, a quarter Corsicans and a quarter Italian, the Calabrian Corps, wearing the battle honour 'Maida' on their caps. Robertson had formed an advisory council of local worthies and imposed import duties and mooring fees in the little Venetian port, which resembled a garrison town, with fourteen taverns and six billiards rooms on its half-mile waterfront, where cricket was also played. Fremantle decided that defence should have been given priority and ordered the building of a small fort, barracks and a battery on the little island off the harbour mouth, which had been named Hoste Island. A castle – to be known as Fort George – was to stand on the headland commanding the entrance and three round towers, which would be named after Bentinck, Wellington and Robertson himself. Within the harbour, the admiral ordered the construction of a simple dockyard with barns converted into warehouses, a careening yard on the beach, where ships could be heeled for repair and cleaning, and sheer-legs mounted on a hulk for the stepping of masts.

While work was beginning, news arrived of two events, which transformed global strategy. On 19 June 1812 the United States of America declared war on Britain, and on the 24th Napoleon invaded Russia. Tension had been mounting between Britain and America because of British attempts to stifle French trade in the Atlantic and the impressment of seamen from American ships on the grounds that they were, in fact, British. The French attack on Russia was the culmination of the long deterioration of relations between the Emperor and the Tsar since the accord of Tilsit five years earlier; among Napoleon's motives was fear of Russian ambitions within Europe and that they might make common cause with the Ottoman Empire that would thwart his own plans. In the Adriatic the impact of the American war was minimal, although naval officers speculated on the threat in the Atlantic to the Royal Navy from the powerful new American warships, classified as frigates and with a frigate's turn of speed but mounting the guns of a ship of the line; hearing of this, Hoste characteristically offered to match his ship against any of the big Americans. The invasion of Russia was another matter; the immediate reaction was optimistic since Russian involvement in the Balkans could now be discounted.

In August, Captain Hoste was back in the Adriatic. On his return to England he had been hailed as a hero, and there had been comparisons with his mentor – 'I never met anyone who possessed such real love for active service, except Lord Nelson'[11] was one comment – but he had not, like Talbot, been knighted for his victory. This disappointment had been compounded by his dismay on finding that the thousands of pounds of prize-money he had sent home in order to buy a country estate in Norfolk had been squandered by his father on electioneering and high living with his rich Whig cronies. However, he was given the pick of the frigates under construction and had chosen the *Bacchante* of 38 guns, nearing completion at Deptford on the Thames downstream from London. She had been launched in November 1811, before 'a joyous and brilliant assembly'[12] and Hoste had no difficulty in finding the men he wanted. When the ship was commissioned, her chaplain remarked, 'This morning, the whole ship's company were drawn up on the quarterdeck. The day was beautiful, the crew, the finest set of young men I ever saw collected together on so small a spot. What pride a man must take in commanding such a party! Hoste is in raptures with them.'[13] O'Brien was his first lieutenant and his midshipmen and 'first-class volunteers' included the sons of three peers, including the Hon. Charles Anson, a direct descendant of the great circumnavigator and grandson of his father's patron Thomas Coke ('Coke of Norfolk'), and Edward Pocock, grandson of the admiral who had taken Havana in the Seven Years War.

On arrival at Lissa he found Port St George transformed and he heard of problems. Fremantle's decision to establish a dock-yard had not been endorsed by higher authority – although it soon came into its own when plague broke out in Malta and ships had to be sent to Lissa for repair – and Hoste fell out with the admiral over trade regulations. Fremantle insisted that Lissa revert to a free port and that merchant ships should trade under a licensing system. Hoste saw that this would be open to abuse and pointed it out in a letter. However, the admiral had already been put out by what he saw as Hoste's presumption in writing to him on arrival that it was a privilege to serve under another 'friend of poor Lord Nelson'. So, instead of thanking Hoste for drawing attention to possible problems, he replied sharply and with sarcasm. Outraged, Hoste wrote back, 'Your asking me if I came here to be complimented and that you would compliment me for an hour if I wished was so insulting to the feelings of a gentleman that I know not how to account for the language.'[14]

Hearing of fighting between the French and Montenegrins near Cattaro, Hoste asked Fremantle for 200 soldiers, or marines, to support the guerrillas but was rebuffed and told that his duty lay elsewhere. This proved to be at the head of the Adriatic, where he sighted another of the Lissa fugitives, the *Danae*, lying snugly under the guns of Trieste; thwarted there, they cruised along the Istrian coast and took a few prizes before crossing to Ancona. There they sighted a convoy of eighteen merchant vessels escorted by nine gunboats, which quickly ran inshore, the merchantmen beaching themselves, while the gunboats anchored in a line offshore. Hoste ordered his boats away with carronades in their bows and under the command of Lieutenant O'Brien. At 50 yards the carronades fired and the boats' crews boarded through the smoke. It was over quickly and all the ships taken. But a storm was brewing to the north-east and that evening a *bora* blew. Leaving small prize crews to bring the captures across to Lissa, Hoste took the *Bacchante* out to sea, steering for Port St George.

One motive in such cutting-out expeditions was, of course, prize-money, particularly for Hoste, keen to make up for the extravagance of his father. Another was the blooding of the boys he was training to become officers. Coolly described as boat-work, such actions were usually less dangerous for them than might have been apparent. One boy sat in the stern of his boat, sometimes taking the tiller; the marines sat on the thwarts between the oarsmen, and in the bows waited the boarders, tough and agile upper-yardmen, with their cutlasses, pikes and often a carronade. Sometimes led by a lieutenant, or an experienced midshipman, they would be first to spring aboard an enemy ship, or plunge ashore through the surf.

Cutting-out expeditions, raids on coastal forts and attacks on convoys became a regular and hazardous task for all British ships in the Adriatic, but their crews never flinched. In September that year the boats of the *Eagle*, commanded by Lieutenant Augustus Cannon, intercepted a convoy of twenty merchant ships escorted by two gunboats, and it was these that they attacked, both striking their colours. Then, as one of Cannon's officers wrote in his diary, although the British had been outgunned,

When were Frenchmen known to oppose with success the Sons of Albion animated with the sublime sentiment of liberty and genuine patriotism! After a tedious but glorious contest the slaves of Buonaparte struck to the British Flag. And here Nature pauses and sheds a tear to the memory of the noblest, the bravest of her sons!! The gallant Cannon, in the hour of victory, while leading on his men to board a gunboat, receiv'd the envious ball. He fell, never to rise again; his agonies were excruciating but his undaunted spirit rose superior. 'Cheer up, my lads, and board them!' were the memorable words of this noble fellow to his companions in arms when his doom was sealed. The Italian fiend, who commanded the gunboat, after striking his colours with treachery unparalleled and ferocious malignancy that ought to stamp the character of Satan alone, fired a swivel [a light swivel-mounted gun] into the gun-barge as she approached to take possession, in which 3 of our brave fellows have died, including the ever lamented Cannon, and 3 badly wounded.[15]

Such actions had become almost routine.

When the *Bacchante* returned to Port St George, Hoste and his chaplain walked up a hillside to watch for the prizes, stopping to inspect the little church of St Cyprian, where the priest showed them the figure of the Virgin, which he said was miraculous.

During the Battle of Lissa, he told them, the Virgin's face had sometimes turned pale and sometimes flushed as the tide of action seemed to ebb and flow As they left, the naval chaplain remarked, 'I do not see why the image should have shown any fears about the matter; a personage endued with such powers ought, I think, to have foreseen the issue.'[16] When they had sighted and counted most of the prizes, they returned to the waterfront and Hoste boarded Fremantle's flagship to report their arrival. While there, he heard the report of a cannon and was told that a round-shot had narrowly missed the head of the flag-captain as he looked out of the quarter-gallery window.

Then he heard what had happened. A lighter had been alongside the *Bacchante* to receive jars of olive oil taken from a prize, and these were being loaded by some of his boys. As O'Brien told it: 'A remarkably fine youth, the son of Viscount Anson, had just quitted my side and had descended into the vessel to see the process employed in loading her. He had scarcely been two minutes on board . . . when one of our main-deck guns, by some inexplicable cause, went off and killed him on the spot.'[17] Hoste was aghast. 'Poor lad', he wrote home. 'Had he been my own son, I could not have been more attached . . . Poor Lady Anson! how much I feel for her.'[18] The boy was buried on the harbour shore beneath a stone slab on which the masons from the building of Fort George carved simply, 'Hon Charles Anson AD 1813'.*

Two more of Hoste's boys were soon to follow him. That January Hoste achieved a double success, capturing five French gunboats bound for Otranto and, two days later, six merchant-men. Again prize crews were ordered away to take the captures to the island of Zante, held by the British. One of the gunboats, the *Calypso*, was to be commanded on passage by Midshipman Edward Pocock. As he and his men clambered aboard, cast off and set sail, the sky to the east darkened with a gathering storm. They were never seen again. Another prize was commanded by

---

* British dead from the Second World War were buried beside him, then moved to a Commonwealth War Graves cemetery on the mainland. His grave remains on Vis.

Mountain hero: Andreas Hofer led the Tyrolese against the French and Bavarians in the Austrian Alps while hoping for British support. Contemporary print

The mountain war: when the Tyrolese rose against Napoleonic rule in 1809, their sharpshooting, ambushes and downhill charges – sometimes led by the monk Haspinger (*right*) – terrified their enemies. Details from the *Panorama of the Battle of Berg Isel, 13 August 1809*, painted by Michael Zeno Diemer at Innsbruck in 1896

Bold sailors: Captain William Hoste, a
protégé of Nelson, who tried to emulate his
mentor in the Adriatic. Painting in oils,
attributed to Samuel Lane

Lieutenant Donat Henchy O'Brien, who
escaped from a French prison to rejoin his
frigate in the Adriatic and fight under Hoste,
seen in this engraving when a captain

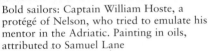

Victory off Lissa: the French copy Nelson's tactics at Trafalgar by attacking the British in
two divisions, only to be out-manoeuvred by Hoste. Print after Robert Dodd

Above: Duel at sea: ships of the line – the British *Victorious* and the French *Rivoli* – fight to the finish at point-blank range in the Adriatic. Contemporary painting in oils

Right: Advocate of fighting ashore: the British commander-in-chief, Lieutenant-General Lord William Bentinck, hoped to fight a peninsular war in Italy. Contemporary engraving

Left: Rear-Admiral Thomas Fremantle, one of Nelson's captains who commanded in the Adriatic capturing Fiume and Trieste. Painting attributed to D. Pellegrini; painted when Fremantle was a vice-admiral

Below: Lieutenant William Pocock of the *Eagle*, who painted Fremantle's attack on Trieste in 1813. Portrait in oils, attributed to Isaac Pocock

Above: The flighty princess: Napoleon's sister Princess Pauline Borghese, who visited and supported him on Elba. This statue by Canova scandalized polite society

Right: The flirtatious soldier: Lieutenant-Colonel Neil Campbell, who was supposed to watch the exiled Emperor on Elba but kept a mistress in Florence and eyed Princess Pauline. Painting in oils by Edouard Pingret

The exiled Napoleon as the British expected him to be, mocked in a caricature of 1814, published in London

Napoleon as he proved to be on escaping from Elba and landing on the coast of France to begin his 'Hundred Days' of victory and defeat. Contemporary French engraving

Midshipman Cornwallis Paley with a British crew of four, the original Italian crew being kept below under hatches. However, while on passage, the Italians ingratiated themselves with Paley, persuading him and all but one of his men to go below to eat. Suddenly the Italians attacked, killing two of their captors, wounding another two and cutting Paley's throat. He survived, to be landed at Corfu, where his wound was dressed but it had turned septic and he too died.

The ship's company of one British frigate mourned the loss of three boys, unaware that at the same time, but in another part of the panorama of war, half a million French soldiers and Napoleon's European conscripts had died in the snowfields of Russia.

13

This place will kill us all

ADMIRAL FREMANTLE was restless at the beginning of 1813, wishing he were in the vortex of the war. As news arrived of the catastrophic failure of Napoleon's invasion of Russia and his retreat from Moscow, British efforts in Spain reached a new intensity. The year before, Wellington had taken the offensive and had stormed the two fortress–cities of Ciudad Rodrigo and Badajoz, defeated Marmont at Salamanca and entered Madrid in triumph. So France was fighting a war on two fronts. But so were the British: while they were still having to contain the French fleets in Toulon and the Atlantic ports, they were at war with the United States. An American attack on Canada had failed and a British counter–offensive had captured Detroit; at sea, the Royal Navy was having to face the powerful American frigates, often manned by skilled crews who had once served under the British flag. Fremantle was appalled and wrote, 'I have just heard of the war with America. Nothing to my judgement can be more impolitic than having drove the Americans to that alternative, the Channel will swarm with American privateers and it will give the French seamen a spirit of enterprise that is not in them at present.'[1] This would have offered a preferable occupation to Fremantle, who complained in his diary, 'This war in the Adriatic is a war of *pots de chambre.*'[2]

He also heard of the arrival of a new superior, one who was all too familiar in the Mediterranean: Vice-Admiral (as he now was)

Sir Sidney Smith. After rescuing the Portuguese royal family from Lisbon and taking them to Brazil, Sir Sidney had enjoyed some adulation in London before his promotion and elevation in command. Flying his flag in the suitably-named battleship *Tremendous*, Sir Sidney had relieved another old friend of Nelson, Vice-Admiral Sir Richard Keats, as second-in-command to Admiral Pellew. As might have been expected, Smith quickly irritated Pellew, a bluff deep-water seaman, by going over his head and writing directly to the headquarters of the British Army in London with his views on how best to co-operate with Spanish guerrillas ashore and asking them to forward his letter to Wellington. He had then shifted his flag to a bigger ship, the *Hibernia*, of 110 guns, and increasingly annoyed the commander-in-chief with his flow of unsolicited advice, particularly in urging him to operate against the Italian, as well as the Spanish, coasts. This prompted Pellew to write that Smith was 'as gay and thoughtless as ever, wants to go with 5 sail to summon Genoa'.[3]

Fremantle's temper was shorter than Pellew's, so that a conflict of temperaments could now be expected, particularly when the former was feeling professionally frustrated. He wrote home from Lissa, complaining that there was 'nothing to do at sea' and 'no society that is at all worth cultivating' ashore, but he congratulated himself on his house, 'which is certainly the most comfortable one in all the island' and that 'my band is now quite perfect, they are not only a military band, but play pieces of music with violins and violin cello, my horns are capital and the trumpeter *speaks music*.'[4] This did not inspire dreams of glory.

When at last there was an opportunity, he was determined to take advantage of it. Not only had large numbers of French troops been withdrawn from Italy but Murat himself had been summoned by the Emperor to command his cavalry in Russia, leaving his court in the hands of Queen Caroline; as Fremantle put it, 'Mrs Murat is Regent.'[5] As King Joachim he had been more successful than expected, for the Neapolitans admired his braggadocio and he had tried to curry favour with both the intelligentsia and the mass of the *lazzaroni*, emulating King Ferdinand's populist style. But now he had ridden away across the steppes and had led the *Grande Armée* to Moscow before the onset of winter and the Russian counter-offensive had forced the retreat. All knew how quickly Napoleon could change his strategy and how easily alliances could fall apart, so, if Fremantle could clear the French from the eastern shore of the Adriatic, he could offer the government in London the option of helping the Austrians or meeting any threat to the Ottoman Empire by striking deep into Central Europe or the Balkans. The force at his command was limited even with the support of General Bentinck, who had had to send troops, arms and ammunition, which he needed for Italy and the Adriatic, to Spain. Bentinck had even been there himself to see Wellington in the hope of retrieving his troops but had had to tell Fremantle, 'I wish we had our corps back. I will do what I can with Lord Wellington. He naturally sees nothing but Spain.'[6]

Early in 1813 an opportunity to play a major part in Continental strategy seemed to have arrived. A British agent in Vienna, John Harcourt King, had reported secretly that the Tyrol was about to rise again. But this time it would not only be the Tyrol, for the rising would include all of what was now called the Alpenbund, the Alpine Union, also involving Vorarlberg, Carinthia and Styria, together with Switzerland to the west and the new Balkan province of Illyria to the south-east. It would be led by Archduke Johann, but it would be without the knowledge and against the known wishes of the Emperor Franz and his Foreign Secretary, Prince Metternich.

The rising was to start on Easter Monday, 19 April 1813. First, the towns and the passes into the lowlands of Bavaria and eastern Austria would be seized and held. That might be all that they could do, but pleas had been sent to Admiral Fremantle and General Bentinck, urging them to take Fiume and Venice and land an expeditionary force at the head of the Adriatic to march north to join them. Another British force should also be landed at Genoa, to prevent Napoleon from sending an army from France into Northern Italy. That was not all. There were hopes of a rising in northern Germany, to be supported by 20,000 Swedish troops landing at Hamburg. In the south, Ali Pasha, the most powerful Balkan warlord, was to invade Illyria. King sent news of all this to Lord Cathcart, the British ambassador in St Petersburg, for forwarding to Castlereagh.

Yet almost as soon as Fremantle and Bentinck had become aware of the limitless possibilities ahead, the plan began to unravel. In February the plot was betrayed to Metternich and a courier to St Petersburg intercepted. Although privately sympathetic to the aim of taking revenge on Napoleon, Austria was still at peace with France and could not afford another war into which they would be launched by such a mass rising. The time was not right. So leaders of the Alpenbund were arrested, Archduke Johann was ordered to abandon his plan; the rising was cancelled. Despite this, both Fremantle and Bentinck hoped that it might be revived and decided to press ahead with their own plans, with the admiral knowing that he could not expect a British expeditionary force in the Adriatic in the immediate future.

One abiding obstacle had been the snake-pit of the Sicilian court and there, at last, Bentinck seemed to have succeeded. With the draconian powers allowed by London, he had bullied Francesco, the heir to the throne, acting as regent in Palermo, to support political reform and persuaded the King to acquiesce. The problem had been the Queen, and Bentinck had conclusive evidence of her intrigues with Murat and was able to force her into exile. On 13 June 1813 she sailed in a British warship for Constantinople, then travelling overland to Vienna, where she was to die on 7 September. Within two months of receiving the news, King Ferdinand had married his mistress morganatically. Bentinck now made it his business to curry favour with the remaining royalty with a series of lavish parties. A sardonic British colonel noted that 'when the royal party entered the saloon, the hustling and jostling to get at the royal paws to kiss by the Sicilian noblesse was perfectly ridiculous and afforded much diversion to the assembled British officers.' Once, the Queen's favourite son was present and the colonel saw 'Prince Leopold the fat, with others of the royal party, playing at leap-frog. Notwithstanding his huge figure, his Royal Highness both danced and leaped most nimbly.'[7] There would be no more problems with the Bourbons of Palermo.

Lacking troops to land, Fremantle studied other possibilities and what action he could take without British military support. There were five principal ports on the eastern and northern shores of the Adriatic, garrisoned by the French and their Croatian allies. The two most southerly, Cattaro and Ragusa, would be left to the frigates based on Lissa. Two larger ports, Fiume and Trieste, would require the presence of the two ships of the line Fremantle kept off Venice and might also involve Austrian land forces. Venice itself, sheltered by its *murazzo*, the Lagoon, islands and marshes and forts on the mainland, would be a far larger undertaking, in which major naval and military forces would have to be employed.

Meanwhile, his frigates continued to round up enemy convoys, with mounting success. The two most successful captains were Hoste and Captain Charles Rowley, commanding a 'seventy-four', the *Eagle*. The latter, a friend of Fremantle, had been flag-captain to Admiral Cotton when he was commander-in-chief and, after the Battle of Lissa, had become senior officer in the Adriatic, much to Hoste's irritation. Rowley ran a tight ship; his officers had to memorize a long catechism of instructions, laying down details of the working and fighting of the ship and clearing for action: 'Wet the decks and have a little sand over them, a match tub and a midshipman to every 4 guns, load the Musquets and put them in the boats with Pikes and Tomahawks . . .' He was strict on etiquette: 'It is my positive order that the officers appear every afternoon in future in their Uniforms and in white pantaloons and boots, as open trousers, or open pantaloons, are not to be worn, or shoes with strings'; 'It is my positive direction that the Officer of the Watch does not permit Midshipmen and Petty Officers to walk the same side of the Quarterdeck as he does'; 'All women are to be mustered by the Master-at-Arms every morning at 10 o'clock, who is to report if any of them are disorderly or blasphemous. Any woman found drunk, blackguarding, or fighting is to be turned out of the ship.'[8]

One of his officers was Lieutenant William Pocock, son of the marine painter Nicholas Pocock and himself an accomplished artist. He was put to work on a panoramic survey of the Dalmatian coast and islands in pencil and watercolour, with each promontory named, to help navigation in the archipelago. Pocock also spoke Italian, French and Spanish, and was often sent ashore on reconnaissance. As he himself noted,

After an attack on Ragonitza on the coast of Dalmatia, which failed from bad information, or recognizance [*sic*], I having been one of the party, observed the nature of the coast and afterwards presented a small sketch of the coast and battery, etc., to Capt. Rowley with my remarks on the best means of getting posses-sion of the port. Capt. Black of the *Alacrity* afterwards obtained possession of the place by following the directions pointed out in my sketch. [9]

Fremantle decided that the first attack should be on Fiume, as a test-case in attempting to take a strongly defended port. It mounted shore batteries and was garrisoned by 350 French troops, so he would employ three ships of the line – two of them from the blockade of Venice – and one or more frigates from Lissa. There was another reason for choosing Fiume: since Napoleon's defeat in Russia and Wellington's success in Spain, Austria had been emboldened to rearm and, it was hoped, again declare war on France, even after having refused to support the Alpenbund. Bentinck was still promoting his strategic ideas, and wrote to the admiral in June that the prospects of risings were good not only in Italy on the eastern shore of the Adriatic but also in the Tyrol. That was still speculation at the beginning of July but Fremantle assem-bled his squadron – the 'seventy-fours' *Milford*, *Eagle* and *Elizabeth*, Hoste's frigate, the *Bacchante*, and a brig – and sailed for Fiume, anchored within sight of the town and cleared for action. Both Fremantle and Hoste had been with Nelson at Tenerife, when loss of surprise had wrecked hopes of a successful assault from the sea, so now strict secrecy was observed. This included such ruses as the musical code devised by Hoste's chaplain, involving the distribu-tion of what appeared to be musical scores, and a simple numerical cipher in which 99, 49, 50 and 78 represented Lissa, Cattaro, Ragusa and Fiume respectively. Yet surprise was to be lost here too, because that first evening the weather broke and the coast was struck 'all night by a tremendous gale with violent peals of thunder and lightning and heavy torrents of rain'. [10]

The attack would have to be a formal, cold-blooded affair. Fiume, lying below mountains rising to 6,000 feet, had mostly been built by the Venetians, before achieving prosperity as an entrepôt for Hungary and for its own exports of timber, figs and wine; it could perhaps now become a base for any British expeditionary force bound for Austria. The forts and shore batteries were fully alert; even so, Fremantle ordered the attack on the morning of 3 July. Having first embarked marines in boats and left them with the brig, the big ships ran inshore to engage the batteries of fifteen heavy guns. They bombarded for two hours, and the *Eagle* and the brig 'sustained the brunt, being both within half a pistol-shot of the principal battery mounting 8 guns'. Then, under cover of drifting smoke, the boats pulled for the shore and, led by Rowley and Hoste, stormed the batteries. The gunners fled, whereupon the seamen heaved the guns around to point inland and themselves opened fire. The French infantry fell back to make a stand in the main square with field-guns, chased by Rowley and Hoste with drawn swords at the head of their men, and 'after a sharp conflict in the streets, drove the enemy out of the town at the point of the bay-onet'.[11] The French made their stand in the square and then disappeared into side-streets, leaving the British in control. 'No prisoners were taken,' it was reported, 'the governor and every offi-cer and man of the garrison having run away.'[12] The bloody, post-storming custom of war was not followed and 'the town, thus actually taken by assault, was neither molested nor plundered, at least as far as every exertion on the part of Capts. Rowley and Hoste could prevent it.'[13] The victors were happy enough with the capture of ninety merchant vessels with their cargoes of olive oil, grain and gunpowder to add to their continuing captures of mer-chant shipping in the Adriatic and the consequent prize-money.

The prospect for future conquests seemed bright. Fiume had proved a relatively easy prize and, farther south, Fremantle's frig-ates had taken smaller ports, so now Trieste could be his next objective. Cattaro and Ragusa would be different for they were deep in the Balkans, far from current Austrian involvement. Both were strongly fortified cities between mountains and the sea, and could probably resist the scale of siege warfare that the admiral could bring to bear. So the only possibility might be blockade, in the hope that sufficient supplies could not reach them overland and that would have to depend on the scale of activity by indige-nous partisans. To assess the situation at both, Fremantle ordered Hoste south but there was still some tension between the two, per-haps rooted in a proprietorial regard for the Nelson they had both known so well and from Hoste having the greater experience of the Adriatic. This was expressed in their social relations. Fremantle noted in his diary, 'Hoste dined with me . . . played two games of chess, both of which I won to my great delight.'[14] Nevertheless, the admiral had a proper regard for the ability of the captain.

Fremantle turned his attention to Trieste, where the prospects were brighter. In August, Austria, seeing the French driven out of Russia with the loss of a huge army and embroiled in Spain, decided to rejoin the war in the latest coalition against Napoleon. Napoleon's stepson Prince Eugène had succeeded Murat in command of the *Grande Armée* in the final stage of its retreat from Russia, but had now resumed his role as Viceroy of Italy, hurriedly raising a new army and preparing to defend the line of the River Isonzo against Austrian attack. So at last the British might be able to fulfil Bentinck's strategic plan to join forces with the Austrians, and this, Fremantle hoped, would begin at Trieste. Before the end of September, he was corresponding with the Austrian field commander in the south, General Laval Nugent, an Irishman in the imperial service, who had been the Austrians' liaison officer with Bentinck in Sicily and with Wellington in Spain. Even though Count Nugent was said to have fewer than 2,000 men under immediate command, he himself had 'great zeal and enterprise',[15] Fremantle had been told, and was already advancing on Trieste.

On 5 October the *Milford* and the *Eagle* anchored off Trieste. It was far more imposing than Fiume: against a range of bleak, bare limestone highlands a parade of mansions ran along the waterfront, including the magnificent new Palazzo Careiotte, ornate with dome, classical pilasters and statuary. High above the twin cupolas of the cathedrals sprawled the great, grey bulk of the citadel. It was said to be defended by 800 French troops, while the 100 guns and mortars on the ramparts of its massive walls and bastions commanded the city and its hinterland. Nugent's little army was encamped inland and out of range, having no artillery that could even pit the walls, let alone batter a breach. That was what Fremantle could now offer. His marines and working parties of seamen were put ashore, and Lieutenant Pocock supervised the landing of some of the main-deck guns from the *Eagle*, to be dragged up the steep streets to a battery being dug opposite the cit-adel. In ten days the British had twelve heavy naval guns in place, in the hope that not even these walls could withstand the impact of 24-pound roundshot. The bombardment began and then Captain Rowley landed his heaviest gun, a long 32-pounder, to hasten the opening of a breach. When it fired, 'the ground gave way and the gun fell six feet below the platform', recorded Fremantle but then, 'it was fine to see Captain Rowley and his people immediately get a triangle above the work and the heavy gun and its carriage run up to its place again in the midst of a shower of grape and mus-ketry.'[16] During the next thirteen days the British lost 10 killed and 35 wounded before the citadel, but on the thirteenth day the French commander, Colonel Rabie, seeing his walls crumble, surrendered.

Could Venice be next? An intelligence agent in the Veneto reported that

By the latest accounts from Venice a general insurrection was expected there against the French party, whose force there was about 4,000 troops, and the Viceroy's army in the neighbour-hood; but the latter was composed chiefly of Italians, who desert in hundreds. The three line of battleships at Venice have taken out their guns [to lighten them in order to enter the basin of San Marco] for the purpose of moving up towards the town to keep the disposition of the city in check.'[17]

Fremantle and Nugent began to plan their attack and the admi-ral was told that, before the end of the year, an Austrian army 100,000-strong should have reached Vicenza in the Veneto. As a result, he announced, 'I hope to be enabled to concert for opera-tions against Venice.'[18]

Operations further south were, however, more immediate. On Fremantle's orders Hoste and Captain John Harper, of the sloop *Saracen*, had sailed past Ragusa, one of the most strongly fortified cities in Europe. Hoste scanned the walls that rose from rocks fall-ing sheer into the sea and the four outlying forts: one, Fort Royal, on the island of Croma (Lokrum), and another, Fort Imperial, 1,200 feet above on the crest of the mountain range that stood

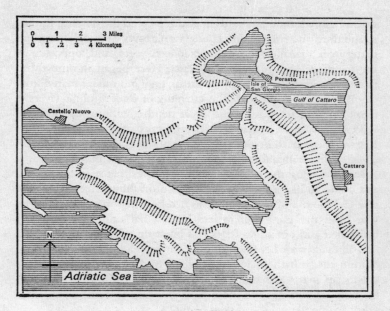

Cattaro (now Kotor)

above the city, commanding it with twenty-one guns. The taking of such a fortress was surely beyond the means of any force the British could bring to bear, let alone a single frigate. He reported to Fremantle, 'The short time I was off Ragusa was sufficient to convince me of the strength of the Ragusan forts', and any idea of besieging it would 'make you laugh if you could see the place, which in the opinion of Captain Harper and myself is impregnable'.[19] So Hoste sailed south, towards the other objective.

The Bocca di Cattaro was by all accounts a place of mythological horror, likely to recall the trials of Odysseus to a naval officer with a Classical education. Set deep in the mountains of Montenegro, its mouth was less than a mile wide and commanded by the fortress and town of Castello Nuovo, with a French and Croatian garrison said to be 600-strong. The fjord ran south from the first basin through narrows into an inner basin, five miles wide. This appeared to be wholly wrapped in mountains, but at the far

183

side a channel some 200 yards in width pierced the heights, leading to the third and final basin. These last narrows were defended by a battery on a small island, immediately beyond, and, opposite, by the fortified town of Perasto (Perast). Here began the most dramatic and sinister scenery of all. Steep, grey mountains reared from deep water, quaking with the currents of underground rivers: a bleak place of steep rock and great depths, without the scent of wild herbs usually carried on the breezes of the Illyrian shore. Eastward, out of sight and at the head of the gulf, lay Cattaro itself, a walled city with a fortress above, also seemingly impregnable.

It was not just the terrain and the defences that made the Bocca di Cattaro so daunting. The weather could show Homeric horror too. Off the mouth of the gulf this had been reported earlier in the year from the *Eagle*. There had been a flat calm, then the sky blackened and out of the darkness burst thunder, lightning and a fireball that struck her maintopmast, flaying eight men on the yard. Within the gulf there was no shelter. Sudden storms could tear sails, snap masts and twirl an anchored ship around her anchor. Rain could blot out the mountains and hurl torrents down their sides. Seamen kept clear if they could.

Aware of this, Fremantle thought that a blockade, perhaps by a single frigate, might be all that would be required to reduce Cattaro. There were thought to be 1,500 French and Croatian troops around the gulf, manning the shore batteries and defending Castello Nuovo and Cattaro itself, where the garrison numbered more than 700 and included French artillerymen to man its 65 guns, commanded by Général de Brigade Etienne Gauthier. However, persistent reports of fighting between the French and both Montenegrin guerrillas and the Bocchese, the more civilized inhabitants of the waterside towns and villages, were encouraging. If the garrisons could be cut off from seaborne support, they would surely surrender.

On 13 October 1813 Hoste took the *Bacchante* into the Bocca di Cattaro to find the unexpected. The Bocchese and the Montenegrins had indeed risen against the French, but had refused to fight as allies because the former owed allegiance to Austria and the latter, as Slavs, to Russia, both of which hoped to dominate Montenegro. Indeed, the factions were violently opposed to one another and, as Hoste wrote to Fremantle, 'The Montenegrins have a penchant for the good things of this world and are not very nice in their means of getting them. The Bocchese detest the Montenegrins . . . and I expect will cut all their throats.'[20] The Bocchese had invested Castello Nuovo but, lacking artillery, could not take it, and the Montenegrins, equally handicapped, were camped around Cattaro at the head of the gulf. So Hoste's immediate problem was political, and he diplomatically hoisted both Austrian and Russian colours to suggest his own impartiality. This soon wore thin. The Montenegrin leader was the Metropolitan Archbishop Petar I, whom Hoste liked, and the Bocchese were represented by Abbot Brunazzi, whom he distrusted. The former, 'the right reverend soldier' as Hoste's chaplain called him, was tall, handsome and white-bearded, dressed in a purple robe with 'manners graceful and easy' but surrounded by '500 desperate banditti'.[21] The latter Hoste found 'an intriguing, self-sufficient priest . . . his tongue never ceases', adding 'If I had my way I'd hang him.'[22] However, Hoste told both that he was not authorized to interfere in their internal affairs and would concentrate on removing the French.

The reduction of Castello Nuovo, Perasto and the defences of the channel to the inner gulf proved easier than expected. When the French commanders demurred at Hoste's summons to surrender, he set about frightening them for he knew that the Montenegrins had 'inspired much terror into the French . . . and give them no quarter . . . they are a ferocious set and no one likes to have anything to do with them',[23] and the reputation of the Bocchese was almost as savage. So having shown the French his heavy guns, which could easily breach their defences, he told them that the consequent assault would be by those they most feared. Capitulation to the British was quickly agreed.

But Cattaro was another matter, the fortress high above the town seemingly beyond the reach of effective bombardment. Hoste reported to Fremantle, 'I don't flatter myself with hopes of taking Cattaro except by blockade . . . Shot are of no use. It is on the pinnacle of a high mountain. General Gauthier has retired there with 600 men and two months' provisions.'[24] Built and occupied successively by Greeks, Romans, Byzantines, Venetians, Slavs,

Serbs, Hungarians, Croatians, Bosnians and Montenegrins with its stone citadel and the castle above, its cathedral, palaces and merchants' houses were surrounded by walls 30 feet high which ran up the steep mountainside to the pinnacle, on which stood the castle. Any siege-works would be subjected to the fire of Gauthier's artillery from above, and in any case Hoste doubted whether any of his own guns were heavy enough to breach the walls. So, writing to Fremantle with a request to be transferred to operations off Trieste, which he knew had begun, Hoste decided to withdraw. But first he was able to unite the feuding Bocchese and Montenegrins. Having put all the captured French artillery under guard, he announced that, unless they united, he would keep the guns himself. Realizing that this would leave them defenceless if the French launched a counter-offensive from Cattaro once Hoste had departed, they finally agreed to co-operate. So he gave them the guns and left for Lissa.

Thankful to be free of the toils of Cattaro, Hoste busied himself with activities he understood and enjoyed, hunting merchant shipping and launching amphibious operations. One of the latter, against Lesina (now Hvar), was a failure despite the participation of British infantry from Lissa, for it demonstrated that fortifications – in this case the aptly named Fort Napoleon – were immune to attack without artillery support and Hoste had to withdraw. But there was hopeful news of the Austrians, who were advancing south along the Dalmatian coast and had already occupied Spalato on the mainland, opposite Lissa. Would they be able to help with the sieges of Cattaro and Ragusa? Cattaro was too far south and too isolated to be considered, but Ragusa was a possible objective, particularly since there was local resistance to the French, led by Count Caboga. The Ragusans welcomed a detachment of the 35th Regiment from Lissa, which Hoste landed at the little port of Ragusa Vecchia (now Cavtat) to the south of Ragusa itself. However, on going ashore, he discovered that this too was a political snake-pit. While professing support for the British, Caboga, mindful of the long history of the Ragusan republic, had no wish to be ruled by them, or by the Austrians or Russians, and had hit on a subtle ruse. He would cede Ragusa to the Ottoman Empire, since this would ensure its independence from both Britain and

Austria, who would, he hoped, oust the French, while the Sublime Porte would be happy to assume sovereignty in name only. Hearing of this, Hoste, without time to consult Fremantle, pre-empted it by sailing into the bay of Ragusa Vecchia, hoisting the Ragusan flag of St Blaise on the campanile, announcing the independence of Ragusa and firing a salute of twenty-one guns. He had checkmated Caboga's scheme with matching subtlety by announcing, 'My sole object is that of aiding and assisting to expel the French from the country . . . With regard to hoisting the Ragusan flag, that is no consideration of mine; it will, of course, be respected by the English.'[25] What he could not guarantee, of course, was that it would be respected by the Austrians, or by anybody else.

With that, Hoste wrote to Fremantle, 'I can give you no hopes of Ragusa soon falling . . . I do not possess the means of reducing it',[26] and again laid course for Cattaro. Entering the grim chasms of the gulf, slowly working his way towards the city against squalls and currents, and finally going ahead himself by boat, he discovered that there had indeed been activity. The Montenegrins, finding the walls impossible to breach with their guns, had tried to blow open and storm the main gates of the city. They had failed, although General Gauthier had withdrawn to the castle of San Giovanni on its peak, 700 feet above the city but still within the outer walls.

Hoste knew that he had to be seen to be taking action, so first he would have to make a reconnaissance. For this he decided to climb Mount Theodore, standing 4,000 feet and across the headwaters of the gulf, opposite the city. In cold, wet and windy weather it was a laborious climb, first through hanging woods, then up gullies leading to the bare, almost vertical slopes and rocks of the summit. Looking down and across to Cattaro, Hoste could see its strength. The thick walls began at the water's edge and zigzagged up the mountain to surround the fort on the fang of rock high above; in the city itself stood the citadel and, clustered around the cathedral of St Tryphon and the churches, the tight-packed roofs of grey stone houses. Artillery would be of little use against such defences and, even if he were able to send for mortars, these would only serve to smash the tiled roofs without affecting the massive walls. The view seemed to confirm his initial pessimism.

It was then that Hoste was touched by inspiration. It was Nelsonian, just as had been the idea for his own inspiring signal before battle off Lissa. It was the memory of Nelson in Corsica nineteen years earlier, faced with another supposedly impregnable fortress at Calvi. Then he had landed his ship's guns in an inlet and had them dragged up steep rocky heights to pound the fortress into submission. Could that be achieved here? It seemed unlikely, for these were high, precipitous mountains. Yet, if he could manage to mount his long 18-pounder guns on those summits, he could subject Cattaro to what would amount to aerial bombardment. He decided to try.

Next morning the *Bacchante* was busy with seamen, riggers and carpenters hoisting tackle to the main yard-arm, looping strops around the barrel of nearly two tons of cannon, hoisting and lowering it into a barge alongside, then setting up sheer-legs and pulleys on the shore and hammering together a heavy wooden sledge to take the gun. More pulleys were rigged to trees and rocks, and teams of seamen landed to haul the ropes. That afternoon the heaving began, and by dark the 18-pounder had been dragged some 400 yards up the mountainside. Across the valley General Gauthier had watched through his telescope but he was not concerned; long before the gun had been hauled to the summit, he felt sure, a French column would have arrived to raise the siege.

At dawn next day the work began again. No Bocchese had offered to help and only a few Montenegrins volunteered to carry stores up the mountain, so the British toiled almost alone. Then it began to rain, cold, steady mountain rain, and as a result, noted Hoste's chaplain, 'the masses of rock proved too loose and unable to support the purchase-strops, which rendered it necessary to cut grooves in the solid rock.'[27] By the end of the third day the gun had been raised 840 yards. There was no question of the working parties returning to the ship for the night; soaked and chilled, their shoes cut open by rocks, they huddled under the shelter of a waxed sail that had been rigged across a gully. The rain still fell, so that, despite emptying sandbags on the slippery slopes, they became mud slides on which the men slithered and there was the danger that they might lose control of the gun and it might slide, bounce and crash down the mountainside. Hoste now ordered that one of his ship's anchors be brought ashore and made fast to the summit to hold the tackle. It began to drag, and only when Hoste ordered a cairn of rocks to be heaped upon it did the anchor hold and the gun was raised another 300 yards. Hoste himself tried to sleep on the mountain, under the sail with his men, cold and exhausted. Finally, on the sixth day, there was a final heave and the gun lurched on to the summit of Mount Theodore.

Hoste ordered that more guns be sent ashore to follow the first and, while a battery was prepared, he managed to write to his mother in Norfolk:

How you would laugh, were you to see me here. I am general, admiral, governor, engineer and complete jack of all trades . . . We have got guns up mountains, which were deemed impassable, and the French general said he would give me six months to get one gun up; I have convinced him of the contrary in six days. He says it is a very *unmilitary* proceeding: I tell him the English sailors do nothing like anyone else but they will *astonish* him before they leave him. We have torn up trees (in getting the cannon up the mountain) that were *planted by Adam*, I should think, and have upset rocks that *were left there since the Deluge.*[28]

On 21 December the first gun was in place. Its arrival was saluted by a long-range shot from Cattaro, which fell far short and was greeted with an ironical cheer by the British gunners. A second 18-pounder and two 11-inch mortars had followed up Mount Theodore while more guns were being hauled up the mountains behind Cattaro; although these were lower than Mount Theodore, they were just as steep and cranes had to be rigged above vertical drops. Blankets for the gun crews were sent up the mountains, with more waxed sails as shelters across gullies. But rain turned the gullies into torrents, and rocks, loosened by rain and the manhandling of the guns, would suddenly tumble without warning, bouncing and bounding down the mountains. Living in relative comfort on board the frigate far below, the first lieutenant of the *Bacchante*, Silas Hood, worried about his captain: 'Frequently for nights would his clothes remain on him, wet as they were, in a climate either at the freezing point, or drenching us all

with torrents of rain. How the people stood it, God only knows!'
Other batteries were set up close to the city walls, including
Congreve's incendiary rockets on launching tripods. Sometimes
Hoste visited the ship and told Lieutenant Hood, 'This place will
kill us all but . . . in a few days I will introduce you to the French
general.'[29]

Three more days were needed to heave the powder, shot and
rations up to the batteries, but at last all was ready. Then Hoste,
surprisingly for a parson's son, decided that the bombardment
should open on Christmas morning. He himself took position at
the head of the valley, from where he could see the city, the gulf
and both ranges of mountains. Soon after first light Hoste gave the
order, saw a stab of flame, a gout of smoke and heard the thump of
the discharge as the first gun fired from Mount Theodore. Soon
flashes and smoke broke from both mountain ranges and the guns
of Cattaro replied; the arena was engulfed in wind-blown smoke
and echoed to the thunder of the guns. For four days the cannonade continued; then a rocket hit a magazine in the city and its
explosion silenced the guns just as Hoste remembered when the
French flagship had blown up and silenced the Battle of the Nile.
By the end of the year one eighteen-year-old British seaman had
been killed by French shot but two more 18-pounders and a carronade had been landed to complete the batteries and, as Hoste said,
'to begin the New Year with them'.[30]

On the morning of 1 January 1814 all the British guns opened
what amounted to broadsides. Buildings in the city were ablaze
and, expecting the end to be near, Hoste sent a bilingual officer to
the city gates under a white flag to summon Gauthier to surrender.
The general received him with the complaint that rockets, which
he had never before seen, were 'a most unmilitary way of proceeding'. But he was again told, 'Why, do you know with whom you
are contending? You are not engaged with soldiers, who do all
these things in a regular technical manner: you are opposed to sailors, people who do nothing like other men and they will astonish
you when they have done with you.'[31] The next and final stage
would be the storming of the city, and Hoste offered the honour
of this to the Archbishop Petar's partisans, the fierce Montenegrins, who would, he knew, relish the task. All that was now

required was for this prospect to be conveyed to General Gauthier, who would know what to expect after such an assault. So on 5 January the French accepted the terms of surrender, and three days later Captain Hoste and his men occupied the town. It was then found that the garrison had consisted of just 300 men, only 37 of them French.

News now arrived that the Austrians were sending an occupying force up the gulf to Cattaro and, as Hoste wanted to avoid involvement in another political confrontation between them and the Bocchese on one hand and the Montenegrins and the distant Russians on the other, he decided to withdraw, and again he did so with relief. There was not time to muster enough men, British, Montenegrin, or Bocchese, to dismantle the batteries, so, as he put it, 'The guns were left in the batteries on the summits as a memorial to the genius and courage of Englishmen.'[32] On 16 January the *Bacchante* passed through the outer narrows of the Bocca di Cattaro and felt the breeze and the lift of the open sea.

14

Nothing like it in history

A S THE *Bacchante* ran north for 30 miles to Ragusa, Hoste completed the report he was sending to Lord Aberdeen, the British ambassador in Vienna, explaining that he had been unable to hand Cattaro over to the Austrians. He complained of his difficulties with the Austrian representative there, Abbot Brunazzi – 'a deceitful, intriguing character . . . he has thrown every obstacle in my way to hinder my gaining Cattaro'.[1] But if he had hoped that he had left political conflict behind him at Cattaro, he found them again at Ragusa. The Austrians had already arrived before the city, albeit in the form of only two battalions under a Count Miliutinovich, with orders to incorporate the French province of Illyria into the Austrian Empire. But when he met Count Caboga, he was told that Captain Hoste of the Royal Navy had already recognized the independence of the Republic of Ragusa. So Miliutinovich had no choice but to recognize the Ragusans as allies and postpone plans for annexation. On 17 January 1814 Count Caboga announced in a formal proclamation the restoration of the ancient Republic of Ragusa.

So Hoste concentrated on the reduction of the city. Looking across at the silvery grey walls, towers and domes rising out of the sea on the rocky headland, it seemed as impregnable as ever. Its walls, he was told, were 70 feet high and 16 feet thick, strengthened by 20 bastions and half a dozen forts. It was defended, he was told, by 170 guns and a garrison of at least 500 men, commanded by the experienced Général de Division Joseph Montrichard. The seaward approaches were commanded by the guns of Fort Royal on the island of Croma and the land approaches by those of the fortress of San Lorenzo to the west and the Revelin to the east and also by Fort Imperial, on the crest of Mount Sergius. The latter commanded the seaward slopes of the mountain range behind the town, so that there would be no hope of dragging his guns to the summits, as at Cattaro. Hoste began to work his way through other possibilities. Could the city be starved by blockade? The garrison had provisions for at least six weeks, he was told. Was there any shortage of water and could the supply be cut? Here, as at Cattaro, it had rained heavily, so the cisterns of the city would be full and there would be no point in trying to cut the flow from the aqueduct that brought water down the mountainsides from a spring six miles away. Yet, since there seemed nothing else that he could do, Hoste decided to inspect the aqueduct anyway.

Built in the fifteenth century by a Neapolitan engineer, the aqueduct was nothing like those built by the Romans on tall arches; this one was, architecturally, understated. From its source it ran down the far side of the mountainous peninsula upon which Ragusa stood before rounding the headland and flowing into the city itself. Except where it had to cross ravines, it ran almost flush with the mountainsides, and the water channel – two feet wide and three feet deep – was roofed with limestone slabs, giving the impression of a paved path some ten feet wide. It struck Hoste that it would be ideal for the passage of a long 18-pounder gun.

With mounting excitement Hoste followed the gentle ascent of the aqueduct from the headland, where it turned inland from the city and up the far side of the *massif*. If a gun could be hauled up the aqueduct for two miles from there to a point directly across the mountain range from the city, it could be manhandled up steep tracks, then across three low, parallel ridges, through thickets of oak and bramble and over rocky, undulating ground to a point he chose immediately above Ragusa. There the gun would be masked by a rocky outcrop from the fire of Fort Imperial further along the crest and he could, after all, repeat what he had done above Cattaro. So on 21 January Hoste landed one of his main-deck guns, had it lashed to a wooden sledge and the long haul began.

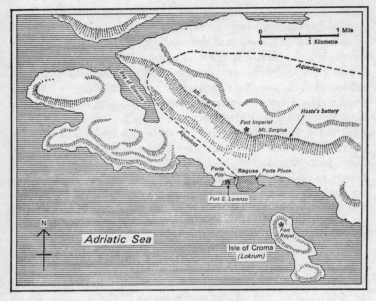

Ragusa (now Dubrovnik)

At first all went well enough, but then it began to rain and the teams of seamen manning the ropes were soaked and chilled with the prospect of again having to sleep on an exposed mountainside. Rain and mud on the aqueduct made the stone slippery, and it was so narrow that extreme care was essential, particularly when crossing ravines, otherwise 'had the gun fallen on either side, nothing could have prevented it from descending into the valley beneath.'[2] Slowly the gun jerked and slid up the aqueduct to the point Hoste had chosen for the cross-country route, and there the heaviest work began. Apart from an occasional goat track, the terrain was of broken rock and across this the sledge had to be dragged. Finally, on 26 January, the cold, exhausted seamen gave a final heave and the gun rocked to the crest. Below was spread the panorama of Ragusa.

Through his telescope Hoste could see the French flag flying from the Orlando column in the main square, the cathedral of St

Blaise and the Rector's Palace, around which clustered the russet roofs of the city. It was at their mercy. The bombardment was due to open on the 27th and would also include guns and mortars on the shore outside the city walls far below, but Hoste decided to try some ranging shots as soon as ammunition arrived. Taking the central piazza as aiming-point and loading the gun with a full charge, he gave the order to fire. Those in the city below, who happened to be looking towards the mountain, would have seen the flash and the smoke, but the report of the gun reached them as the shot whirred over the roofs and smashed into the front of a house on the main street. All eyes were now on the mountain and the drifting smoke, as the gun fired again and this time the shot struck one of the columns of the portico of the church of San Ignatio.★

The effect was dramatic. Ragusans poured into the streets, hoisted the flag of St Blaise and called on the French to surrender. General Montrichard held an excited meeting with his staff, some of whom said that the city was now doomed but others that its defences were still intact and surrender unthinkable. Even so, on the 26th Montrichard sent an officer under a flag of truce to the Austrian positions outside the walls, asking for a cease-fire so that terms could be discussed. Hoste now came down the mountain to be immersed in the politics he loathed. During his absence a more senior naval officer had arrived in a ship of the line, Captain Edward Leveson-Gower of the *Elizabeth*, and Hoste feared that his laurels were to be snatched from him. But, although he found that Leveson-Gower 'growls and is dissatisfied with everything', the latter showed sensibility and anchored well away from Ragusa rather than 'pluck away a single feather of those glories, which he could have no claim to'.[3]

General Montrichard agreed to the terms offered by Hoste and Miliutinovich, which were for the city to be surrendered on the 28th and its garrison shipped across to Ancona. Ragusa was then to be occupied by the Austrians. Count Caboga felt betrayed, with good reason, and determined to pre-empt the occupation by seizing the city himself. But the citizens of Ragusa themselves, fearing

★ The star-shaped scar can still be seen.

looting by Caboga's irregulars and possibly fighting with the Austrians, opted for a quieter, if less glorious, future and betrayed his plan. So when the irregulars burst through the city gates on the morning of the 28th, they found themselves facing the bayonets of Austrian infantry and British marines. Shouting with frustrated fury, they poured out of the city again, some of them to return later in the day to sell produce in the market. So Ragusa fell.

Hoste, keen to get away and leave Leveson-Gower in command, busied himself with getting the long 18-pounder down from Mount Sergius and then setting sail for Trieste to report to Admiral Fremantle. But, he admitted, 'the fatigue and labour we have all had has almost knocked me up.' He was a sick man; indeed his health was, as the ship's surgeon reported, 'alarmingly bad'.[4] He rallied on arrival at Trieste, where the admiral, now living in the grand Palazzo Careiotte, gave him stirring news of the war far to the north, beyond the Alps. The allied generals, taking advantage of the shock inflicted on the French by the disaster in Russia, had finally co-ordinated their strategy. On 16 October 1813 the armies of Austria, Russia, Prussia and Sweden had brought Napoleon to battle at Leipzig and had driven him back, with the loss of 70,000 men; the French had thereupon lost control of Germany and the Bavarians turned against them. In the same month Wellington's expeditionary force in Spain had followed his climactic victories at Vitoria in June and San Sebastian in August by marching through the Pyrenees and invading France.

Hoste was ill and exhausted but, so as not to alarm his family in England, wrote home cheerfully that 'this city appears a paradise. It is carnival time and you would suppose all the people were mad: nothing but masked balls every evening and operas and plays without end.'[5] Admiral Fremantle concentrated on enjoying himself, noting in his diary, 'Had a gay ball on shore, some tolerable looking damsels there' and 'A grand ball . . . one remarkably pretty Venetian woman there, amused myself very much'; but there were annoyances here, too: 'My band with their instruments deserted to the enemy, the devil go with them.'[6]

The admiral was also piqued that the Admiralty seemed to do no more than acknowledge news of his repeated successes in the Adriatic and himself adopted a somewhat similar attitude to Hoste, who noted sarcastically that Fremantle had been 'pleased to express his *approbation* of *Bacchante's* conduct on all occasions'.[7] But Hoste was gratified by the news that the Emperor of Austria had awarded him the Order of Maria Theresa. Despite his state of health, the admiral now ordered him south to join the blockade of Corfu.

After calling at Lissa, the *Bacchante* steered south-east and then her captain's health finally broke: he could not stand and the surgeon diagnosed rheumatic fever. Even so, he decided to look into the harbour of Corfu, and there he sighted a French frigate and fifteen gunboats in the harbour. Deciding he could not face such odds close inshore, he had turned away when the ship, sailing at 8 knots, ground on to a shoal and stuck fast. Hoping that the French had not noticed this, Hoste at once made the pretence of coming to anchor, taking in sails, while throwing stores over the side that could not be seen from the shore, to lighten the ship. Also, to give the impression that his presence was deliberate, he made signals as if he were reporting French movements to a ship on the horizon. The slight Adriatic tide did not help and still the ship did not move, so the first guns had to be heaved overboard. Three days passed and 24 of her 38 guns had been jettisoned, leaving her hardly able to defend herself. If the French frigate came out, would Hoste have had to surrender? 'I had prepared my mind for that', he said later. He would have sent the sick and the boys away in some of the boats and then:

> I would have taken every other man with me in the ship's boats, well armed with cutlasses, pistols and tomahawks. I would have laid a train to the *Bacchante's* magazine; have waited the approach of the enemy on the off-side of the ship till they were close to me; then, setting fire to the port-fire of the train, I would have pulled off at once to the Frenchman and, I have not the slightest doubt, we should have had her in Malta with us in a very few days.[8]

Finally, by moving roundshot from the magazine forward to the bows, so raising the stern, her boats finally managed to tow the frigate into clear, deep water and she was away. On 20 April the *Bacchante* reached Malta.

Hoste was now 'more dead than alive' and was ordered ashore. As he was lowered into the boat to take him away from the *Bacchante*, his ship's company gave three cheers and 'in a moment, as from a sudden impulse, he rose on his legs for the first time for three months and returned the compliment; then dropping into the arms of the surgeon as if in a fit, was rowed on shore regretted by all'.[9] Too ill to return to duty, Hoste was told that his only hope was his immediate return to England and he embarked in the *Cerberus*, which had fought under his command at Lissa.

Before leaving Malta, he had heard more news of the wider war. In December the Austrians had entered France through Switzerland, and there was extraordinary news from Naples. Murat, on his return from Russia, had resumed his role as King Joachim but had become apprehensive about his future and begun secret negotiations with the British in Sicily and with the Austrians about the possibility of his changing sides in return for a guarantee of his continued sovereignty. He feared that the allies might restore King Ferdinand to Naples, so he did all he could to ensure the separation of what had been the Kingdom of the Two Sicilies, leaving Ferdinand to reign in Palermo; he even introduced a law imposing the death penalty for anybody trying to usurp the throne of Naples. Even so, hearing of the Emperor's coming confrontation with the allies in central Europe, he had returned to his side and had fought at Leipzig.

It was obvious that the end was near, and Murat told Napoleon that he would now go to Naples for reinforcements but in fact to continue secret negotiations with the latter's enemies. So at the beginning of 1814, he offered the allies the reinforcements he had just offered Napoleon – 30,000 men to fight against France – in return for an assurance of the security of his own throne and possessions. His offer was accepted and his Neapolitan army was soon fighting Prince Eugène in the north of Italy. Now he conceived an even more extravagant ambition. Instead of just remaining King of Naples, he would harness the unrest throughout the peninsula that had so excited General Bentinck to his own cause and become monarch of a united Italy. However, the latest news to reach Malta was that Napoleon was still fighting and he had shown before how he could spring back to command the stage.

The Emperor was said to be incandescent with rage at the treachery of Murat.

Yet there had been an ironical turn of fortune because it seemed that, at last, Lord Bentinck might be able to put his great hope into action and open another peninsular campaign in Italy. Having secured Sicily, he turned his attention to the mainland and was given permission by the British government to land an expeditionary force in the north to support the Austrians, possibly with Murat as an unexpected ally.

On 9 March 1814 Bentinck landed at Leghorn with 6,000 British troops and a Sicilian force and issued a stirring proclamation urging Italians to unite and 'resume her ancient splendour among independent nations'.[10] More like an impassioned patriot than a British general, he went further with a call to arms, 'Warriors of Italy . . . call upon us and our united forces will make Italy become what Italy was in its finest hours and what Spain is.'[11] A month later he had captured Genoa and proclaimed the restoration of its ancient republic. But this ran contrary to British plans for Genoa to become part of the Kingdom of Piedmont and Sardinia, as a buffer between France and Italy. 'It is not insurrection that we need now', wrote Castlereagh to Bentinck. 'We need disciplined forces, dependent upon sovereigns whom we can trust.'[12] Unable to implement his dream and reprimanded by Lord Castlereagh, Bentinck returned to Sicily, crestfallen, that June and a month later was recalled to London, his Mediterranean adventures ended.

The naval war in the Adriatic seemed to be over, and it was time for Captain Hoste to return home. But before making for the Straits of Gibraltar, homeward bound, the *Cerberus* was to call at Genoa with despatches for Admiral Pellew. As she sailed up the Italian coast past scenes of former triumphs and disasters at Maida, Capri and Ischia, they passed close to the hills of the island of Elba and, sighting a British frigate lying at anchor, closed with her to exchange signals. 'We have just spoken by telegraph to an English frigate, the *Undaunted*, lying at Porto Ferrajo', wrote William Hoste to his father in Norfolk; 'She has telegraphed to us, "The Emperor *Bony* is here". Only conceive what ideas such an event must create . . . The man who made all Europe tremble is now a prisoner . . . There is nothing like it in history.'[13]

15

Keep me in your memories!

ON THE afternoon of 3 May 1814 the sails of a frigate had been sighted from the fortifications of Portoferraio, the capital of Elba, the island six miles off the north-western coast of Italy. She had signalled that she was preparing to enter the harbour, but the wind had dropped and she lay becalmed. However, a boat was launched and was pulled for the landing steps to put ashore a party of officers in diverse and multicoloured uniforms, one in the scarlet and gold of a colonel in the British Army. This was Lieutenant-Colonel Neil Campbell, a soldier–diplomat with the title of British Commissioner. Colonel Campbell was about to introduce himself to the military and civil authorities of Elba and explain his mission. He was to present them to their new monarch, the deposed Emperor Napoleon I of France.

At the beginning of the year the prospect had been very different for both men. Colonel Campbell had been a liaison officer with the Russian army advancing on Paris. A Scot, aged thirty-seven and a bachelor who had begun his military career in the light infantry, he was tough and athletic; he had beaten Sir John Moore and his officers in a running race at Shorncliffe camp during the wait for expected French invasion. He had fought in the Peninsular War, commanding a Portuguese infantry regiment and fighting at Salamanca, where Wellington had defeated Marmont and broken the French in northern Spain. There he had been wounded. Seconded to the staff as a linguist and because of his intelligence, easy manners and striking presence – tall, classical good looks and curling, dark hair – he was seconded to the Russian military staff as liaison officer. But he was a man of action and in March 1814, as the Russian, Prussian and Austrian armies were invading France from the east and Wellington from the south, he himself led a Russian cavalry charge. In the tumult of men and horses the cossacks mistook him for a French officer and he was slashed by a sabre and speared by a lance. Then, while recovering from his wounds, his name was put to Lord Castlereagh, the Prime Minister, for an extraordinary diplomatic appointment.

Lord Castlereagh was in Paris and ordered Campbell to report to him in person to receive his instructions to 'attend the late chief of the French Government'.[1] That meant Napoleon. While the colonel had been riding towards Paris with the Russians, the Emperor had been commanding his depleted army with his old flair in eastern France in the hope of cutting the allies' communications and forcing them to fall back from the capital. He was too late and on 30 March they had entered Paris. So Napoleon had made for his palace at Fontainebleau, outside the capital. His position was hopeless. Not only had several of his marshals deserted him but his foreign secretary, Talleyrand – 'A villain, a revolutionary,' he declared – and his minister for police, Fouché, had gone over to the returning Bourbons. There had been no choice but abdication. To this he had agreed on 6 April, renouncing his throne in favour of the fat, middle-aged Louis XVIII. Banishment was the only option, and Napoleon was alarmed by talk of exile on St Lucia in the Caribbean, or the Azores or, what he dreaded even more, the remote island of St Helena, even farther into the emptiness of the South Atlantic. So when offered the sovereignty of the island of Elba, he accepted with relief. It was only 150 miles from France, 30 from his native Corsica and close to the mainland of Italy. Exile might not be permanent.

Colonel Campbell was to attend Napoleon into exile as one of four allied commissioners but when the others returned to Austria, Prussia and Russia, he was to remain on Elba, not only to watch and report on the exile but also to monitor events in Italy as best he could. Murat still reigned as King Joachim of Naples and he, having once changed sides, might do so again in concert with his brother-in-law, if the British tried to restore King Ferdinand to his lost kingdom. This was the fear that had prompted Murat to make the death sentence mandatory for those he saw as pretenders to the throne of Naples. Campbell, his head still bandaged and his arm in a sling, hurried to Fontainebleau, where he found the other commissioners preparing for the journey to Elba. On 17 April he was presented to Napoleon.

'It was a strange feeling that came over me,' he wrote in his diary,

> when the aide-de-camp, after announcing my name, retired shutting the door, and I found myself suddenly closeted with that extraordinary man, whose name had been for so many years the touchstone of my professional and national feelings and whose appearance had been presented to my imagination in every form that exaggeration and caricature could render impressive. I saw before me a short, active-looking man, who was rapidly pacing the length of his apartment like some wild animal in his cell. He was dressed in an old green uniform with gold epaulets, blue pantaloons and red topboots, unshaven, uncombed, with the fallen particles of snuff scattered profusely upon his upper lip and breast. Upon his becoming aware of my presence, he turned quickly towards me and saluted me with a courteous smile.'[2]

As British visitors to Paris during the Peace of Amiens had discovered, Napoleon could quickly change his mood and manner and be charming or bullying, arrogant or inquisitive. Now he talked to Campbell as a fellow soldier, asking him about his wounds, his decorations and his family. Told that the colonel was Scottish, he remarked, 'I like them very much, there is something very martial about them',[3] and of the British in general, 'Yours is the greatest of all nations . . . I have been your greatest enemy – frankly such; but I am so no longer. I have wished likewise to raise the French nation but my plans have not succeeded.'[4]

During the coming week Campbell was to see two contrasting aspects of Napoleon. On the morning of 20 April he left Fontainebleau. Campbell watched and recorded, 'he passed us all with a salute and a smile' to where soldiers of the Old Guard were drawn up in the courtyard and where his carriage waited. 'I bid you farewell', he told them. 'For 20 years I have found you ever brave and faithful, marching in the path of glory . . . You are all my children. I cannot embrace you all but I will do so in the person of your general', and he kissed General Petit on both cheeks and was handed the standard of the *Garde Impériale*. Napoleon hugged the flag, then gave it back, saying, 'Farewell! Keep me in your memories!' He then stepped into his carriage, which 'was carried off at a gallop' to the clatter of its cavalry escort and to shouts from the Old Guard of 'Vive l'Empéreur!'[5] Then he was gone.

A different Napoleon had become apparent on the journey south. The road passed through towns and villages that showed increasing hostility; some were royalist; others, simply tired of war, conscription and the loss of their young men. Shouts of abuse and derision were heard, and stones were thrown at the carriage. However brave Napoleon might have been on the battlefield, he had a horror of the mob and the assassin and sometimes he 'sat within the carriage . . . apparently very much frightened, without attempting to stir from the corner'.[6] He even put on a Russian cloak and 'a common round hat' with a white royalist cockade and mounted the horse of one of his own outriders. At an overnight halt he changed hats and coats with Colonel Campbell and assumed his name. Hostility mounted as they passed through Provence, and in one village Napoleon saw his own effigy smeared with blood and hung with a placard reading, 'There is the odious tyrant! Sooner or later crime is punished!'[7] It was a relief when the cavalcade finally rode into the coastal village of Fréjus and there, offshore, rode the British frigate that was to carry him into exile; a pale, almost portly figure, he no longer looked the conqueror. At sunset on 28 April Captain Thomas Ussher ordered the gunner of the *Undaunted* to fire a royal salute of twenty-one guns and Napoleon came on board.

Once under sail, Napoleon relaxed. He enjoyed discursive conversations with Campbell, the Austrian commissioner (the other two had remained ashore) and the ship's officers. He talked about various campaigns, allies and enemies, complaining that Spain should be a natural friend to France and could easily take Gibraltar from the British by bombarding it for a year; he criticized the British for attacking and making an enemy of Denmark and for bungling the Walcheren expedition; and he asked about British visitors to Paris whom he had met during the Peace of Amiens. He was 'extremely inquisitive as to all points respecting our Navy, its establishment, discipline, etc.,'[8] and showed surprise when told that Vice-Admiral Sir Sidney Smith was now second-in-command in the Mediterranean when the latter's nephew Midshipman William Sidney Smith, who was serving in the frigate, was presented to him. He also talked about trade, economics and politics. He even spoke of his wife, the Empress Marie-Louise, who was returning to her native Vienna with their son, whom he had proclaimed King of Rome; he hoped they would join him on Elba. But he did not discuss his Polish mistress, Countess Maria Walewska, by whom he had also had a son, Alexandre. He laughed at caricatures of himself published in London and was told that there were as many of the British monarch and politicians. He remarked that his present voyage would give rise to more, and Captain Ussher replied that that 'would immortalize the *Undaunted*'.[9]

Campbell was not convinced when Napoleon also 'expressed the desire to pass the remainder of his life at Elba, studying the arts and sciences'.[10] Indeed he reported to Castlereagh, 'He possesses no command over himself in conversation and . . . has given frequent proof of the restlessness of his disposition and his expectation of opportunities arising, which will give scope to the exercise of it in France.'[11] He was aware that the geographical position of Elba could pose Napoleon as a threat to the peace of Italy as well as that of France.

Ashore in Portoferraio, Colonel Campbell explained his mission. The French officer commanding the depleted garrison of the island, General Jean-Baptiste Dalesme, had indeed heard of the Emperor's abdication and prudently hoisted the Bourbon flag on the two forts above the town. He had also heard that Napoleon was on his way to exile on Elba, and Campbell now explained that he had arrived to take possession of the island as his kingdom. Dalesme was then reassured when a compatriot, General Antoine Drouot, who enjoyed a reputation in the French army for courage and incorruptibility, now introduced himself as Napoleon's chief minister and court chamberlain and read the formal letter of the new King of Elba's accession. He also announced that the King would receive the general and a civic delegation on board the frigate that evening. There they were received by Napoleon at his most dignified and benign, wearing the medal of the *Légion d'honneur* on the green uniform coat of a cavalry officer. One of the delegation, the manager of the island's open-cast coal mines, later recounted, 'He was calm, his eyes were bright, he had a kindly look on his face and he smiled in a dignified manner.' Napoleon then spoke of his love for France and the circumstances that had brought him to their island; from now on he would 'consecrate himself to the welfare of the Elbans'.[12]

Next morning, Napoleon was on deck at first light, eager to inspect his kingdom. From books and questioning he already knew something about Elba. 'It is certainly a very small island',[13] Napoleon remarked to Campbell on first seeing it. The island was 16 miles long and 3 to 10 miles in width, its coast all rocky headlands and bays. The predominant colour was the dark green of its pines, evergreen oaks and scrub, from which rose bare, grey peaks of mountains at its western end, rising to more than 3,000 feet. Its population of some 12,000 lived from subsistence farming, cultivating vineyards, olives and sweet chestnuts, or from tuna-fishing, iron-mining and salt-panning, the only other natural resource being marble and granite used for building, A quarter of Elbans lived in the capital, Portoferraio, a little walled town, fortified against raiding North African corsairs. Its huddled, red-roofed houses and steep, often stepped, streets were dominated by two castles and, while it looked pretty, even handsome, from the sea, the narrow streets around the harbour stank of fish and sewage.

Elbans were hardy people, akin to Napoleon's fellow Corsicans, living rough lives, still aware of the danger from corsairs, who, even now, raided European shores for slaves. Partly for this reason, and to guard against political assassins, Napoleon was to be allowed a defence force of 600 men shipped from France, mostly members of the Old Guard and his favourite Polish lancers, backed by a militia of some 1,200 Elbans. The cost of his court and his little army would have to be met by an annual subsidy paid by the new French government and taxes he would raise on the island. One detail that absorbed Napoleon was the design of his royal standard and he consulted the Elban worthies, who sent him a book of local heraldry. From this he chose a white flag with a red diagonal stripe, which had been flown when Elba had been ruled by Florence, and to this he added three golden bees from his own coat of arms; this was quickly stitched together by the frigate's tailor.

Unable to wait for the official reception planned for the afternoon, Napoleon asked to be rowed ashore, accompanied by Campbell and Ussher, to take a closer look at a large farmhouse he thought might make a suitable royal residence. In the boat he remarked that he had left his sword behind, worried not by any breach of etiquette but by his fear of assassination. They walked on the beach and looked at the house for two hours before returning to the frigate in preparation for the formal arrival at two o'clock. It was then obvious that the Elbans enjoyed ceremony as much as any other Mediterranean people. Boats crowded with musicians, and sightseers put out from the shore; the yards of the *Undaunted* were manned and a royal salute fired. Ashore waited his subjects with the golden keys of Portoferraio and a guard of honour in the familiar uniform of French infantry from General Dalesme's garrison. Then, as Campbell recorded:

> At the beach, he was received by the prefect, clergy, etc., and the keys were presented upon a plate amid exclamations of 'Vive l'Empéreur!' We next proceeded to the church in procession and from thence to the *Hôtel-de-Ville*, where all the authorities and principal inhabitants were assembled, with each of whom he conversed. After this, he mounted his horse, attended by about a dozen persons, and visited part of the fortified outworks. Dinner was at 7 pm.[14]

King Napoleon had taken possession of his realm.

Despite Portoferraio being *en fête*, the squalor of its narrow streets and mean houses within its walls was apparent. Napoleon quickly determined to opt for a residence away from the smells and chose a pleasant house on the ridge of the saddle between forts above the town, the Villa Mulini, named after windmills that once had stood there. A long, low, two-storey house, yellow-washed with green shutters and, standing high, not only did it command views of both the harbour and the open sea but any breeze would blow through its open windows. However, it was small for a royal residence and Napoleon ordered that a ballroom be built on the upper floor, so requiring the central section of the roof to be raised. He himself would occupy a suite on the ground floor, with a tiny study and library beside a long, pink-walled reception room with French windows opening on to the garden and its terrace above the sea.

With the enthusiasm he applied to all new projects, he set about ruling the island. Inspection was necessary and this now began, mostly on horseback. Napoleon had brought more than a hundred horses with him and, noted a British officer, 'his white Arabs were very handsome and a favourite one he had brought from Egypt.' In the stables 'every horse had his name placed above the manger and several of them were named after his great battles such as Marengo, Austerlitz, etc. A very fine charger, which carried his master during the last fatal campaign in France, was jet black and called Borodino.'[15] Riding these, he visited fortifications, storehouses, villages and vantage-points, where summer houses might be built, and he inspected the open-cast iron mines. He sailed across to the small island of Pianosa, 15 miles to the south-west; this was not under his jurisdiction but he decided it should be and gave orders for its occupation, joking, 'All Europe will say I have made a conquest already.'[16] He ordered that a battery should be mounted there as an additional defence against corsairs.

One of the first British visitors to Elba was one of Bentinck's staff officers, Major Montgomery Maxwell, who came out of curiosity to see what he called 'this now caged bird', who would, he forecast, 'some day or other spread his wings to the astonishment of the world'.[17] Told that Napoleon was on one of his inland excursions, Maxwell and several brother-officers set out in search and found him riding in the mountains with two equerries and an escort of two Polish lancers. 'I frankly confess I felt much disappointed', Maxwell recalled.

I peeped at his round, thick, short thighs and pot-belly. 'Is this the great Napoleon?' Moreover, the countenance, in which I expected to behold a union of the demon and the soldier, appeared soft and mild in the extreme; there was nothing striking in it, not a line to trace the warrior or the politician on his large and polished brow; nothing but the high, smooth forehead, partly shaded when he took his hat off by the jet-black matted lock of hair I had so often heard of . . . The nose was regular, the mouth beautiful and about it seemed to play a most contented and engaging smile. His eye . . . possessed so many qualities and attributes and seemed so chameleon-like, changing its hues every moment that I can scarcely say what colour it is but on a venture I should say it was light blue but at all events it was filled with expression and genius . . . I now became enraptured by his lively, bewitching air . . . No wonder the French soldiers adored him.[18]

Speaking in French, Napoleon engaged the British officers in conversation, mostly about military matters. After expressing his admiration for Sir John Moore – '*Brave général! Brave général!*' – he showed anger 'with a lowering brow and malice in his mouth' when told that one of his visitors had been with Wellington's army at Bordeaux. Then his expression lightened and he asked a Scottish officer, 'Is it really true that you wear the petticoat and do you not find it very cold?'[19]

Meanwhile the Austrian commissioner had returned to the mainland, leaving Colonel Campbell as the sole representative of the allies. He and Napoleon had struck up what appeared to be an easy friendship, the latter calling him 'Combell', conversing in French and establishing a degree of intimacy with the words, 'We are here as soldiers.'[20] He spoke frankly about the past, complaining of the cost of espionage against the British, confirming that he had seriously intended to invade England ten years earlier; he himself would have led 100,000 soldiers and had expected to march from the coast to the capital in three days. Although the occupation of London would have ruined British trade and commerce, he did not believe that that alone would have subdued the country; after his victory, he would have given independence to Ireland. Had fate not intervened, in three or four years France would have built 300 ships of the line – 'What a difference that would have made!' he declared — prompting Campbell to reply, 'We do not know why Your Majesty has wished to annihilate us.'[21] But now, Napoleon added, 'For 20 years at least no power can make war against England and she will do as she likes.'[22]

Still his thoughts returned to France and the future. When Captain Ussher returned to Elba from a visit to Fréjus, Napoleon 'enquired with great eagerness, what was the news? What said the people at Fréjus? Did he see any French troops, or troops of the Allies?' When Ussher replied that many people there had 'enquired anxiously for His Majesty' and that 'he had many adherents still in France,' Napoleon 'showed the strongest exultation . . . and chuckled with joy'[23] but then added without conviction, 'Oh, the Emperor is dead. I am no longer anything.'[24]

After a month King Napoleon had established a little court at the Villa Mulini but, although he gave receptions attended by his officers' wives and the daughters of Elban worthies eyed him with provocative curiosity, he missed female company. His wife, the Empress Marie-Louise, showed no sign of wishing to join his exile for she was enjoying a liaison with a dashing Austrian general, who had been chosen by his government as the controller of her household but was, in fact, fulfilling the same covert duties as was Colonel Campbell at her husband's court. One who was thought to be the love of his life, the divorced Empress Josephine, had died of diphtheria at Malmaison, outside Paris, on 29 May, with a theatrical aptness that made her departure seem almost in sympathy with his own; she had never borne him the heir he required, she had been unfaithful to him and yet she continued to occupy an elusive but central part of his life. But his loneliness was soon to be relieved.

Three women were about to arrive on Elba. The first to come was his favourite sister, Pauline. Beautiful and flirtatious, her high charge of sexuality had carried her beyond scandal into amorous mythology, described by one of her lovers as 'the greatest hussy you can imagine but also the most tempting'.[25] Napoleon had tolerated her innumerable love affairs, just writing to her, 'I hope you are behaving yourself.'[26] Her first husband, a general, whom she had married at the age of seventeen, had died of yellow fever in the West Indies, leaving her with an infant son, but she had soon married again. Her second husband was Prince Borghese and, it was said, she was attracted more by his title, money and palaces in Rome and Florence because she described him as 'such a eunuch'.[27] She quickly aroused more scandal by posing naked to Canova for a statue of a reclining Venus, answering criticism by saying that there had been nothing to worry about as there had been a stove in his studio. She was now aged thirty-four, and had kept her looks, which were enhanced by her experience in the power of roving eyes, knowing smile and gestures of the hands which set her bracelets jingling.

Pauline arrived on Elba on 1 June, on passage for Naples, where she was to stay with her sister Queen Caroline. She now stayed with her brother at the Villa Mulini and, when he suggested he build a summer residence at San Martino, in the hills, she, with characteristic generosity, gave his chamberlain a handful of diamonds to pay for it. Then, to the surprise of all but Napoleon, she departed two days later for Naples and rumours spread. One was that she had refused his incestuous advances, but it was more probable that she had been entrusted with a mission to Murat. Napoleon had become increasingly worried about the danger of abduction as much as by the threat of assassination, not so much by corsairs as by a variety of enemies to the north, agents of the Bourbons, the allies, or indeed Jacobins. Although he had distrusted Murat since his defection, he may have been hoping that they still had a mutual interest in survival, since King Joachim was in increasing fear of being deposed in favour of the returning Bourbons. Murat had naval and military forces available to protect Napoleon; beyond that, might there be the possibility of an alliance to promote the survival in Naples of one and a return to France by the other?

The second woman visitor was Napoleon's mother, who was given passage from Leghorn in a British brig in company with Colonel Campbell, who had been on the mainland to soothe the pain of his wounds in the medicinal baths of Lucca. Letizia Bonaparte – known officially as Madame Mère – was now sixty-four and had so astutely managed the income granted by her son that she was rich. She was vivacious yet imperious, small, 'stout . . . dressed in the pink of fashion and highly rouged' and was said to 'play billiards four hours every day'.[28] They sailed on 2 August, at the height of the summer heat, and dined on deck, where Campbell, accustomed to charming grand ladies, led her to confide in him; on one occasion she told him that she had had to dissuade the fourteen-year-old Napoleon from choosing a naval career, telling him, 'My son, in the navy you have to contend with both fire and water!'[29] On arrival off Portoferraio, she was mortified that her son was not there to meet her because he had been expecting her the day before and, noted Campbell, 'she seemed greatly agitated and mortified . . . turning quite pale and huffed.'[30] When her son returned from a day in the mountains she was mollified, particularly when shown the house he had rented for her near his own and then by the firework display he had arranged in her honour that night. She quickly took to life on the island. Campbell reported that 'on walking round the ramparts, she jumped up on a gun-carriage and stood on it for ten minutes, viewing the present dominions of her favourite son.'[31] Elba reminded her of Corsica, which she could sometimes see like a cloud on the western horizon. Finding the Elbans akin to Corsicans and conversing with them in Italian, she began to lead a gentle, genteel social life, holding receptions in her drawing-room and riding about the island in an open carriage. She would dine with her son every Sunday, when they would play cards and she could accuse him, 'You're cheating, son!' and he would reply, 'You're rich, mother!'[32] This was much more comfortable than having to worry about his latest campaign and whether he might be overwhelmed by the latest coalition raised against him.

A month later the third woman visitor arrived: his Polish mistress, Countess Marie Walewska, now aged twenty-eight, with their four-year-old son Alexandre. A fair-haired, fresh faced young woman with lively, trusting eyes, she was clearly looking forward to settling down in the island with her lover. At Fontainebleau she had been ready to join his exile but had been spurned; now she was to try again, calling at Elba on passage from France to Naples, where she hoped to dissuade Murat from appropriating land that Napoleon had given to their son. But the King of Elba had other plans, partly dictated by his determination not to allow his mistress to meet his mother. Indeed, he insisted that she come ashore at a lonely cove and stay at a former hermitage in a chestnut grove on a remote hillside, which he had had converted into a simple guest house. She landed on 1 September and spent two nights with Napoleon at the hermitage. Then a note arrived from General Drouot in Portoferraio, telling him that his secret was about to be exposed: there was gossip that the Empress Marie-Louise had arrived secretly and was staying with him at the hermitage; indeed, the mayor of a small town near by had climbed the hillside to pay his respects to the supposed Empress. There was only one way out: Marie Walewska would have to leave that night, despite the danger of trying to reach her ship in a rough sea. Leave she did, but sadly. Perhaps he had confided in her too, and asked her to report to him from Naples, because she said later, 'He considers his exile temporary and the information he demands is what he needs to choose the most propitious moment to bring it to an end.'[33]

Despite Napoleon's fears of exposure, the secret of her visit had been well kept. Even Campbell could only note in his diary more than a fortnight after her departure that:

About three weeks ago, a lady with a child, apparently five or six years of age, arrived here from Leghorn. She was received by Napoleon with great attention but a certain degree of conceal-ment and accompanied him to a very retired small house in the most remote part of the island. After remaining two days she re-embarked and is said to have gone to Naples. Everyone in Elba believes that this is Marie-Louise with her son . . . but my infor-mation leads me to believe that it is a Polish lady from Warsaw, who bore child to Napoleon a few years ago. It is probable that the concealment used and her speedy departure for the Continent proceed from delicacy towards Marie-Louise and the fear of this connection becoming known to her.[34]

Then on 31 October Pauline, Princess Borghese, returned; Campbell noted that her Elban corvette was escorted by a Neapolitan frigate. Napoleon awaited her eagerly, not only as his favourite but for the news she would bring from Naples. It was known that the victorious allies had convened a post-war confer-ence in Vienna under the auspices of the Austrian Foreign Sécretary, Prince Metternich, and this was about to begin. In all probability Murat had heard reports of what might be decided, particularly whether or not he, King Joachim, was to be replaced by King Ferdinand. She was able to tell her brother that word from the Congress of Vienna was that the future of the kingdom of Naples was still in the balance. The Austrians, to whom Murat had allied himself, supported him but the new kings of France and Spain were calling for the return of their fellow Bourbon Ferdinand from Palermo and the restoration of the Kingdom of the two Sicilies. Yet one lesson that had been learned over the past two decades was that not only nations changed sides but individuals, too, and that could always, yet again, include King Joachim.

Napoleon was delighted by the return of Pauline and that she set up her own household for a prolonged stay. She was loyal, generous and exciting company; indeed, the gossips of Portoferraio again put it about that theirs was an incestuous relationship, which, given the amorality of both, was not impossible. Her presence cheered the social life of Elba as she set about arranging parties. When Napoleon had a deconsecrated church rebuilt as a theatre, she arranged concerts and theatrical performances, amateur and professional, hiring actors from Florence to perform racy plays with such titles as *Les folies amoreuses* and *Les fausses infidélités*, and giving three masked balls there that winter, persuading Madame Mère to wear even more make-up.

Napoleon entered into these jollities with a purpose for, aware of Campbell's watchful eye, he hoped that his immersion in social revelry would lessen his suspicions; indeed the colonel did comment that 'these were amusements such as common mortals might indulge in.'[35] Had he been present, on one occasion, Campbell might have noted that, when in the company of some attractive young women, Napoleon was playing the party game of evasion 'Blind Man's Bluff'.

All were agog for news from the Congress of Vienna, where the leading diplomats of Europe mixed with celebrities of smart society to enjoy the balls, concerts and soirées if not to take part in the conference itself. Perhaps to nobody's surprise, Sir Sidney Smith also materialized, with the self-imposed duty of persuading the politicians that their next cause should be the abolition of slavery in North Africa. His old adversary was still on his mind and he told

Hyde de Neuville, an emissary from Paris, that he expected
Napoleon to escape from Elba, adding, 'Your countrymen are
under a great illusion if they believe that the prestige that sur-
rounds his name is destroyed by France's recent defeats.'[36]

Yet, on Elba, Campbell was bored and wondering whether his
prolonged stay was worthwhile. In October his knighthood had
been announced and it was unlikely that his duties as commissioner
would bring any further reward. So, despite his suspicions, the arrival of Pauline and Napoleon's apparent involvement in social diver-
sions did not suggest imminent problems. His vigilance relaxed.
Napoleon's own flotilla, consisting of the brig *Inconstant* and three
smaller craft, were allowed to ply freely to and from the Italian mainland and Rear-Admiral Benjamin Hallowell, Nelson's friend, now
the naval commander in the area, decided, or had been instructed,
that a frigate was no longer necessary as permanent guardship off
the island. It had also been decided, for diplomatic reasons, that the
British should not appear to be Napoleon's only gaolers, so naval
precautions were reduced to an occasional visit by a brig.

The feeling that Napoleon's exile was final had been reinforced
by a new poem by Lord Byron, '*Ode to Napoleon Buonaparte*',
which John Murray had published that year as a pamphlet. This
began,

> 'Tis done – but yesterday a King!
> And arm'd with Kings to strive–
> And now thou art a nameless thing
> So abject – yet alive!

and continued,

> Then haste thee to thy sullen Isle,
> And gaze upon the sea;
> That element may meet thy smile,
> It ne'er was ruled by thee!

Colonel Campbell had been enjoying his conversations with
Napoleon, which might last for three or four hours and ranged as
widely as ever. The talk was often military and political. 'He

praised the Italians and ridiculed the Germans', Campbell remembered; 'He would engage always to beat 30,000 Germans with
20,000 Italians.'[37] He considered the appointment of the Duke of
Wellington as British ambassador in Paris, which had just been
announced, to be 'an open insult to the feelings of the French
people' and deplored the restoration of the Bourbons to Paris,
declaring that 'there would be a violent reaction of the whole
nation before five years were over, similar to what took place at the
Revolution, in consequence of their humiliation.' He ridiculed
the apparent vagueness of the Congress of Vienna: 'How could so
many sovereigns remain together for any length of time? Their
separation without a final settlement of Europe . . . would have a
dreadful effect.' Of his own situation, Napoleon was 'agitated by
the want of money' because the promised subsidy from the allies
had yet to be paid and he was worried by reports that it was
'intended to remove him to St Helena, or St Lucia'. He complained to Campbell of being 'shut up in this *bicoque* [shanty] of a
house, separated from the world with no interesting occupation,
no *savants* [intellectuals] with me, nor any variety in my society,
excepting when I have occasionally the pleasure of conversing
with yourself – even without money'.[38] There had been delays in
paying the substantial pension agreed by the new King in Paris.

Although none of this suggested that Napoleon planned an
immediate escape from Elba, Campbell came to believe

> that Napoleon was not sufficiently watched; that I had no means
> of preventing him from escaping; that he was still of a most rest-
> less disposition; that discontented persons of an adventurous
> spirit, from France and Italy, frequent Elba . . . that a conspiracy
> might be formed in Napoleon's favour at Toulon . . . and that
> the first intelligence might be his being in possession of that
> important place and the fleet.[39]

Towards the end of the year the colonel noticed that Napoleon
no longer welcomed his company as he had: 'He has gradually
estranged himself from me and various means are taken to show
me that my presence is disagreeable. Of this, however, I could not
be certain for a long time as it was done by hints, which could well

not be noticed.' No explanation was given; Napoleon simply became more regal, erected barriers of protocol, surrounding himself with 'courtly forms of etiquette' so that interviews had to be requested and were often delayed, although when they did meet he was civil. Campbell put this down to the widespread belief that Britain was responsible to her allies for guarding Napoleon's exile and, as he put it, 'that I am the executive agent for this'.[40] It does not seem to have struck him that Napoleon's aloofness might have been designed to encourage him to make more frequent visits to the mainland so to give himself more freedom to receive clandestine visitors, who might have attracted the colonel's attention; for such visitors from the mainland there were.

Among his openly received visitors was an English tourist, John Macnamara, whom Napoleon agreed to receive because he had just arrived from France. After the usual *tour d'horizon* that he offered to privileged visitors with apparent stoicism – 'Napoleon is always Napoleon and always will know how to be content and bear any fortune' – he asked about the state of France and received an oblique reply. 'We had a storm last night', said Macnamara. 'Now there is no wind but the sea is agitated.' Napoleon understood and just said, 'Well answered.'[41]

The French and Polish soldiers, who at first would, as one British visitor put it, 'whiff their cigars and drink their beer under an olive tree and vote Portferraio *leur petit Paris*',[42] were becoming bored with Elba, as was Colonel Campbell. After a lonely Christmas on the island he found another excuse to absent himself for a few weeks to 'consult some medical man in Florence on account of the increasing deafness supposed to arise from my wounds', there was another motive: a mistress, a Countess Miniacci, he had acquired in Florence but would describe as his cousin. There seemed to be no immediate risk of any attempted escape by Napoleon but, even so, he asked Captain John Adye of the brig *Partridge* 'to cruise around the island during my absence',[43] He told him that 'in case of Napoleon quitting Elba, or any of his vessels being discovered with troops on board, military stores, or provisions . . . to intercept and, in the case of their offering the slightest resistance, to destroy them'.[44] On 16 February he sailed for Leghorn.

While on the mainland, Campbell formed a new theory. If Napoleon tried to escape from Elba, he would make for Italy. Murat, he heard, was now certain that the allies would try to replace him with King Ferdinand and, to pre-empt this, planned to call for a rising throughout the Italian peninsula to eject the Austrians from the north and proclaim a united Italy under his own sovereignty. If he were joined in this by the great Napoleon, all Europe would again be thrown into disarray. There were specific clues that something was afoot. The colonel was told that chests of plate belonging to Princess Pauline had secretly been shipped to Leghorn and that the Polish lancers on the island were busy repairing and soaping their saddles.

So when, on 26 February, the *Partridge* anchored off Leghorn and Captain Adye came ashore, Campbell eagerly asked him for news of Elba, which he had left two days before. 'I neither saw nor heard of anything extraordinary',[45] replied Adye: Napoleon had been there and he had seen men of the *Garde Impériale* planting trees in front of their barracks. However, after he had sailed later that day, he had noticed activity by the small ships of Napoleon's flotilla: *Inconstant* had put to sea, then returned, and he remembered that the smaller vessels also seemed to have been preparing for sea. This was enough for Campbell to sound a warning, writing to Lord Burghersh, the British ambassador in Florence, asking him to advise the senior British naval officer at Genoa to send a warship to Elba in case some plot was coming to a head. The letter should reach Florence quickly, but it would be several days before his request could arrive in Genoa. Meanwhile Campbell determined to return at once to Elba and embarked in the *Partridge*.

Next morning, the 28th, the brig lay becalmed some miles to the north of Portoferraio and Campbell asked for a boat to take him ashore. Before leaving, he told Adye that, if he had not returned in two hours, he could be assumed to be in trouble and an urgent message was to be sent to Lord Burghersh, saying that Napoleon had escaped. As the boat approached the harbour, Campbell saw that sentries were still on duty but, as he drew closer, he realized that they were not French but Elban. He landed and walked towards the French military headquarters, on his way meeting an English visitor named Grattan, who had come ashore from the *Partridge* on her last visit. He told the colonel that on the afternoon of the 26th there had been 'a sudden bustle', the gates of the town had been shut and the rumour spread that Napoleon was about to leave for Italy – Naples or Milan – or for France, to land at Antibes. At seven o'clock that evening 'the troops marched out of the fortifications without music, or noise, embarked in small boats and were taken out to the *Inconstant*.' That morning, the Emperor had left the Villa Mulini and walked down the lane and the pink marble steps to attend Mass in the dark little church of the Misericordia. Then at nine that evening he and his staff had gathered on the quay to embark. There was no wind, so the flotilla had to be towed out of the harbour by its boats to lie offshore, awaiting a breeze. Grattan had himself hired a boat and was rowed towards the ships and saw 'Napoleon in his grey surtout and round hat pacing the quarterdeck of the brig, which, as well as all the other vessels, was crowded with troops'. Grattan was challenged, explained that he had 'come merely to see the Emperor'[46] and was ordered away. There was no wind until next day and it was not until the afternoon of the 27th that the flotilla of seven vessels was out of sight. Napoleon had escaped.

Campbell now sought an Italian doctor, whom he knew, and was told that the commandant of the island's National Guard had been appointed governor of the island. He was easily found and when asked who had appointed him governor, replied, 'The Emperor Napoleon'. Campbell replied that he should 'hold no more connection with Napoleon, or Murat, and surrender the island to the Allies, perhaps even give intelligence of importance.' The one person on the island who should know where Napoleon had gone was his sister Pauline, so he walked to her house and asked for an audience on the pretext of offering to take letters to Leghorn for her. He was invited into the *salone* and then, as he wrote in his diary, 'she came out and made me sit down beside her, drawing her chair gradually still closer, as if she waited for me to make some *private* communication.'[47] The colonel came to the point: where was her brother? She then began to 'protest her ignorance of Napoleon's departure until the very last moment and of his present destination; laid hold of my hand and pressed it to her heart that I might feel how much she was agitated. However, she did not appear to be so and there was rather a smile upon her countenance.' But there was one clue. 'During this conversation, she dropped a hint of her belief in his destination being for France: upon which I smiled and said, 'O non! Ce n'est pas si loin, c'est à Naples'; for I fancied (for the moment) she mentioned France purposely to deceive me. Two or three minutes afterwards, I took my leave.'[48]

Taking Grattan with him., Campbell returned to the *Partridge* to write urgent despatches to Lord Castlereagh, Lord Burghersh and the senior British officers at Genoa and also to be forwarded to London, Paris and Vienna. Escaping with Napoleon had been nearly 1,200 others: his staff, including three French generals, 600 men of the Old Guard, 100 Polish lancers, 300 Corsicans and about 100 civilians. Although Captain Adye believed Napoleon had gone to Naples, Campbell now thought it must be France because

the horses and guns, which he was said certainly to have embarked, could be of no use at Naples but only an incumbrance; although, to be sure, it might be a mask to make one believe that he had not gone there and he might afterwards have thrown them overboard. Would he, however, also have encumbered himself with so many civil followers and with all the Corsicans if he was destined for Naples? He could not throw *them* overboard.[49]

So the colonel and captain agreed to crowd sail and set course for Antibes, as Campbell decided, 'I think his destination is for the frontier of Piedmont next France and that he will take possession of some strong place near Nice, or between that and Turin, dispersing his civil followers all over North Italy, of which he will proclaim independence, raising the disaffected there, while Murat does the same in the south.'[50] The outlook was, he thought, ominous: 'I had long thought Napoleon so restless and unprincipled a person that he would lose no opportunity of employing himself in war upon the Continent.'[51] Even so, Colonel Campbell was well aware that Napoleon had taken him, the representative of all the allies, by surprise. It was not until 5 March that he heard that

Napoleon and his miniature army had disembarked in Golfe Juan near Antibes, and had disappeared into the interior of France.

The news reached Major Maxwell in Genoa on 2 March and he jotted in his diary, 'This evening the astounding intelligence has arrived here that the restless, ruthless Napoleon has left his abiding-place and again broken loose upon the world. From all I saw and heard when I visited Elba I made sure such would be the case.'[52] Two days later, excitedly mixing his metaphors, he added 'Bonaparte had landed in France, the torch is in his reckless hand, ready to light up the flames of civil war . . . He has got the devil's dice-box in his hand and is about to play hazard with a vengeance.'[53]

16

The fortune of war

Exactly sixteen weeks after the escape from Elba two men sought an interview with the Duke of Wellington. Both had served in the Mediterranean, playing their parts over the decade during which the British had sought to prevent Napoleon from striking east towards the Ottoman Empire and India, but they had not met; nor did they do so on this day. On the evening of 18 June 1815 they were among thousands, living, dead and dying, on two square miles of farmland south of Brussels which had on that day become another of the great battlefields that had scarred Europe during the past quarter-century. Smoke and the smell of burned gunpowder, eviscerated men and horses, trampled, wet grass and rye hung in the air over what would become known as the battlefield of Waterloo.

Sir Neil Campbell had been seeking the commander-in-chief for three days. On his return to London from Elba he had received a mixed reception. Both Lord Castlereagh and the Prince Regent had congratulated him on watching Napoleon and cleared him of any blame for the escape. Others thought differently and asked why he had been absent at the crucial time and there was even the canard that he had accepted a bribe from Napoleon to stay away on the final day. On hearing of the escape, Lord Burghersh had written to Castlereagh:

From an unwillingness to act unkindly towards an officer of Sir Neil Campbell's merit, I have abstained from bringing under your lordship's consideration the improper manner in which, I felt, he did the duties of the situation in which he was placed. His absences from Elba were constant. . . . Sir Neil felt that his situation about Bonaparte was unpleasant and that the duty was better done by occasional visits. This opinion was at variance with mine.'[1]

But Castlereagh defended Campbell:

Our Government never undertook a police operation on Elba. Colonel Campbell was certainly there for the purpose of occasionally communicating with our Government upon such matters as might pass under his observation both there and in Italy . . . but nothing more was ever contemplated. It would have been out of Colonel Campbell's power to have attempted anything further – he could not have done it.[2]

But, while thus exonerated, Campbell's role remained sufficiently controversial for him to be denied another posting as liaison officer with the allied armies. Instead, he was given permission to rejoin his regiment, the 54th Foot, currently in Flanders with the army under the Duke of Wellington, although he would have to resume his substantive rank of major.

In the past weeks Europe had been shaken by the second coming of Napoleon. After landing in France, he had marched north through Grenoble until faced by French troops sent by the Bourbons to arrest him. Striding up to them, he had opened his coat and invited them to shoot him; instead they cheered. From that moment he was triumphant: his old soldiers flocked to his standard and even his renegade marshals turned their coats again. Before he entered Paris, King Louis XVIII had fled. The allies abandoned their talking and revelry in Vienna, mobilized their armies and marched them towards France. The British, who had shipped most of their Peninsula veterans to North America to fight in the continuing war with the United States, put together a small army for the Duke to command. This, together with Belgian, Dutch and German troops, who made up two-thirds of the allied army, had concentrated on Brussels, while Marshal Blücher led the Prussians west to reinforce them.

Campbell travelled to Brussels and, after reporting at headquarters on 15 June, was invited to dine with Wellington that evening and promised an interview with him the following morning. He attended the dinner but it was constantly interrupted by reports of the moves and counter-moves of the armies, and this was clearly not a time to ask Wellington about his own military future; an aide-de-camp suggested he report to headquarters again next day. Hoping to be rejoining his regiment, the major (as he again was) set about acquiring field equipment and horses, but all was chaos and he was only able to buy one mount. Then news arrived of the clash between the French army and the Dutch and British at Ligny and the apparent defeat of the Prussians at Quatre Bras. The British army was, he heard, south of Brussels near the village of Waterloo and there he might find the commander-in-chief. So, before dawn on 17 June, he rode out of Brussels on the road south and, on the morning of 18 June, he saw through the rain the allied army drawn up on a low ridge above a wide, shallow valley planted with rye.

There, half a mile apart, the 72,000 men of the allied army – one third of them British – faced the same number of French. While the former hopefully awaited the arrival of 89,000 Prussians, the latter hoped for reinforcement by 33,000 French under Marshal Grouchy, both these armies still 10 or more miles to the east. In the centre of the allied line, at the hamlet of Mont St Jean, were the headquarters, a cavalcade fifty strong: the Duke in his black cocked hat and blue coat, with his field commanders and aides-de-camp, foreign liaison officers, all in gorgeous uniforms; also the 22-year-old Prince of Orange, who for political reasons, had had to be appointed to the command of all but the British troops and, in name, subordinate only to Wellington himself. Campbell could see the Duke on his horse, Copenhagen, at the centre of activity as gallopers rode up with reports and aides wheeled away with his orders. Again, this was not a time to ask about his own affairs and he could not bring himself to 'press for an interview in a way that was not agreeable to himself'.[3]

So he rode at a discreet distance from the Duke's staff and from there he would watch the battle. It began after the rain had stopped, shortly before midday. He heard the opening of the

French cannonade and the shot whirr overhead; the volleys that threw back the first assault by massed French infantry; the drumming of hoofbeats of charge and counter-charge and when French cavalry rode against the British infantry squares; he heard the drums of the *Garde Impériale* as they made their final advance and the crash of the British volleys that cut them down. All was veiled by gunsmoke. There was nothing he could do but watch and wait.

He had no idea that others, who had also played their parts in the Mediterranean, were within hundreds of yards of him; Major-General Sir James Kempt, who had led the light brigade at Maida, took over command from General Picton when the latter was shot dead as his division rose from behind a hedge in two ranks to hurl back the first mass attack by French infantry with a volley such as had decided the day at Maida and then by the bayonet; Colonel Sir John Colborne, who had also fought at Maida, was now commanding the 52nd Foot, which enfiladed the flank of the Imperial Guard in their last charge; among their opponents General Baron Pierre Cambronne, once a drummer boy and a sergeant-major, who had escaped from Elba with Napoleon, was with the Guard. Campbell had been told that his own regiment, the 54th, was held in reserve to the rear in a position to block the road to Brussels in case of a French victory. He could not ride away from the battle and he did not do so until, in late afternoon, the Prussian army finally appeared on the French flank to the east and the Duke of Wellington waved his hat to order a general advance.

This again was certainly not the moment to seek a private interview. But no such scruples affected another senior officer from the Mediterranean theatre of war: Sir Sidney Smith. He had left Vienna, as had most of those attending the congress, having tirelessly promoted his anti-slavery campaign, founding what he called the Knights Liberators of the Slaves in Africa, rattling homeward in a coach emblazoned with his coat of arms. Accompanied by his wife of five years and his three attractive stepdaughters, he had reached Brussels just as the climactic battle was imminent. Leaving the women at an hotel on the afternoon of the 18th, he rode south towards the sound of the guns and, as he put it, 'stemmed a torrent of the disabled and *givers-in*' that suggested the battle might be over. Passing a wounded British officer, whom he recognized, he borrowed his cavalry sabre; he had a duel with Napoleon in mind, for he said later that he was

> thinking his sword a better one to meet my old antagonist on horseback . . . I was now and then jammed among broken wagons of disarmed Napoleonist janissaries and finally reached the Duke of Wellington's person. Though I was not allowed to have any of the fun, I had the heartfelt gratification of being the first Englishman that was not in the battle who shook hands with him before he got off his horse.

There was no getting away from Sir Sidney, who followed the Duke to his quarters in the village of Waterloo and was soon 'drinking his health at his table'.[4]

Like Campbell, Smith had seen the slopes before the British positions heaped with corpses and wounded bodies of what was later said to be 63,000 men and 10,000 horses. He heard the cries of the wounded, who were already being robbed and murdered for valuables, or even their clothes, by marauding peasants. So with the sensitivity with which his insensitivity was sometimes mixed, he determined to do what he could. On returning to Brussels next day, he hired a wagoner to take his carts to the battlefield and bring as many wounded as possible to a Jesuit hospital in the city. In this way 134 wounded soldiers, half of them French, were carted to rudimentary medical care. Then, after returning to the village of Waterloo, Sir Sidney again accosted the Duke, who found a task for him away from his headquarters, asking him to accompany the advancing army as an interpreter to arrange the surrender of fortified towns along the road to Paris.

★ ★ ★

In the third week of July 1815 Captain William Webley, who had fought under Nelson in Aboukir Bay and spent storm-racked months off Toulon, was commanding the first-rate *Swiftsure* in the Atlantic, on patrol off the Vendée and the ports of La Rochelle and Rochefort. On the 15th of the month he sighted another British sail of the line, the 'seventy-four' *Bellerophon*, which he knew to be commanded by his friend Captain Frederick Maitland. The ship was lying off the Ile d'Aix in the wide sound of the Basque Roads and through his telescope, he could see unusual activity on her upper deck. Calling for his barge, Webley was pulled across to the *Bellerophon*, climbed her side and shook hands with Maitland on her quarterdeck. Then, as he recalled, 'Captain M. explained in a mysterious tone, "I've got him." "Got him? Got who?" "Why Bonaparte to be sure."'[5] 'You are a lucky fellow',[6] Captain Webley had said.

Napoleon had ordered a ship to be prepared for his escape to America. One idea was to board a Danish sloop; once she had sailed, he would, in case of interception, hide in a cask stowed in the hold and breathe through a tube. This plan was abandoned because, if the ship was boarded and detained for more than a day by the British, he would have to make an ignominious surrender. There was one more chance: perhaps the British might allow him to sail for America, or even take him there themselves? Several emissaries came out to the *Bellerophon* at anchor off the Ile d'Aix. One, Count Las Cases, tried to persuade Captain Maitland that 'The Emperor is so anxious to spare the further effusion of blood that he will proceed to America in any way the British Government chooses to sanction, either in a French ship of war, a vessel armed *en flute* [an armed auxiliary], a merchant vessel, or even a British ship of war.'[7] Maitland asked another, General Savary, why Napoleon did not seek asylum in England, and was told, 'The climate is too damp and cold; it is too near France; he would be, as it were, in the centre of every change and revolution that might take place there and would be subject to suspicion; he has been accustomed to consider the English as his most inveterate enemies and they have been induced to look upon him as a monster without one of the virtues of a human being.'[8] There was no alternative to unconditional surrender.

On 15 July, after ensuring that he could be accompanied by a retinue of thirty-three, Napoleon embarked in a boat to be carried from Ile d'Aix to the anchorage in the Basque Roads. Dressed in an olive-green greatcoat over his *chasseurs'* uniform and a small cocked hat with a *tricolore* cockade, he climbed up the side of the *Bellerophon* and surrendered to Maitland on the quarterdeck, saying, 'I am come to throw myself on the protection of your

Prince [the Prince Regent] and laws,' The captain led him to the great cabin, from the window of which he could see the masts of French and neutral ships that might have taken Napoleon to America. 'Une belle chambre', he said, and Maitland replied, 'Such as it is, sir, it is at your service while you remain on board the ship I command.' Napoleon noticed a portrait on the bulkhead and asked, 'Qui est cette jeune personne?' 'My wife.' 'Ah! Elle est très jeune et très jolie'.[9] Napoleon was once again the charmer.

On board the *Bellerophon* the fallen Emperor was treated as royalty. He spoke little English and Maitland struggled with French but they managed to converse and Napoleon expressed his wish to watch the ship's company weigh anchor and make sail. At first he had begun to boast, 'I can see no sufficient reason why your ships should beat the French with so much ease . . . a French ship is heavier in every respect than one of yours, she carries more guns and has a great many more men.'[10] The captain replied that it was because of greater British experience at sea and constant training in gunnery. But when the ship had sailed, Napoleon remarked, 'What I admire most in your ship is the extreme silence and orderly conduct of your men; on board a French ship, everyone calls and gives orders and they gabble like so many geese.'[11] Then, after inspecting a guard of marines, he mused, 'How much might be done with a hundred thousand such soldiers as these.'[12]

On his voyage to captivity the fallen Emperor continued to dine with the captain. At table, while the conversation ranged over the past, Napoleon confirmed the forecast of his old enemy Sir Sidney Smith nearly a decade earlier. 'If it had not been for you English,' he said, 'I should have been Emperor of the East. But wherever there is water to float a ship, we are sure to find you in our way.'[13]

★ ★ ★

News of the first abdication of Napoleon and his exile to Elba had spread across France in a week, down Italy in a fortnight and across the Mediterranean within a month. When it reached Murat, he was no longer King Joachim and he was in Corsica, not Naples. At the beginning of the year, he and Caroline had still been reigning from the Palazzo Reale, worried about their future but their imaginations whirling with dreams of ruling a united Italy. Both appeared confident of their popularity, she the most regal of all the Bonaparte women, ruling an extravagant court, gliding through the seemingly endless succession of painted, gilded salons of their four great palaces in a flock of two or three dozen ladies-in-waiting – including a dozen princesses and another dozen duchesses – all dressed in flowing yellow and white. He, on the other hand, was a swaggering populist in his curls, plumes, gorgeous uniform and clanking sabre. Both disguised their fears with gaiety. A visiting Englishman, the poet Samuel Rogers, reported that at a palace ball she was 'wreathed in diamonds from head to foot' and 'danced like a gentlewoman', whereas he 'danced like a dancing-master, perfect in his steps and affecting an ease not natural to him'.[14]

Then came news of Napoleon's escape from Elba and the rallying of France to his cause. Hearing that other renegade marshals had returned to the imperial standard, Murat wrote to Napoleon, also offering his services. Confident of being welcomed, he decided that this was the moment to turn on Austria and arouse all Italy to drive them out and unite under his rule. 'The hour has come for the accomplishment of the great destinies of Italy', he proclaimed. 'All Italians are summoned to belong to an independent nation . . . 80,000 Italians from the Kingdom of Naples will march north, led by their King.'[15] Murat did march north, took Rome, Florence and Bologna and then met the Austrian army at Tolentino on 2 May 1815. He was routed. A fortnight later King Joachim was back in Naples, admitting, 'All is lost except honour. There is nothing left for me but death',[16] whereupon he left for the fortress of Gaeta, leaving Caroline and their children to follow. Before she could sail away, the Austrian vanguard had entered the city. It was commanded by Lieutenant-General Count Adam von Neipperg, who was, ironically, the officer with whom the Empress Marie-Louise had been dallying while her husband was exiled on Elba. With him was Prince Leopold, the heir to the Bourbon dynasty, to ensure that his father, Ferdinand, was again proclaimed King of the Two Sicilies.

At Gaeta the deposed King Joachim and his former queen parted: she to Trieste and he to Corsica. Murat had now heard that Napoleon had spurned his offer to return to his side, so he

would have to act alone. His one hope was an Italian rising that
would overwhelm the Austrians and eject King Ferdinand. So,
inspired by Napoleon's escape from Elba and his rallying of
France, Murat determined to emulate him and began to recruit
his own little army of Corsicans. It was then that news arrived of
an event of such overwhelming historical importance that, by
contrast, it showed the dilemma of the former King and Queen of
Naples as the tragi-comic opera it was. When Murat heard the
news from Waterloo, his immediate reaction was that Napoleon
would have been victorious if he himself had commanded the
cavalry. But, if he too accepted defeat, there was no future for him
and his family but exile, and this he rejected, although the British
had offered a frigate to carry him to Trieste and Metternich had
generously sent him a passport and the offer of safe haven in
Austria. He was confident of his popularity with Neapolitans,
who so enjoyed his swagger, and he decided that it was now or
never. With a small entourage of loyalists and some 250 armed
Corsicans he sailed in seven feluccas for the Bay of Naples on the
night of 28 September. On passage an autumn gale blew and scattered the flotilla, driving Murat's ship far down the coast until
they saw the mountains of Calabria. Off the long, pale beach of
Sant' Eufemia, Murat's companions urged him to abandon his
plan and make for Trieste but the skipper added that, whatever he
decided, they would have to go ashore for food and water. The
nearest port was Pizzo, on a rocky headland a dozen miles to the
south, and that became their destination. Now, he hoped, he
could emulate Napoleon's return from Elba. Although full of
confidence, he did allow himself the aside: 'At worst? I shall die a
king.'[17]

In his days of glory Murat had ridden through Calabria with his
glittering cavalcade, directing operations of war, leaving the rou-
tines of occupation and suppression to his generals. He went below
to change into one of his magnificent uniforms and a plumed hat
with a diamond clasp. Sailing towards the little town of Pizzo, on
its crag above the sea, commanded by a squat little castle, they
launched a boat, and he and sixty-eight followers were ferried
ashore, landing on the beach below the town at eleven o'clock in
the morning. Up the steep road and through the gates they

marched and into the busy market-place, where the theatrical figure of their former king was met with blank, astonished stares. Murat's companions waved their hats and cheered King Joachim, but the crowd backed away. Seeing a file of soldiers ahead, Murat ordered the sergeant to follow him, promoting him captain on the spot; but they turned and ran. This was not the welcome he had expected, so he decided to head for Monteleone, the next town, which had formerly welcomed the French. Horses were needed and as they asked for a posting-house where they could be hired, the crowd emerged from the shadows of the side-streets, and a police officer approached and demanded their business. Murat had lost confidence, and he replied that he was on his way to Trieste and had a valid passport from Prince Metternich. The officer ordered their arrest; one of Murat's men fired his pistol, dispersing the crowd, and they ran for the beach. But their boat and the felucca had disappeared.After finding a beached fishing boat, they were trying to drag it down to the water when the crowd caught up with them. One of Murat's men fired again and was himself shot dead; the others were manhandled back into Pizzo.

In the town the crowd, losing its fear, was now a lynch mob and as Murat, bleeding from scratches, his clothes torn, was dragged into the square, a woman screamed, 'You had four of my sons shot!'[18] They were marched to the castle and herded into a vaulted cell. From there they could see the sea through a small, barred window in the thick walls.

News of Murat's arrest was rushed to Naples, where the newly returned King Ferdinand was informed as he sat in the royal box at the San Carlo opera house. He left at once for the Palazzo Reale, where he climbed the great marble staircase to hold an emergency council of state. Ferdinand was told that, under a law introduced by the former King Joachim, the mandatory penalty for attempting to usurp the throne was death. So there was nothing more to be said, except that 'General Murat will be brought before a military commission. The condemned will have half an hour to receive the consolations of religion.' In Pizzo a court-martial of seven officers was convened with an adjutant-general, who owed his promotion to Murat, as president. Murat himself guessed the outcome when he was separated from his fellow prisoners and given a meal of roast pigeon cut into small pieces, to be eaten with a spoon so as to deprive him of a weapon for suicide.

At first Murat refused to acknowledge or appear before the court martial – 'I am your King, get out, don't crowd my prison' – but he had no option. He became philosophical, and told a guard,

> What have I done to the Neapolitans to have them as enemies? Anything which is liberal in their codes is my work . . . I should have thought King Ferdinand more human and more dignified. I should not have acted thus towards him if, landing in my states, the fortune of war had put him into my hands.[19]

He was brought before the court on 13 October and their verdict was, as expected, unanimous. After he was condemned, he was led up a narrow stone staircase and across a cramped courtyard to a cell within the ramparts, where a priest awaited him. He had been allowed half an hour more life, and most of this he spent in writing a letter of farewell to Caroline and their children:

> My last hour has come, in a few moments I shall have ceased to live . . . Show the world that you are worthy of me. I leave you without a kingdom and without means in the midst of my numerous enemies. Show yourself superior to misfortune; think of what you are and what you have been . . . Do not curse my memory. I declare that my greatest grief in the last moments of my life is to die far away from my children.

He then folded into the letter a lock of his curling black hair.

The door opened and an officer entered to say that it was time. Murat walked out into the sunlight. Although the courtyard was on the roof of the castle and open to the sky, it was so confined as to appear little bigger than a knacker's yard behind a butcher's shop. It was half filled with the twelve men of the firing-squad and their officer so that, when Murat was stood against the opposite wall, the muzzles of their long muskets almost touched his chest. He refused a blindfold and a proffered chair, pulling his shirt open and ordering, 'Soldiers, do your duty, fire at the heart but spare my face.'[20] Orders were given, the muskets raised and fired, their smoke drifting over the walls of the castle like smoke from a chimney. Six musket-balls hit his chest and one his right cheek; his body still moved and the officer drew a pair of pistols and fired them into Murat's handsome head.

★ ★ ★

The mail arrived unexpectedly at a comfortable country house near the Buckinghamshire village of Swanbourne on Sunday, 25 June 1815, and Betsey Fremantle, the admiral's wife, opened a letter from her husband. She wrote excitedly in her diary, 'The mail brought the account of a grand victory obtained by the Duke of Wellington at Waterloo . . . The slaughter of officers and men quite tremendous, my husband was obliged to break to Ld. Ponsonby the death of his brother Gen. Ponsonby, who was kill'd in the action.'[21] Admiral Fremantle had heard the news first because he was closer to the Continent, although no longer in the Mediterranean. On his return to England he had been appointed Knight Commander of the Bath (but was put out by being in the second class of the order) and had accepted the command in the Channel Islands, while hoping for his final ambition to become commander-in-chief in the Mediterranean, which he considered 'the only one a gentleman can take in time of peace.'[22]

The Channel Islands station, although a few miles from France, was quiet and, when he arrived, there was little work for the two frigates and two sloops under his command. But since Napoleon's escape from Elba he had been restive and, after Waterloo, keenly concurred with a French royalist emigré on Jersey, the Duc d'Aumont, in plans to launch a small, freelance attack on the mainland, as had so often been tried in earlier years, with disastrous consequences. Napoleon was said to be heading for Paris and the war continued, so this might be the moment to strike and Fremantle offered to ship the duke and his men to Normandy. On 7 July, nearly three weeks after Waterloo, he put them ashore on a long, sandy beach near Arromanches and they plunged inland. The royalists muddled their way south and had reached Bayeux, where they were surrounded by troops loyal to Napoleon and who had not heard that he had again abdicated. D'Aumont was about to surrender when news arrived that, on the day they had landed, the allies had entered Paris and King Louis XVIII had returned to his capital on the following day. This fiasco marked the end of Sir Thomas Fremantle's two decades of war.

★ ★ ★

All Europe began to relax as the fleets and armies began to disperse and the sailors and soldiers returned home. Admiral Fremantle's hopes were, even now, for the Mediterranean command, so he let the house in Buckinghamshire and took his wife and children on the journey south. It would be a grand tour of Europe, beginning in France and lasting months, or even years, and would unwind his memories of the years since Trafalgar. From the political antagonisms of Normandy they headed for Paris, where they arrived as tourists and visited the Louvre, to see what Betsey described as 'the plunder of all Europe' while they still could because 'some of them have been already removed by the Prussians and ·those belonging to Belgium are to be taken down by order of the Duke of Wellington'.[23] They toured museums, the Invalides, the Montparnasse catacombs, fountains installed by Napoleon and shops in the arcades of the Palais Royal – 'the most tempting I ever saw' – but there she also found 'everything most depraved in Paris'. They also went 'to the review near Montmartre, where Ld. Wellington reviews 80,000 men, nearly all English'.[24]

Across France they travelled and into Italy and the theatre of war Fremantle had known. Entering Venice for the first time, he found it a husk of the glorious city he had imagined when seeing it through his telescope from beyond the *murazzo*. 'Venice is not what it was', he wrote to his brother. 'It is melancholy to see the decadence of a place formerly so renowned, the population does not now exceed 9,000, of which one fourth are certainly mendicants . . . and not 20 men are now employed in the Arsenal, which . . . formerly occupied 4,000 daily, it is said that the ships remaining are to be disposed of.'[25] There they met the sculptor Canova and his former model Princess Pauline, whose mother-in-law confided that she regretted Pauline's marriage to Prince Borghese: 'My son found that marrying 10,000 bayonets was not a bed of roses.'[26]

In March 1818 Sir Thomas achieved his ambition and was

appointed Commander-in-Chief, Mediterranean Fleet, as Nelson had been, and could look forward to years of pleasurable cruising in that sea. They returned to Naples, where they had married in the Hamiltons' embassy twenty years earlier, and there they found King Ferdinand back on the throne. He was not the only ghost of the war years. Vice-Admiral Sir Sidney Smith was there too, with his wife, gratified that his campaign against North African slavery had inspired the attack on Algiers in 1816 by Lord Exmouth, as Admiral Pellew had now become. Sir Sidney might still appear in Betsey's eyes 'a conspicuous figure', but his old style was muted and, she noted, 'he had been to the King and came off in a shore boat with all his orders and four dingy stars and a round hat. He is looking old and talks much less than he did.'[27] There, too, Fremantle again met the Austro-Irish General Nugent, beside whom he had fought at Trieste. Visiting his house near Portici to the east of Naples, Betsey found his priorities just what they might have been before the long war. 'The situation is very fine between the sea and Vesuvius, which rises from their lawn as if it belonged to their pleasure ground. There is a wood at the bottom of the mountain and he is cutting walks through it and improving it very much. The house is built on a layer of lava and may any day be buried under it again.'[28] This might have been a metaphor for all of Europe, but on that day the sun was shining and the world was at peace.

Afterwards

People

Lieutenant-General Lord William Bentinck was appointed Governor-General of Bengal in 1827. There he introduced Indians into the administration and instituted financial reforms, and in 1833 became the first Governor-General of India before returning home two years later to become Member of Parliament for Glasgow. He died in 1839.

Napoleon Bonaparte, having surrendered to the British after Waterloo, found that his fears were realized when he was exiled to St Helena in the South Atlantic. There his exile was supervised by the Governor, Major-General Sir Hudson Lowe, who had once commanded on another island, Capri. The deposed Emperor died in 1821 under circumstances that are still debated.

Princess Pauline Borghese (*née* Bonaparte) retired to Rome, although both she and her husband had openly taken lovers: hers being the composer Giovanni Pacini. She suffered from tuberculosis and moved to Lucca for the cleaner air, but died in 1825.

Colonel Sir Neil Campbell was invalided from the Army in 1816 because the wound by the cossack's lance, which had penetrated his lungs, caused a recurrence of respiratory problems. But he was promoted to major-general and travelled on the Continent before, in 1826, being appointed Governor of Sierra Leone. In Africa he was intensely active despite poor health aggravated by the heat and humidity. The following year he died of fever.

Captain Richard Church resumed an exotic career after the loss of Capri in 1808, commanding Greek troops in the Ionian Islands before becoming a liaison officer with the Austrians in 1815. He became a general in the Neapolitan service and then commander of the Greek insurgents fighting the Turks, before finally becoming a leader of the Greek rebellion of the 1820s. He retired to Athens as a general in the Greek army in 1854 and died in 1873.

Admiral Sir John Duckworth was given no further naval command after the Dardanelles fiasco but was appointed Governor of Newfoundland in 1810 and a baronet on his retirement three years later; he died in 1817.

King Ferdinand of the Two Sicilies outlived his queen, Maria Carolina, by eleven years, holding his throne with Austrian support and continuing to suppress liberal opinion. He died in Naples in 1825.

Major-General Alexander Fraser returned to Sicily after the disaster in Egypt. He commanded a brigade in the force landed in Portugal under Sir John Moore and was eventually evacuated from Corunna. Promoted lieutenant-general, he commanded a division in the Walcheren expedition of 1809 and died of fever on his return the same year, to be described in the *Gentleman's Magazine* as having been 'mild as a lamb and as a lion strong'.

Vice-Admiral Sir Tom Fremantle was appointed Commander-in-Chief, Mediterranean, in 1818 and enjoyed much social life ashore, accompanied by his family until, in 1819, he died suddenly at Naples.

Captain Sir William Hoste, having been made a baronet in 1814, married Lady Harriet Walpole, daughter of the Earl of Orford, and fathered three sons and a daughter. Although he was still in poor health after his exertions in the Balkans, his naval career continued: he conducted sea trials with steamships and later commanded the royal yacht. But he was now suffering from tuberculosis and died in 1828 at the age of 48.

Major-General Sir James Kempt was awarded the Grand Cross of the Order of the Bath for his gallantry at Waterloo and was appointed Governor of Nova Scotia in 1820 and of Canada in 1828. After returning to Britain in 1830, he was appointed Privy Counsellor and then Master-General of the Ordnance. He died in 1854.

Mehemet Ali strengthened his position as ruler of Egypt under nominal Ottoman sovereignty by his massacre of the Mamelukes in 1811. After conquering Arabia and the Sudan, he aided the Ottoman suppression of Greece but was forced to abandon his conquest of Syria by Britain and Turkey. His rule was made hereditary and he died in 1849.

Caroline Murat (née *Bonaparte*), formerly Queen of Naples, took refuge in Austria after the death of her husband. Her two sons emigrated to America, where she hoped to join them, but both daughters married Italians and she finally settled in Florence, where she died in 1839.

Lieutenant William Pocock retired from the Navy at the end of the war and devoted himself to naval research and development, writing papers on the use of tanks rather than barrels for storing liquid on board ships, to give them additional buoyancy; on the use of steamships in war, particularly in towing sailing warships into action when becalmed; on reform of the impressment of seamen; and on the search for 'traversing the Arctic Sea' to the Pacific. He died in his native Berkshire in 1836.

Vice-Admiral Sir Sidney Smith continued his campaign against North African slavery and was gratified by the naval attacks on Algiers in 1816 and 1824, although disappointed not to be in command; he was, however, promoted full admiral. In 1815 he and his wife had moved to Paris, where he had many French royalist friends. When he died in 1838, he was buried in the cemetery of Père Lachaise.

Lieutenant-General Sir John Stuart, Count of Maida, resigned his commission in 1815 in protest at what he considered lack of support from the British government when he commanded in the Mediterranean; he died in the same year.

Field Marshal the Duke of Wellington began a political career after his victory at Waterloo, with a seat in the Cabinet and carrying out diplomatic missions. In 1828 he became Prime Minister and later, in addition, Home Secretary and Foreign Secretary, before retiring in 1846. A friend and supporter of the young Queen Victoria, he promoted the Great Exhibition of 1851 but hindered some reforms of the British Army, which he had led with such brilliance. He died in 1852 at the age of eighty-three and was buried in St Paul's Cathedral beside Nelson.

Places

Capri is now, of course, a famous holiday island but traces of the events of 1806–8 can still be found. The Palazzo Inglese still stands just below the town of Capri, close to the funicular railway, and the Phoenician Steps to Anacapri exist, although so crumbled that they cannot be climbed; a road now runs to Anacapri.

Elba remains remarkably unspoiled by mass tourism and essentially remains much as it was in 1814. In Portoferraio the Villa Mulini is open to visitors, and performances and recitals are sometimes staged at Napoleon's little Teatro Accademia. Inland, his summer residence, the Villa San Martino, can also be visited.

Gaeta remains a massive fortress, with part of the town within the outer walls above the sea, much of it now used by military and penal institutions.

Innsbruck retains pride in the rising of 1809 with a monument to Andreas Hofer and a museum on Berg Isel, as well as a spectacular panorama of the battle of 13 August, painted in 1895, on permanent display at the other side of the city. In the Hofkirche, Hofer is buried beneath a splendid marble monument, with Speckbacher buried to his right and Haspinger to his left. In the Italian-ruled South Tyrol, the birthplace of Hofer near St Leonhard also maintains a museum of 1809.

Lissa, or Vis as it is now known, has several reminders of British occupation during the Napoleonic War. Fort George and forts Bentinck, Robertson and Wellington (spelt *Vellington* on some local maps, since British sailors of that time transposed w and v) still stand, although ruinous, and the lonely grave of Midshipman Anson can still be seen near the harbour mouth. In 2003 the islanders founded the William Hoste Cricket Club, having read about the British playing the game there in the early nineteenth century in the author's biography of Captain Hoste.

Palermo is now a large industrial city and its waterfront was much damaged by bombing during the Second World War. The Palazzo Normanni, where the Bourbons held court, remains much as it was, as does the Palazzina Cinese and other palaces and churches.

Pizzo is frequented by tourists, and the castle is now a museum with waxworks of Murat, his companions and his captors.

Sant' Eufemia seems to have changed surprisingly little, although the runway of an airport lies just inshore of the northern end of the long beach. The centres of Maida and the other villages retain much of their early nineteeth-century appearance.

Trieste is part of Italy, although remaining somewhat Habsburg in character. The massive citadel above the town is open to visitors and the Palazzo Careiotte, where Admiral Fremantle once lived, still dominates the waterfront.

Notes

ABBREVIATIONS

BL   British Library
BM   British Museum
BRO Buckinghamshire Record Office
NAM National Army Museum
NC   *Naval Chronicle*
NMM National Maritime Museum
NRS Navy Records Society
PRO Public Record Office

PROLOGUE

1. Nicolas, Sir Harris (ed) *Dispatches and Letters of Lord Nelson* (London, 1844–6), vol. 7, p. 417
2. Sparrow, Elizabeth, *Secret Service: British Agents in France, 1792–1815* (Woodbridge, 1999), p. 277
3. Howard, E.G.G., *The Memoirs of Sir Sidney Smith* (London, 1839), vol. 1, p. 309
4. Howard, E.G.G., *The Memoirs of Sir Sidney Smith* (London, 1839), vol. 1, p. 309
5. NMM, ADM L 137
6. Windham, vol. 2, pp. 290–4
7. Barrow, vol. 2, p. 474

1: THE SPIRIT OF LORD NELSON

1. Hemlow, Joyce (ed), *Letters of Fanny Burney* (Oxford, 1972–84), vol. 5, p. 313

2. Brownlow, Countess of, *Reminiscences* (London, 1867), p. 8
3. Newnham Collingwood, G.L., *The Correspondence of Lord Collingwood* (London, 1827), p. 205
4. Petrides and Downes (eds.), p. 127
5. Petrides and Downes (eds.), p. 131
6. Crawford, p. 119
7. NMM, Hoste Papers
8. Mackesy, Piers, *History Today* (1960), vol. 10, p. 203
9. Acton, pp. 484–6
10. Acton, p. 141
11. Acton, p. 536
12. Barrow, vol. 2, p. 195
13. Acton, p. 572
14. Petrides and Downes (eds.), p. 127
15. Bunbury, p. 182
16. Petrides and Downes (eds.), p. 122
17. Petrides and Downes (eds.), p. 124
18. Barrow, vol. 2, p. 160

2: Tally-ho, said I!

1. Acton, p. 566
2. Acton, p. 566
3. Bunbury, p. 70
4. Mackesy, p. 126
5. Russell of Liverpool, Lord, *Knight of the Sword: The Life and Letters of Admiral Sir Sidney Smith* (London, 1964), p. 123
6. Russell of Liverpool, Lord, *Knight of the Sword: The Life and Letters of Admiral Sir Sidney Smith* (London, 1964), pp. 125–6
7. Russell of Liverpool, Lord, *Knight of the Sword: The Life and Letters of Admiral Sir Sidney Smith* (London, 1964), p. 123
8. Boothby, pp. 65–6
9. Hopton, p. 92
10. Pocock, *A Thirst for Glory*, p. 195
11. PRO, WOI/305, 489ff
12. BL, Bunbury Papers, Add. MS 370
13. Hopton, p. 180
14. Stewart, David, *Sketches of the Highlanders* (Edinburgh, 1822) vol. 2, p. 260
15. Russell, pp. 127–8

3: The glitt'ring bayonets shine

1. NMM, Hoste Papers
2. Petrides and Downes (eds.), p. 131

3. Boothby, p. 68
4. Hopton, p. 100
5. Knowles, p. 83
6. Boothby, p. 69
7. Boothby, p. 70
8. Bunbury, p. 66
9. Russell, p. 129
10. *Proceedings of the Royal Artillery Institution*, vol. 23, pp. 401–2
11. *Proceedings of the Royal Artillery Institution*, vol. 23, pp. 401–2
12. Cole, M.L., and Gwynn, Stephen (eds.), *Memoirs of Lowry Cole* (London, 1934), pp. 44–50
13. PRO, ADM51 1691
14. Anderson, Joseph, p. 12
15. *Proceedings of the Royal Artillery Institution*, vol. 23, pp. 401–2
16. Stewart, vol. 2, p. 263
17. Cole, p. 46
18. Boothby, p. 77
19. *Proceedings of the Royal Artillery Institution*, vol. 23, pp. 401–2
20. Anderson, Joseph, pp. 12–23
21. *Proceedings of the Royal Artillery Institution*, vol. 23, pp. 401–2
22. Boothby, p. 73
23. Boothby, p. 79
24. Boothby, p. 74
25. Boothby, p. 75
26. *Proceedings of the Royal Artillery Institution*, vol. 23, pp. 401–2
27. Bunbury, p. 62
28. Bunbury, p. 63
29. Boothby, p. 81
30. Boothby, p. 82
31. NAM 718/02
32. Boothby, pp. 35–67
33. Bunbury, p. 63
34. NAM 6807/453
35. NAM 6807/453
36. NAM 7102/33/236

4: CHILDISHNESS, WICKEDNESS AND FOLLY

1. Bouchier, Lady (ed.), *Memoir of the Life of Admiral Sir Edward Codrington* (London, 1873), pp. 116–7
2. Boothby, pp. 85–6
3. PRO, ADML/137
4. BL, Add. MS 37053

5. Bunbury, p. 47
6. PRO, WO/6/150/10
7. Maurice, vol. 2, p. 125
8. Bunbury, p. 79
9. PRO, ADM/51/1691
10. Maurice, vol. 2, pp. 126–9
11. Bunbury, pp. 272–3
12. Maurice, vol. 2, p. 128
13. Maurice, vol. 2, p. 128
14. Maurice, vol. 2, p. 129
15. Russell, p. 142
16. Maurice, vol. 2, p. 132
17. NMM, Hoste Papers
18. Acton, p. 582
19. Acton, p. 570
20. Acton, p. 569
21. Maurice, vol. 2, p. 129
22. PRO, WO/1/305, p. 55
23. Barrow, vol. 2, p. 178
24. Maurice, vol. 2, p. 148
25. Russell, p. 133
26. Collingwood, 1828, pp. 258–9
27. Shankland, Peter, *Beware of Heroes: Admiral Sir Sidney Smith's War against Napoleon* (London, 1975), p. 180
28. Shankland, Peter, *Beware of Heroes: Admiral Sir Sidney Smith's War against Napoleon* (London, 1975), p. 181

5: AN EASTERN TURN

1. Kaye, p. 396
2. Mackesy, p. 157
3. PRO, FO/42/9/97
4. Collingwood, p. 203
5. Windham, vol. 1, p. 306
6. PRO, WO/6/150/94
7. James, vol. 4, p. 230
8. Maurice, vol. 2, p. 148
9. Petrides and Downes (eds.), p. 100
10. Clowes, vol. 5, pp. 220–1
11. *NC*, vol. 26, pp. 367–8
12. Crawford, p. 128
13. James Richardson's journal, private collection
14. Petrides and Downes (eds.), p. 102

15. James Richardson's journal, private collection
16. Clowes, vol. 5, p. 224
17. *Gazette* (1807), p. 595
18. Petrides and Downes (eds.), p. 105
19. James, vol. 4, p. 223
20. James, vol. 4, p. 223
21. Crawford, p. 133
22. Crawford, p. 136
23. Crawford, p. 137
24. James Richardson's journal, private collection
25. Crawford, p. 138
26. Petrides and Downes (eds.), p. 107
27. Petrides and Downes (eds.), p. 101
28. Barrow, vol. 2, p. 229
29. Barrow, vol. 2, p. 244

6: A CALCULATED RISK

1. Hughes, p. 209
2. Bunbury, pp. 96–7
3. Bunbury, p. 95
4. Petrides and Downes (eds.), p. 43
5. Bunbury, pp. 101–2
6. Bunbury, p. 102
7. Anderson, Joseph, p. 20
8. Anderson, pp. 22–3
9. Bunbury, p. 111
10. Hughes, p. 209
11. Anderson, p. 25
12. Bunbury, p. 112
13. Anderson, pp. 25–6
14. Anderson, p. 26
15, Fortescue, vol. 6, p. 27
16. Anderson, p. 17
17, BM, Add. MSS. 20189*fn*. 128

7: THE EMPEROR AND THE QUEEN OF THE SEA

1. Fugagnollo, p. 16
2. Fugagnollo, p. 22
3. Fugagnollo, pp. 29–30
4. Fugagnollo, p. 55

Notes

5. Fugagnollo, p. 41
6. Fugagnollo, p. 42
7. Plant, p. 62
8. Collingwood Correspondence, NRS (London, 1957), p. 321

8: This island of despair

1. Maxwell, vol. 1, p. 277
2. Finlay, G., *History of the Great Revolution*, 2 vols. (Oxford, 1877), vol. 1, p. 418
3. Knowles, p. 89
4. Knowles, p. 132
5. Money, p. 19
6. Knowles, p. 90
7. Knowles, p. 92
8. Knowles, pp. 102–3
9. Knowles, pp. 109–10
10. Knowles, p. 138
11. Knowles, p. 155
12. Knowles, p. 170
13. Knowles, p. 171
14. Knowles, p. 198*fn*
15. Prole, p. 20
16. Maggs' catalogue, no. 1331, 2002

9: To arms!

1. Oman, Carola, p. 594
2. Oman, Carola, p. 596
3. BM, Add. MS 37884, fol. 109
4. BM, Add. MS 20190, fols. 115–120
5. Gregory, p. 74
6. Hall, pp. 2–3
7. Gedye, G.E.R., *Introducing Austria* (London, 1955), p. 40
8. Hall, p. 10
9. Hall, p. 25
10. Hall, p. 37
11. Hall, p. 29
12. Hall, p. 26
13. Hall, p. 32
14. Hall, p. 98

Notes

10: AN ABYSS OF MISFORTUNE

1. Bunbury, pp. 165–6
2. Bunbury, p. 162
3. Bunbury, p. 162
4. Bunbury, p. 165
5. Petrides and Downes (eds.), p. 126
6. Bunbury, pp. 163–4
7. Bunbury, p. 164
8. Bunbury, p. 167
9. Bunbury, pp. 173–7
10. Bunbury, p. 178
11. Bunbury, p. 180
12. Bunbury, p. 179
13. Hall, p. 107
14. Hall, p. 105
15. Hall, pp. 156–7
16. Hall, pp. 156–7
17. *Gentleman's Magazine* (1810), vol. 80, pt 2, p. 157
18. Hall, p. 159
19. *Gentleman's Magazine* (1809), vol. 79, pt 2, pp. 1067–8
20. Hall, pp. 166–7
21. Hall, p. 168
22. Hall, p. 173
23. Hall, p. 173
24. *Gentleman's Magazine* (1810), vol. 80, pt 2, pp. 159–60
25. Buckland, p. 224
26. Historic Manuscripts Commission (London, 1923), Bathurst MSS, pp. 131–2
27. *Gentleman's Magazine* (1809), vol. 79, pt 1, p. 873
28. Hall, p. 177
29. *Gentleman's Magazine* (1809), vol. 79, pt 1, p. 873
30. Hall, pp. 183–4
31. Hall, p. 185
32. Hall, p. 192
33. Gedye, p. 41

11: ECHOES OF TRAFALGAR

1. Bunbury, p. 186
2. Bunbury, p. 188
3. Warner, p. 223
4. Hughes, Letter 162

5. Hughes, Letter 176
6. Hughes, Letter 162
7. Hughes, Letter 184
8. Hughes, Letter 185
9. Warner, p. 228
10. Warner, pp. 228–9
11. Nicolas, vol. 1, p. 393
12. NMM, Hoste Papers, MRF/88/100
13. Petrides and Downes (eds.), p. 117
14. Pocock, *Remember Nelson*, p. 144
15. NMM, Hoste Papers
16. NMM, Hoste Papers
17. O'Brien, vol. 2, p. 199
18. NMM, Hoste Papers
19. NMM, Hoste Papers
20. O'Brien, vol. 2, p. 205
21. Pocock, p. 167
22. O'Brien, vol. 2, p. 471
23. O'Brien, vol. 2, p. 474
24. O'Brien, vol. 2, p. 205*fn.*
25. Pocock, p. 168
26. Pocock, p. 168
27. O'Brien, vol. 2, p. 211
28. O'Brien, vol. 2, p. 219
29. O'Brien, vol. 2, p. 219–20
30. O'Brien, vol. 2, p. 222
31. O'Brien, vol. 2, p. 473
32. Pocock, p. 177
33. NMM, Hoste Papers
34. Pocock, p. 179

12: NATURE PAUSES AND SHEDS A TEAR

1. Buckland, p. 234
2. Buckland, p. 247
3. Fremantle, vol. 3, p. 94
4. Fremantle, vol. 3, p. 347
5. PRO, FO/7/111
6. BRO, Fremantle Papers, D/FR/40/9/3
7. PRO, FD/FR/40/9/5
8. Parry, p. 113
9. James, vol. 5, p. 341
10. BRO, Fremantle Papers, D/FR/35/6/15

11. Pocock, p. 181
12. O'Brien, vol. 2, p. 234
13. Pocock, p. 181
14. NMM, Hoste Papers
15. H.M.S. *Eagle* MSS journal, private collection
16. Pocock, p. 189
17. O'Brien, vol. 2, pp. 253/4
18. NMM, Hoste Papers

13: THIS PLACE WILL KILL US ALL

1. Parry, p. 114
2. Fremantle, vol. 3, p. 365
3. Parkinson, C. Northcote, *Edward Pellew* (London, 1934), p. 406
4. Fremantle, vol. 3, pp. 362–3
5. Parry, p. 103
6. Fremantle Archive (private collection)
7. Maxwell, vol. 1, p. 30
8. Bryan MSS (private collection)
9. Pocock MSS (private collection)
10. *Eagle* MSS (private collection)
11. *Eagle* MSS (private collection)
12. James, vol. 6, p. 31
13. Pocock MSS (private collection)
14. Fremantle, vol. 3, p. 362
15. Parry, p. 119
16. Brenton, vol. 2, p. 485
17. Fremantle Archive
18. Fremantle, vol. 3, p, 123
19. Pocock, p. 209
20. Fremantle Archive
21. NMM, Hoste Papers
22. Pocock, pp. 206–8
23. Pocock, p. 205
24. Pocock, p. 209
25. NMM, Hoste Papers
26. NMM, Hoste Papers
27. NMM, Hoste Papers
28. NMM, Hoste Papers
29. NMM, Hoste Papers
30. NMM, Hoste Papers
31. NMM, Hoste Papers
32. NMM, Hoste Papers

Notes

14: NOTHING LIKE IT IN HISTORY

1. NMM, Hoste Papers
2. NMM, Hoste Papers
3. NMM, Hoste Papers
4. NMM, Hoste Papers
5. NMM, Hoste Papers
6. Fremantle, vol. 3, p. 366
7. NMM, Hoste Papers
8. NMM, Hoste Papers
9. NMM, Hoste Papers
10. Muir, p. 306
11. Bologna State Archives; cf. Capograssi, *Gl'inglesi*, p. 196
12. Londonderry, Marquess of (ed.), *Correspondence of Viscount Castlereagh*, 12 vols. (London, 1851), vol. 9, p. 427
13. NMM, Hoste Papers

15: KEEP ME IN YOUR MEMORIES!

1. MacKenzie, p. 39
2. Campbell, pp. 157–8
3. Campbell, p. 158
4. Campbell, p. 159
5. Campbell, p. 183
6. Campbell, p. 191
7. Campbell, p. 192
8. Campbell, p. 207
9. Campbell, p. 212
10. Campbell, p. 200
11. MacKenzie, p. 63
12. MacKenzie, p. 70
13. MacKenzie, p. 85
14. Campbell, p. 216
15. Maxwell, vol. 1, p. 193
16. Campbell, p. 217
17. Maxwell, vol. 2, p. 162
18. Maxwell, vol. 1, pp. 172–3
19. Maxwell, vol. 1, pp. 180–1
20. Campbell, p. 217
21. Campbell, p. 225
22. Campbell, p. 224
23. Campbell, p. 237
24. Campbell, p. 239

25. Hibbert, p. 62
26. Hibbert, p. 233
27. Hibbert, p. 229
28. Maxwell, vol. 1, pp. 188–9
29. Campbell, p. 277
30. Campbell, pp. 278–9
31. Maxwell, vol. 1, p. 189
32. Christophe, p. 138
33. MacKenzie, p.129
34. Campbell, pp. 303–4
35. Christophe, p. 144
36. Pocock, *A Thirst for Glory*, p. 218; Hyde de Neuville, *Mémoires*
37. Campbell, p. 313
38. Campbell, pp. 314–30
39. Campbell, p. 323
40. Campbell, p. 349
41. MacKenzie, p. 189
42. Maxwell, vol. 1, p. 161
43. Campbell, p. 362
44. Campbell, p. 368
45. Campbell, p. 369
46. Campbell, p. 375
47. Campbell, p. 376
48. Campbell, p. 377
49. Campbell, p. 378
50. Campbell, pp. 378–9
51. Campbell, p. 380
52. Maxwell, vol. 2, p. 39
53. Maxwell, vol. 2. p. 43

16: THE FORTUNE OF WAR

1. *History Today* (1994), vol. 44, issue 2, p. 34
2. Campbell, p. 106
3. Campbell, p. 114
4. Barrow, vol. 2, p. 273
5. Maritime Museum, Newport News, Virginia, USA, Webley MSS
6. Maritime Museum, Newport News, Virginia, USA, Webley MSS
7. Maitland, p. 43
8. Maitland, p. 35
9. Maitland, pp. 71–2
10. Maitland, p. 76
11. Maitland, p. 96

12. Maitland, p. 88
13. Maitland, p. 99
14. Hibbert, p. 244
15. Hibbert, p. 244
16. Hibbert, p. 246
17. Acton, p. 670
18. Acton, p. 671
19. Bear, p. 280
20. Bear, p. 281
21. Fremantle, vol. 3, p. 375
22. Parry, p. 131
23. Fremantle, vol. 3, p. 383
24. Fremantle, vol. 3, p. 385
25. Parry, p. 131
26. Fremantle, vol. 3, p. 391
27. Foxell, p. 42
28. Foxell, p. 82

Bibliography

Acton, Sir Harold, *The Bourbons of Naples* (London, 1990)

Allmyer-Beck, Johann C., *Der Tiroler Volksaufstand im Kriegsgeschichte, 1809* (Innsbruck, 1960)

Anderson, Joseph, *Recollections of a Peninsula Veteran* (London, 1913)

Anderson, R.C., *Naval Wars in the Levant* (Liverpool, 1952)

Barrow, John, *The Life and Correspondence of Admiral Sir William Sidney Smith*, 2 vols. (London, 1848)

Bear, Joan, *Caroline Murat* (London, 1972)

Boothby, Charles, *Under England's Flag* (London, 1900)

Brenton, Edward Pelham, *The Naval History of Great Britain*, 2 vols. (London, 1837)

Buckland, C. S. B., *Metternich and the British Government* (London, 1932)

Bunbury, Henry, *Narrative of Some Passages in the Great War with France* (London, 1854)

Campbell, Major-Gen. Sir Neil, *Napoleon at Fontainebleau and Elba* (London, 1869)

Cerio, Edwin, *The Masque of Capri* (London, 1957)

Chandler, David, *Dictionary of the Napoleonic Wars* (London, 1993)

Christophe, Robert, *Napoleon on Elba* (London, 1964)

Clowes, W.L., *The Royal Navy: A History*, 7 vols. (London, 1900)

Crawford, Abraham, *Reminiscences of a Naval Officer* (London, 1999)

Emsley, Clive, *Napoleonic Europe* (London, 1993)

Espitalier, Albert, *Napoleon and King Murat* (London, 1998)

Fortescue, J.W., *A History of the British Army*, vols. 5 and 6 (London, 1910–30)

Foxell, Nigel (ed. and trans.), *Betsey Fremantle: viaggio nelle Due Sicilie, 1817–1820* (Palermo, 2001)

Fremantle, A. (ed.), *The Wynne Diaries* (London, 1935–40)

Fugagnollo, Ugo, *I dieci giorni di Napoleone 1 a Venezia* (Venice, 1982)

Bibliography

Gregory, Desmond, *Sicily: The Insecure Base* (London, 1988)

Hall, Charles, *Memoirs of the Life of Andrew Hofer* (London, 1820)

Hall, Christopher, *British Strategy in the Napoleonic War* (Manchester, 1992)

Hibbert, Christopher, *Napoleon: His Wives and Women* (London, 2002)

Hopton, Richard, *The Battle of Maida* (London, 2002)

Hughes. Edward (ed.), *The Private Correspondence of Admiral Lord Collingwood* (London, 1957)

James, William, *The Naval History of Great Britain*, 6 vols. (London, 1878)

Kaye, J.W., *The Life and Correspondence of Major-General Sir John Malcolm* (London, 1956)

Knowles, Sir Lees, *The British in Capri, 1806–1808* (London, 1918)

Kramer, Hans, *Andreas Hofer* (Brixen, 1994)

Mackenzie, Norman, *The Escape from Elba* (Oxford, 1982)

Mackesy, Piers, *The War in the Mediterranean, 1803–1810* (London, 1957)

Maitland, Captain, F.L., *Narrative of the Surrender of Buonaparte* (London, 1826)

Maurice, Sir J.M.(ed.), *The Diary of Sir John Moore*, 2 vols. (London, 1902)

Maxwell, Col. A. Montgomery, *My Adventures*, 2 vols. (London, 1845)

Maxwell, Sir Herbert (ed.), *The Creevey Papers* (London, 1912)

Money, James, *Capri, Isle of Pleasure* (London, 1986)

Muir, Rory, *Britain and the Defeat of Napoleon, 1806–1815* (London, 1996)

Musulin, Stella, *Vienna in the Age of Metternich* (London, 1975)

Newnham, G.L. (ed.), *The Public and Private Correspondence of Vice-Admiral Lord Collingwood* (London, 1828)

O'Brien, Donat Henchy, *My Adventures during the Late War* (London, 1902)

Oman, Carola, *Sir John Moore* (London, 1953)

Oman, Sir Charles, *Studies in the Napoleonic Wars* (London, 1929)

Parry, Ann, *The Admirals Fremantle* (London, 1971)

Paulin, Karl, *Der Tiroler Freiheitsjahr, 1809* (Innsbruck, 1959)

Petrides, Anne, and Downes, Jonathan (eds.), *Sea Soldier: Letters and Journals of Major Marmaduke Wybourn, R.M., 1797–1813* (Tunbridge Wells, 2000)

Pilot, Antonio, *Napoleone 1 a Venezia nel 1807* (Venice, 1914)

Plant, Margaret, *Venice: Fragile City* (London, 2002)

Pocock, Tom, *Remember Nelson: The Life of Captain Sir William Hoste* (London, 1977)

——, *A Thirst for Glory: The Life of Admiral Sir Sidney Smith* (London, 1996)

Poole, S. Lane, *Life of Sir Richard Church* (London, 1890)

Puryear, Vernon, *Napoleon and the Dardanelles* (Los Angeles, 1951)

Warner, Oliver, *The Life and Letters of Vice-Admiral Lord Collingwood* (London, 1968)

Windham, William, *The Windham Papers*, 2 vols. (London, 1913)

Woodman, Richard, *The Victory of Seapower* (London, 1998)

Woodward, David, *The Russians at Sea* (London, 1965)

Zanlorewzi, Claudio, *I forti di Mestre* (Venice, 1997)

INDEX

Index